PROGRAMMABLE CONTROLLERS

PROGRAMMABLE CONTROLLERS
WORKBOOK AND STUDY GUIDE

Second Edition

L. A. Bryan
E. A. Bryan

An Industrial Text Company Publication
Atlanta • Georgia • USA

Editor Stephanie Philippo
Art Director Gina Kory
Associate Editor Deborah Suwala

Due to the nature of this publication and because of the different applications of
programmable controllers, the readers or users and those responsible for applying the
information herein contained must satisfy themselves to the acceptability of each
application and the use of equipment therein mentioned. In no event shall the publisher
and others involved in this publication be liable for direct, indirect, or consequential
damages resulting from the use of any technique or equipment herein mentioned.

The illustrations, charts, and examples in this book are intended solely to illustrate the
methods used in each application example. The publisher and others involved in this
publication cannot assume responsibility or liability for actual use based on the
illustrative uses and applications.

No patent liability is assumed with respect to use of information, circuits, illustrations,
equipment, or software described in this text.

CONTENTS

INTRODUCTION

This book has been designed with a dual purpose in mind: to stand on its own as a study guide and to accompany *Programmable Controllers: Theory and Implementation*, Second Edition as a workbook.

In its role as a study guide, this book enables practicing professionals to refresh their memories and sharpen their skills in traditional and cutting-edge PLC technologies. With its extensive, universal content, this text allows professionals to immediately apply the information presented to a variety of industrial automation problems.

As a workbook, students and technical personnel can use this text to reinforce the information presented in *Programmable Controllers: Theory and Implementation*, Second Edition, beginning with the principles of PLC operation and culminating with the selection of the right programmable controller for an application.

Experience shows that the conscientious use of a supplemental workbook like this one can lead to faster learning and better knowledge retention. However, to reap these benefits, the reader must thoroughly review the material presented in the study guide section of each chapter and then work all of the associated review questions. Section 2 of the book provides the answers to all the review questions, including explanations of the solutions, so that the reader can check his/her answers.

Whether it is used as a structured part of a total PLC curriculum or as a brief refresher course for PLC users, *Programmable Controllers: Workbook and Study Guide* will enable its readers to gain valuable insights into current industrial automation technology.

STUDY GUIDE AND REVIEW QUESTIONS

INTRODUCTION TO PROGRAMMABLE CONTROLLERS

CHAPTER 1 STUDY GUIDE

- Programmable controllers, also called *programmable logic controllers* or *PLCs*, are solid-state device members of the computer family. They are capable of storing instructions to implement control functions, such as sequencing, timing, counting, arithmetic, data manipulation, and communication, to control industrial machines and processes.

- The design criteria for the first programmable controller was specified in 1968 by the Hydramatic Division of the General Motors Corporation.

- The primary goal of programmable controllers was to eliminate the high costs associated with inflexible, relay-controlled systems. The specifications required a solid-state system with computer flexibility able to (1) survive in an industrial environment, (2) be easily programmed and maintained by plant engineers and technicians, and (3) be reusable.

- Early programmable controllers were used in applications requiring ON/OFF (discrete) control .

- The first PLCs were an improvement over relays since they were easily installed, used less energy and space, and included diagnostic indicators to aid in troubleshooting.

- Today's programmable controllers offer faster scan times, lower cost, and greater computational capability. Enhancements in hardware include high-density I/O systems and intelligent I/O modules.

- A programmable controller is composed of two basic sections:
  - the central processing unit (CPU)
  - the input/output (I/O) interface

- The CPU is composed of three main parts: the processor, the memory, and the power supply.

- During its operation, the CPU completes a process known as *scanning*, which includes:
  - reading the input data or status of field devices via the input interfaces
  - executing the control program stored in the memory system
  - writing, or updating, the output devices via the output interfaces

- The input/output (I/O) system forms the interface that connects the field devices to the controller. Devices that send input signals to the processor (e.g., push buttons, limit switches, thumbwheel switches) are wired to terminals of the input interfaces. Devices that will be controlled by the processor (e.g., motor starters, solenoid valves, pilot lights) are wired to terminals of the output interfaces.

- A programming device is used to enter the control program. Typical programming devices include personal computers and miniprogrammers.

- PLCs are an improvement over relays since they eliminate the wiring involved with interlocking control relays; therefore, program changes may be made without rewiring.

- Programmable controllers are computers that are specifically designed for an industrial environment. PLCs can function under harsh conditions (e.g., electrical noise, mechanical vibration, extreme temperatures) and use a ladder programming language familiar to plant personnel.

- PLCs are segmented into five major categories:
  - micro (up to 32 I/O)
  - small (32 to 128 I/O)
  - medium (64 to 1024 I/O)
  - large (512 to 4096 I/O)
  - very large (2048 to 8192 I/O)

- Between each of the five PLC categories exist overlapping areas, which contain products that exhibit characteristics of the smaller category while featuring enhancements of the larger product range.

- The ladder diagram has been the traditional method for representing electrical sequences of operations. These diagrams represent the interconnection of field devices in such a way that the activation, or turning ON, of one device will turn ON another one according to a predetermined sequence of events.

- A PLC implements hardwired interconnections in its CPU using software instructions. During this process, it uses familiar ladder diagrams in a manner transparent to the engineer or programmer.

- The programmable feature of PLCs is the single greatest benefit in the use and installation of programmable controller systems.

REVIEW QUESTIONS

1-1 Define a programmable logic controller.

1-2 Sketch a conceptual diagram of a PLC application.

1-3 In what year and by what company was the first programmable controller specified?

1-4 List five initial specifications of the first PLC design.

1-5 In the early years of their existence, PLCs were primarily used for:
a–ON/OFF control
b–position control
c–analog control
d–all of the above

1-6 For the following list of PLC enhancements, put an *H* next to the hardware enhancements and an *S* next to software enhancements:

_____ machine diagnostics

_____ fast scan time

_____ intelligent I/O

_____ functional block instructions

_____ peripheral equipment

_____ floating-point math

_____ small, low-cost PLCs

1-7 The _____ and the _____ are the two basic sections of a programmable controller.

1-8 Sketch a block diagram showing the relationship between the central processing unit, inputs, and outputs of a PLC.

1-9 Sketch a block diagram showing the relationship between the three components that form the CPU.

1-10 Sketch a block diagram illustrating the three parts of a scan.

1-11 *True/False.* The input/output system forms the interface through which field devices are connected to the controller.

1-12 *True/False.* A PLC is an industrial computer with specialized hardware and software.

1-13 A _____ device is required to enter the control program into memory.

1-14 Name two typical programming devices.

1-15 What are some distinct differences between PLCs and other computer controls?

1-16 *True/False.* Relay controls are better than PLCs for applications that require rapid modification.

1-17 The _____ standard is the graphic representation language used by control software manufacturers to implement a PLC-like environment with PCs.

1-18 Real inputs and output devices controlled by a PLC are connected to it via _____.

a–personal computers
b–I/O interfaces
c–copper wires
d–ladder diagrams

1-19 *True/False.* A PLC does not need to be rewired to make changes to its control program.

1-20 Programmable controllers with between 32 are 128 I/O are known as _____.

1-21 *True/False.* Categorization of programmable controllers is based primarily on I/O count.

1-22 *True/False.* There are five major categories of PLC products. These categories overlap to include products that have enhancements to standard features of the major categories.

1-23 The ladder program in a PLC is _____ inside the PLC's CPU.
a–interfaced
b–reversed
c–hardwired
d–softwired

1-24 *True/False.* PLC systems require as much space in an enclosure as relay systems.

1-25 Explain why the use of remote input and output subsystems is beneficial in large applications.

1-26 *True/False.* Programmable controllers can be used to diagnose field device malfunctions.

1-27 Match each of the following features of programmable controllers with the benefit that it offers:

_____ solid-state components   a–minimal space requirements

_____ small size   b–reduced troubleshooting

_____ software timers/counters   c–expandability

_____ microprocessor-based   d–high reliability

_____ modular architecture   e–easily changed presets

_____ diagnostic indicators   f–multifunction capabilities

1-28 A PLC's _____ feature provides the single greatest benefit over hardwired control.

1-29 *True/False.* Programmable controller systems are used to improve system performance and reliability and to produce quality products at reduced costs.

1-30 Personal computers may be used as a(n) _____ to display information about a process or machine.

1-31 List three PLC applications in the metals industry.

1-32 List three PLC applications in the automotive industry.

NUMBER SYSTEMS AND CODES

CHAPTER 2 STUDY GUIDE

- Every number system:
  - has a base or radix
  - can be used for counting
  - can be used to represent quantities or codes
  - has a set of symbols

- The base of a system determines the total number of unique (different) symbols used by that system. The largest-valued symbol in any number system is equal to the base minus one.

- The number systems most commonly used in programmable controllers are:
  - binary (base 2)
  - octal (base 8)
  - decimal (base 10)
  - hexadecimal (base 16)

- All digital computing devices use the binary number system, which consists of only two digits: 0 and 1.

- Each digit of a binary number is known as a *bit*. A group of eight bits is known as a *byte*, and two or more bytes form a *word* or *register*.

- The octal number system has a base of 8 and, therefore, consists of 8 digits—0, 1, 2, 3, 4, 5, 6, and 7.

- The decimal number system, which is the most widely used numbering system, consists of 10 digits: 0, 1, 2, 3, 4, 5, 6, 7, 8, and 9.

- The hexadecimal number system, base 16, consists of 16 symbols—the numbers 0 through 9 and the letters *A* through *F*.

- The decimal equivalent of any number system can be computed by multiplying each digit by the weighted value of its position and then summing the results.

- A decimal number may be converted into any base number system by performing a series of divisions by the desired base. The conversion process starts by dividing the decimal number by the base and placing the remainder in the least significant digit position. This process continues until there is no remainder. The last remainder is the most significant digit.

- The only operation a digital computing device can perform is addition. To perform subtraction, a binary number must be *complemented* (changed to a negative number) and then added. A binary number can have two types of complements: a one's complement and a two's complement.

- The *one's complement* places an extra bit in the most significant (right-most) position and lets this bit determine if the number is positive or negative. If the number is negative, all of the other bits are inverted.

- The *two's complement* also puts an extra bit in the most significant position; however, each bit, from left to right, is inverted after the first 1 is detected.

- The most common binary codes are:
  - ASCII
  - BCD
  - Gray

- ASCII (the *American Standard Code for Information Interchange*) is the most common code for alphanumeric representation. This code has 128 characters which represent letters, numerals, mathematical and punctuation symbols, and control codes.

- The binary coded decimal (BCD) system is a convenient way to represent decimal numbers in binary. This code uses four bits to represent each decimal digit.

- The Gray code is one of a series of cyclic codes known as *reflected codes* and is suited primarily for position transducers. In this code, there is a maximum of one-bit change between two consecutive numbers.

- Programmable controllers store data in their registers in either binary or BCD format.
  - In binary format, the maximum positive decimal equivalent number that can be represented in a 16-bit register is 65,535. If the most significant bit is used as a sign bit, the maximum and minimum numbers are +32,767 and -32,767, respectively.
  - Using a BCD format, a 16-bit register can hold decimal values ranging from 0000 to 9999.

REVIEW QUESTIONS

2-1 Which of the following statements is <u>not</u> true of any number system?

a–Every system has a base.

b–Every system can be used for counting.

c–Every system can be used to represent quantities.

d–Every system has the same number of symbols.

2-2 *True/False.* The base of a number system determines the total number of unique symbols used by that system.

2-3 The largest-valued symbol in a number system is equal to _____.

2-4   Match the following bases with their appropriate number systems:

_____ hexadecimal   a–base 10

_____ binary   b–base 8

_____ octal   c–base 16

_____ decimal   d–base 2

2-5   Indicate the largest-valued symbol for each of the following number systems:

(a) decimal

(b) octal

(c) binary

(d) base 11

(e) hexadecimal

(f) base 3

2-6   *True/False.* In any number system, every digit has a weight associated with its position.

2-7   The number 14_{10} is:

a–14 in any number system

b–14 in decimal

c–14 in octal

d–all of the above

2-8   Why is the binary number system used in digital devices such as programmable controllers and computers?

2-9   What is the decimal equivalent of the number 72351_8?

2-10 Convert the following binary numbers to their decimal equivalents:

(a) 10011011

(b) 01100101

2-11 In binary, one plus one equals:

a–one (1)

b–zero-one (01)

c–one-zero (10)

d–two (2)

2-12 Define the following:

(a) bit

(b) nibble

(c) byte

(d) word

2-13 Fill in the blanks of the binary number diagram in Figure 2-1 using the following list of terms:

- bit
- word
- most significant byte
- least significant byte
- most significant bit
- least significant bit

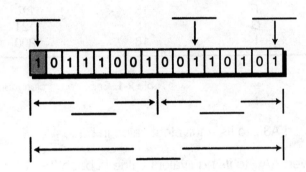

Figure 2-1. Binary number diagram.

2-14 *True/False*. A word can be three bytes long.

2-15 *True/False*. In the octal system, it is not possible to count to an equivalent of eight decimal.

2-16 The largest octal number that can be represented in one byte with all binary ones is _____ octal.

2-17 Match the following octal numbers with their decimal or binary equivalents:

_____ 5 octal	a–10 decimal
_____ 10 octal	b–1111 binary
_____ 12 octal	c–0101 binary
_____ 17 octal	d–8 decimal

2-18 The largest octal number that can be represented in a two-byte binary word is _____ octal.

2-19 What is the hexadecimal equivalent of 16 decimal?

2-20 How many bits are required to represent 2B9 hexadecimal in binary?

2-21 What is the largest hexadecimal number that can be represented in a two-byte binary word?

2-22 Convert $IG4_{27}$ to an equivalent number in base 3 given the conversion information in Table 2-1.

Base 27	Decimal	Base 3	Binary
0	0	0	0
1	1	1	1
2	2	2	10
3	3	10	11
4	4	11	100
5	5	12	101
F	15	120	1111
G	16	121	10000
I	18	200	10010

Table 2-1. Base conversion table.

2-23 Convert $A3_{16}$ to its equivalent value in base 4.

2-24 Convert AA_{16} to its equivalent value in base 3.

2-25 Convert the following numbers:

(a) 153 octal to binary

(b) F35 hexadecimal to octal

(c) 28 decimal to binary

(d) 35 decimal to octal

(e) 101101 binary to decimal

(f) 46 octal to decimal

(g) 57 octal to hexadecimal

2-26 *True/False.* The one's and two's complements are used to convert a number to its negative equivalent.

2-27 _____ is the only mathematical operation a digital computing device can perform.

2-28 *True/False.* The number +20 (decimal) would require five bits to be represented as its -20 binary equivalent.

2-29 For the decimal number +24, find:

(a) the binary one's complement

(b) the binary two's complement

2-30 *True/False.* ASCII codes use alphanumeric and control characters to represent data.

2-31 Standard ASCII character sets use a(n) _____ code, which provides room for lower case and control characters, as well as standard alphanumeric characters. A(n) _____ code is used when parity is required.

a–5-bit
b–6-bit
c–7-bit
d–8-bit
e–9-bit

2-32 What does the acronym ASCII stand for?

2-33 Illustrate the ASCII code representation of the letter A (65_{10}), including the parity bit.

2-34 Illustrate the ASCII transmission of the letter A with start and stop bits and odd parity.

2-35 The BCD system requires _____ bits to represent the decimal number 7.

2-36 What is the decimal equivalent of the BCD number 8796?

2-37 How many bits can change state as the number increases in a Gray code scheme?

2-38 Name a type of field device that uses the Gray code.

2-39 *True/False.* A programmable controller word is also called a register.

2-40 *True/False.* It is possible to have a four-bit word.

2-41 A 16-bit register can hold up to _____ BCD digits, each having a maximum decimal value of _____.

Study Guide and Review Questions

LOGIC CONCEPTS

CHAPTER 3 STUDY GUIDE

- The binary concept refers to the idea that many things can be thought of as existing in only two states. For instance, a light can be ON or OFF and a switch OPEN or CLOSED.

- A binary 1 represents the presence of a signal or the occurrence of some event (i.e., ON, OPEN, or TRUE), while a binary 0 represents the absence of a signal or the nonoccurrence of an event (i.e., OFF, CLOSED, or FALSE).

- The two binary states are represented by two distinct voltage levels, with one being more positive than the other.
  - Binary logic that uses a 1 to represent the more positive voltage level and a 0 to represent the lower voltage is called *positive logic.*
  - Binary logic that uses a 0 to represent the more positive voltage level and a 1 to represent the lower voltage is called *negative logic.*

- Programmable controllers and other digital equipment use logic functions to form statements that determine the outcome of an input. The three basic logic functions are AND, OR, and NOT.
  - The output of an *AND function* is TRUE (1) only if all inputs are TRUE (1).
  - The output of an *OR function* is TRUE (1) if one or more inputs are TRUE (1).
  - The output of a *NOT function* is TRUE (1) if the input is FALSE (0) and FALSE if the input is TRUE.

- The NOT function is also called an *inverter* because it negates (or reverses) the output of a function. When used in conjunction with the AND and OR functions, the NOT function forms NAND and NOR gates, respectively.

- Boolean algebra provides a simple way of writing complicated combinations of logical statements that can either be TRUE or FALSE. Boolean algebra uses symbols to represent the AND, OR, and NOT functions.

- Hardwired logic refers to logic control functions (timing, sequencing, and control), which are determined by the way devices are physically interconnected.
  - PLCs replace hardwired logic relays by using the three basic logic functions (AND, OR, and NOT), either singly or in combination to form instructions that determine whether a device will be switched ON or OFF.
  - PLC contacts and hardwired relay contacts operate in a similar manner—both provide power when their contacts are closed.

- Ladder diagrams, also called *contact symbology*, are relay-equivalent contact symbols (i.e., normally open and normally closed contacts and coils) used in the programming of PLC control logic. The symbols in ladder diagrams can be in series, parallel, or a combination of both.

- A complete ladder diagram can be thought of as being formed by individual circuits, or *rungs*, each having one output.

- Each element in a ladder diagram has a reference number, or label, known as the *address*.
  - The address for a given input/output can be used throughout the program as many times as required by the control logic.
  - In a PLC, each set of available coils and their respective contacts have a unique address by which they are identified.

REVIEW QUESTIONS

3-1 The idea that many things exist in two predetermined states is called the _____ concept.

3-2 Which logic type is more conventional?
a–positive logic
b–negative logic
c–Boolean logic
d–depends on the application

3-3 The logic functions used in PLCs include:
a–the AND function
b–the OR function
c–the NOT function
d–all of the above

3-4 *True/False.* In a two-input AND operation, if one input is TRUE (1) and one input is FALSE (0), the output is FALSE (0).

3-5 For the OR function, how many inputs need to be TRUE for the output to be TRUE?

3-6 Referencing the alarm horn circuit in Figure 3-1, what must take place for the alarm horn to sound?

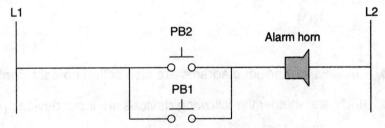

Figure 3-1. Alarm horn circuit.

3-7 The contacts in an AND function circuit are located:
a–in parallel
b–in series
c–in a combination of both parallel and series
d–in a configuration dependent on the application

3-8 The NOT function is also called a(n):

a–false-to-true converter

b–changer of states

c–inverter

d–translator

3-9 A NOT symbol is used when a logic 1 signal must _____ some device.

a–activate

b–deactivate

c–change

d–protect

3-10 The gate shown in Figure 3-2 is the symbol for the _____ function.

a–NAND

b–OR

c–NOR

d–NOT

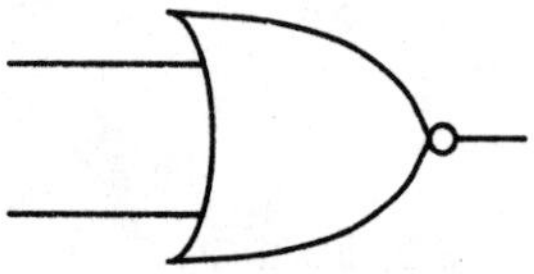

Figure 3-2. Logic gate.

3-11 *True/False.* Logic gates and Boolean gates do not represent the same functions.

3-12 The Boolean expression $Y = A \cdot B$ is read:

a–Y equals A NOT B

b–Y equals A ORed with B

c–Y equals A times B

d–Y equals A ANDed with B

3-13 Indicate the order in which the following Boolean operators are performed in an equation.

_____ AND

_____ NOT

_____ OR

3-14 *True/False.* Ladder diagrams are also called contact symbology.

3-15 Indicate whether the following devices are input devices *(I)* or output devices *(O)*:

_____ timer contact

_____ push button

_____ pilot light

_____ control relay

_____ timer

_____ limit switch

3-16 Define the term *rung*.

3-17 *True/False*. In most PLCs, a rung can contain more than one output.

3-18 Each symbol in a PLC ladder rung has a(n) _____ by which a connected device is referenced.
a–unique reference number
b–address
c–I/O interface reference terminal connection
d–all of the above

3-19 For the electromechanical circuit shown in Figure 3-3, implement the PLC-equivalent circuit using addresses 100, 101, 102 for inputs and 110 for the output.

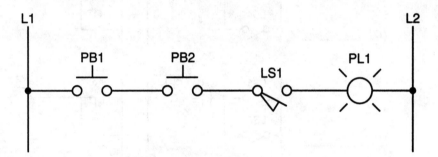

Figure 3-3. Electromechanical circuit.

3-20 In a ladder diagram, the output coil symbol is located:
a–at the far left
b–at the far right
c–in the center
d–anywhere in the diagram

3-21 *True/False*. There are a fixed number of normally open and normally closed contacts available in a PLC.

3-22 The NOT function, as implemented in contact symbology, is a(n):
a–normally closed contact
b–normally open contact
c–internal output
d–series circuit

3-23 A(n) _____ circuit is equivalent to the Boolean OR operation.

3-24 The _____ output or coil is used to deactivate an output device when any left-to-right path of input conditions are TRUE.

3-25 *True/False*. An input or output can be used as many times as necessary in the control program.

3-26 Indicate the type of circuit for each of the following logic sequences. Use the following labels: *S/P*–series/parallel circuit, *P/S*–parallel/series circuit, *S*–series circuit, *P*–parallel circuit.

Relay Ladder Diagram	Contact or Ladder Diagram

(a) _____

LS1 LS2 SOL1   X1 X2 Y1

(b) _____

LS3 SOL2   X3 Y2
LS4   X4

(c) _____

LS5 CR1 PL1 (G)   X5 Y3
LS6   X6

(d) _____

LS7 CR2 PL1 (G)   X7 C2 Y4
LS10 CR3   X10 C3

(e) _____

LS11 LS12 AL1   X11 X12 Y5
LS13   X10

(f) _____

LS14 LS15 CR1   X14 X15 Y6
LS16 LS17   X16 X17

(g) _____

LS14 CR1-1 SOL3   X14 C1 Y7

3-27 Express the following equation as a ladder diagram rung:

$$Y = [(A + B)C] + [(DE) + F]$$

3-28 Minimize the following equation using Boolean algebra laws:

$$Y = [(A + AB) + (\overline{\overline{A} + \overline{B}})][\overline{B} + (A + \overline{A}B)]$$

CHAPTER
FOUR

PROCESSORS, THE POWER SUPPLY, AND PROGRAMMING DEVICES

CHAPTER 4 STUDY GUIDE _____

- The central processing unit (CPU), which encompasses all the elements that form the intelligence of a PLC, is composed of three main sections:
    - the processor
    - the memory system
    - the power supply

- In the CPU, the processor continually interacts with the system memory to interpret and execute the control program, while the power supply provides all the necessary voltage levels to ensure proper operation of the processor and memory components.

- Microprocessors, which are categorized according to their word length, provide the intelligence for today's PLCs. The larger the word length, the more sophisticated the PLC.

- The principle function of the processor is to command and govern the activities of the entire PLC system. The processor performs this function by interpreting and executing a collection of system programs known as the *executive*.

- *Multiprocessing* is an approach that divides the total system tasks among several microprocessors, thus distributing the control and processing responsibilities.

- The basic function of a PLC is to read all of the field input devices and then execute the control program, which turns the field output devices ON or OFF. This process of reading the inputs, executing the control program, and updating the outputs is known as the *scan*.

- The scan time is the total time the PLC takes to complete the program and I/O update scans.

- If an input signal changes states twice in one scan, the PLC will not be able to "see" the signal. To remedy this situation, many PLCs use either immediate instructions or pulse stretchers.
    - *Immediate instructions* interrupt the continuous program scan to receive an input or to update an output immediately.
    - A *pulse stretcher* stretches the input signal so that it will last for at least one complete scan.

- The processor uses error-checking techniques to confirm the validity of transmitted data. Common error-checking techniques include:
    - parity check
    - checksum

- Parity check is a technique that checks for an even or odd number of 1s in a word, depending on whether the check is for even parity or odd parity. An extra bit, called the *parity bit*, is added to each byte or word to make the word contain an odd or even number of 1s.

- Parity error checking is a single-error detection method; if more than one bit changes value, the error will not be detected.

- The checksum error detection method provides a means of checking a block of data. The last word of the block, the block check character (BCC), contains a pattern that describes the bit organization of the whole block.

- The most common checksum error detection methods are:
  - cyclic redundancy check (CRC)
  - longitudinal redundancy check (LRC)
  - cyclic exclusive-OR checksum

- The Hamming code is the most common error detection and correction code. It can detect two or more bit errors and correct one-bit errors.

- The processor runs CPU diagnostics, such as memory, processor, battery, and power supply checks, to detect communication failures and other PLC malfunctions.

- The system power supply plays an important role in the total PLC system operation. It not only supplies all the necessary voltages to the system, but also ensures system reliability and integrity by warning the processor about improper voltage levels.

- Power systems often incorporate constant voltage and isolation transformers to regulate power fluctuations.
  - *Constant voltage transformers* are used when line voltages frequently vary beyond the limits of the power supply.
  - *Isolation transformers* are used when surrounding equipment introduces considerable amounts of electromagnetic interference (EMI) into the power lines.

- A PLC's power supply should be adequate to accommodate the current requirements of all system devices.

- PLC's require programming devices to enter the control program into the system memory. The most common programming devices are *miniprogrammers* and *personal computers*.
  - Miniprogrammers, also known as *hand-held* or *manual programmers*, are inexpensive, portable tools for starting up, changing, and monitoring a PLC's control logic.
  - Personal computers use specialized software to perform ladder programming, editing, documentation, and real-time monitoring of the PLC's control program.

REVIEW QUESTIONS

4-1 The three components that form the central processing unit (CPU) are the _____, _____, and _____.

4-2 The term *CPU* is often used interchangeably with the term _____.

4-3 *True/False.* The CPU encompasses all the elements that form the intelligence of a PLC system.

4-4 The _____ provides the intelligence of today's programmable controllers.
a–I/O interface
b–miniprogrammer
c–memory system
d–microprocessor

4-5 The processor governs all system activities by interpreting and executing a collection of system programs known as the _____.

4-6 The approach used to divide the total system duties among several processors that share the control and processing responsibilities is known as _____.

4-7 _____ allow independent control tasks to take place outside of the CPU.

4-8 *True/False.* The speed at which a microprocessor can solve a program is a function of word length.

4-9 The total scan time of a system includes the _____ scan time plus the _____ scan time.

4-10 The use of remote I/O _____ the scan time as a result of the remote subsystem transmission.
a–increases
b–decreases
c–inverts
d–does not affect

4-11 If a PLC with a total scan time of 7 milliseconds receives an input signal that changes state _____, the controller will never "see" the signal.
a–once in 14 msec
b–twice in 9 msec
c–twice in 5 msec
d–once in 3 msec

4-12 *True/False.* Most programmable controllers generate a signal signifying the end of the program scan.

4-13 Software instructions that allow the interruption of a scan to receive inputs or to update outputs are known as:
a–immediate instructions
b–midscan instructions
c–interrupt instructions
d–update instructions

4-14 A _____ is used to lengthen extremely fast inputs.

4-15 *True/False.* The communication between the main CPU and remote I/O subsystems takes place in serial binary format.

4-16 _____ techniques are normally incorporated in the communication between the CPU and a remote subsystem to confirm the validity of transmitted data.

4-17 Parity check is sometimes called _____.

4-18 Parity error checking examines the transmitted data for an _____ or _____ number of 1s.

4-19 The _____ is the extra bit that is incorporated in a data transmission that uses parity check.

4-20 What must the parity bit be for the 7-bit ASCII character E (105_8) if:

(a) odd parity is required

(b) even parity is required

4-21 Parity error checking can detect:

a–single errors
b–single errors and correct them
c–multiple errors
d–multiple errors and correct one

4-22 *True/False.* If during even parity transmission of the ASCII character A (1000001), ASCII B (1000010) is received instead, an error will be detected.

4-23 *True/False.* Checksum is an error detection technique that is used in the transmission of multiple words.

4-24 The last word in a checksum computation is known as the:

a–end check character
b–character check
c–block check character
d–block character check

4-25 Which of the following is <u>not</u> a checksum method?

a–cyclic redundancy check (CRC)
b–horizontal redundancy check (HRC)
c–longitudinal redundancy check (LRC)
d–cyclic exclusive-OR checksum

4-26 *True/False.* Most error detection methods are performed by a software routine in the executive program.

4-27 *True/False.* In the exclusive-OR operation, more than one input must be 1 (ON) for the output to be 1.

4-28 The _____ is the most commonly used error detection and correction code.

4-29 For the four-word data transmission shown in Figure 4-1, find the BCC using:

(a) longitudinal redundancy check

(b) cyclic exclusive-OR checksum

Word 1	111001
Word 2	101011
Word 3	011010
Word 4	100001

Figure 4-1. Four-word data transmission.

4-30 Error-correcting codes can detect _____ bit errors and can correct _____ bit errors.

a–one or more

b–two or more

c–one

d–two

e–three

4-31 Name at least four CPU diagnostics that are performed by the controller.

4-32 PLC relay contacts that act as fault contacts operate in a _____ timer fashion.

a–backup

b–preset

c–watchdog

d–bridge

4-33 *True/False.* PLCs cannot use input voltages from a DC power source.

4-34 A PLC power supply must be able to tolerate a _____ variation in line voltage conditions.

a–5–10%

b–10–15%

c–10–50%

d–20–35%

4-35 The power supply issues a _____ command to the processor when the line voltage exceeds the upper or lower limits for a specified duration.

4-36 A constant voltage transformer compensates for changes in the _____ to maintain a steady voltage in the _____.

a–secondary

b–load end

c–primary

d–input module

4-37 A constant voltage transformer's rating should be selected based on the _____ of the load.

    a–average power requirements
    b–worst-case power requirements
    c–primary rating
    d–best-case power requirements

4-38 When are isolation transformers required?

4-39 *True/False.* The cause of a power supply overloading problem can usually be easily detected.

4-40 What should be done if the total current requirement for an I/O configuration is greater than the total current supplied by the power supply?

4-41 A PLC's processor requires 1.125 amps to support 40 digital inputs and 28 digital outputs. The input modules consume 280 mA, while the output modules require 250 mA. The modularity of the I/O is eight points per module. What is the minimum amount of current that the power supply must be able to supply?

4-42 Name the two most common programming devices used with programmable controllers.

4-43 Miniprogrammers are most commonly used to program _____ PLCs.

    a–small
    b–medium
    c–large
    d–very large

4-44 List three PLC programming functions of miniprogrammers.

4-45 Some miniprogrammers have removable _____, which can store a complete program.

    a–LEDs
    b–microchips
    c–LCDs
    d–memory cards

4-46 List three PLC programming functions of personal computers.

CHAPTER

FIVE

THE MEMORY SYSTEM AND I/O INTERACTION

CHAPTER 5 STUDY GUIDE

- The memory system is the area of the PLC's CPU where all of the programs are stored and executed by the processor to provide the desired control of field devices.

- The memory system in a PLC is composed of two memory sections:
  - executive memory
  - application memory

- The executive memory is a collection of permanently stored programs that are considered a part of the system itself. These supervisory programs direct all system activities, such as execution of the control program, communication with peripheral devices, and other system housekeeping activities.

- The application memory stores user-programmed instructions that form the applications program.

- There are two types of memory: *volatile* and *nonvolatile*.
  - Volatile memory will lose its programmed contents if all operating power is lost or removed. The contents of volatile memory may be altered easily.
  - Nonvolatile memory will not lose its programmed contents if all operating power is lost or removed. The contents of nonvolatile memory usually cannot be altered.

- The executive memory's permanent system programs are stored using nonvolatile memory. Application memory is stored using volatile memory with a battery backup.

- There are many different kinds of volatile and nonvolatile memory, including:
  - read-only memory
  - random-access memory
  - programmable read-only memory
  - erasable programmable read-only memory
  - electrically alterable read-only memory
  - electrically erasable programmable read-only memory

- Read-only memory (ROM) is a nonvolatile memory that stores information permanently. Programs stored in ROM can be examined, but not altered.

- Random-access memory (RAM) is a volatile memory commonly used for application memory. RAM, also known as *read/write (R/W) memory*, provides an excellent means for creating and altering a program.

- Programmable read-only memory (PROM) is a nonvolatile ROM that can be programmed only once and never altered again.

- Erasable programmable read-only memory (EPROM) is a type of PROM that can be erased using ultraviolet light. EPROM is used to store application programs that don't require additional program changes or on-line data entry.

- Electrically erasable programmable read-only memory (EEPROM) is a nonvolatile PROM that can be erased by electrical pulses.

- All memory consists of three basic units: *bits*, *bytes*, and *words*.
  - A bit is the smallest structural unit of memory. Each bit stores information in the form of binary 1s and 0s, where a 1 represents the presence of a voltage charge and a 0 represents the absence of a voltage charge.
  - A byte is a group of bits handled simultaneously by the processor. A byte usually contains 8 bits.
  - A word is a group of bytes handled simultaneously by the processor. Typical word lengths are 8, 16, and 32 bits.

- Memory capacity is nonexpandable in small PLCs and expandable in larger PLCs. Memory is measured in K units, where each K unit represents 1024 word locations.

- The amount of memory required by each instruction in a PLC is known as *memory utilization*. Each instruction in a PLC uses a predetermined number of bytes or words.

- A memory map details the organization of a PLC's memory, which has two main sections:
  - the system memory
  - the application memory

- The system memory contains the *executive area* and the *scratch pad memory area*. The system memory is hidden from the user.
  - The executve area contains permanently stored system supervisory programs.
  - The scratch pad memory area is a temporary storage area that holds small amounts of data for interim calculations.

- The application memory contains the *data table area* and the *user program area*. These areas are accessible to the user for control applications.
  - The data table area stores all data associated with the control program and retains status information for both inputs and outputs.
  - The user program area holds user-programmed data and the control program.

- The data table area can be further broken down into three sections: the *input table*, the *output table*, and the *storage area*.
  - The input and output tables store data about the status of input and output devices.
  - The storage area stores information about internal bits, which are used for interlocking in the control program, as well as input and output data stored as groups of bits.

- Each I/O device connected to terminal points in a PLC's I/O module has an *address* mapped to the I/O table. This address defines the device's physical location, as well as where data related to that device will be stores. Addresses are used in the control program to name each of the contact or coil symbols.

REVIEW QUESTIONS

5-1 The total memory system in a PLC is composed of the _____ and the
_____ memories.

5-2 Which area of the total memory system stores user-programmed instructions?

5-3 *True/False.* The executive software in most PLCs has a battery backup.

5-4 Volatile memory will _____ its programmed contents if all operating
power is lost or removed.

5-5 *True/False.* The contents of nonvolatile memory are easily altered.

5-6 Indicate whether the following memory types are volatile (V) or nonvolatile (N):

_____ electrically alterable read-only memory (EAROM)

_____ random-access memory (RAM)

_____ programmable read-only memory (PROM)

_____ erasable programmable read-only memory (EPROM)

5-7 _____ is the most commonly used application memory and is
generally backed up by a battery.

5-8 _____ is designed to be reprogrammed after being erased with
ultraviolet light.

5-9 *True/False.* Erasable programmable read-only memory (EPROM) is unsuitable in
applications requiring on-line changes.

5-10 _____ is a nonvolatile memory that exhibits the programming characteristics of RAM.

5-11 PLC memories can be visualized as an array of single unit cells, each storing
information in the form of _____ or _____.

5-12 *True/False.* A byte is the smallest structural unit of memory.

5-13 The ON/OFF information stored in a memory cell is known as the
_____.

a–device data
b–bit status
c–bit rate
d–information status

5-14 *True/False.* Memory capacity can be expanded in all PLCs.

5-15 Each K unit represents _____ word locations of memory.

5-16 What is the maximum word address (decimal) for a 4K memory system?

5-17 How many bits of memory will aPLC system with an 8-bit microprocessor, a 16-bit memory structure, and a 4K memory capacity have?

a–4,096 bits
b–32,768 bits
c–65,536 bits
d–131,072 bits

5-18 _____ refers to the number of memory locations required to store each PLC instruction.

a–memory map
b–memory configuration
c–bit utilization
d–memory utilization

5-19 Determine the memory requirements for an application with specifications as listed in Table 5-1, given that the PLC requires 30% extra memory for future expansion:

- 10 outputs, each driven by 8 contact elements
- 20 timers, each driven by 6 contact elements
- 30 counters, each driven by 1 contact elements
- each output coil instruction uses 2 words of memory
- each timer and counter instruction uses 3 words of memory

Table 5-1. Application specifications for Problem 5-19.

5-20 *True/False.* Enhanced instructions, such as data manipulation and mathematical operations, require more memory than basic instructions.

5-21 Memory organization, which defines how certain areas in a PLC's memory are used, is formally referred to as a _____.

5-22 Match the following PLC memory areas with their uses:

_____ executive   a–control program area

_____ scratch pad   b–constant/variable storage area

_____ application memory   c–system software area

_____ data table   d–interim calculation area

5-23 The executive and scratch pad areas are part of the _____.

a–system memory
b–application memory
c–data table
d–user program memory

5-24 The _____ memory area stores user-programmed instructions and the control program.

5-25 The _____ memory area retains the status information for inputs and outputs.

5-26 Sketch a total PLC memory map labeling the following areas:

- application memory
- data table area
- executive area
- scratch pad area
- system memory
- user program area

5-27 *True/False.* The input table is an array of bits that stores the status of digital inputs connected to the input interfaces.

5-28 *True/False.* Each connected input has a bit in the input table that corresponds exactly to the terminal where the input is connected.

5-29 A controller with a maximum of 128 outputs would require an output table of:

a–128 bits
b–128 bytes
c–64 bits
d–32 bytes

5-30 A controller with 64 connected I/O devices, a capacity for 128 I/O, and an 8-bit byte size would require an I/O table of:

a–128 bytes
b–64 bits
c–16 bytes
d–64 bytes

5-31 The status of the bits in the output table is controlled by the _____ as it interprets the control program.

5-32 The output table is updated during the _____, while the output field devices are updated during the _____.

a–I/O update scan
b–processor scan
c–data scan
d–program scan
e–I/O device scan

5-33 The storage area is divided into the _____ area and the _____ area.

5-34 *True/False.* Internal outputs directly control output devices.

5-35 In what formats can the data in the register/word area be stored?

5-36   Specify which of the following are constants (C) and which are variables (V):

_____ timer preset values

_____ analog input values

_____ BCD outputs

_____ set points

_____ counter accumulated values

_____ ASCII messages

_____ decimal tables

5-37   The user program memory is reserved for storage of the _____.

5-38   The interpretation of the user program is accomplished by the processor's execution of the _____ program.

5-39   Sketch a memory map indicating the beginning and ending word addresses of each section of a PLC with specifications as shown in Table 5-2. Arrange the memory sections from top to bottom in the following order:

- input table
- output table
- internal storage
- register storage
- user program area

- total application memory of 2K words with 16 bits
- capability of connecting 256 I/O devices (128 inputs, 128 outputs)
- 64 available internal outputs
- 64 storage registers
- octal numbering system
- user memory uses the remaining part of the 2K memory

Table 5-2. PLC specifications for Problem 5-39.

5-40   How much memory (i.e., word locations) is left for the user memory in Question 5-39?

5-41   If a limit switch connected to an input module is closed for one scan only, its reference address would be:

a–latched ON
b–ON for one scan
c–normally closed
d–OFF for one scan

5-42   _True/False._ An address can be used as many times as needed in the control program.

THE DISCRETE INPUT/OUTPUT SYSTEM

CHAPTER 6 STUDY GUIDE

- Discrete input/output (I/O) interfaces provide the physical connection between the digital, outside world (field equipment) and the central processing unit. Discrete input modules transmit digital data from field devices to the processor, while discrete output modules transmit digital signals from the processor to field devices.

- Rack enclosures hold and organize a PLC's I/O modules. Each module has an *address*, which specifies its rack location. The three types of rack enclosures are *master racks*, *local racks*, and *remote racks*.

  - Master racks are enclosures that hold the CPU or processor module. Some master racks have I/O housing capabilities.
  - Local racks are enclosures, placed in the same area as the master rack, that house a local I/O processor.
  - Remote rack enclosures, which are located far away from the CPU, contain a remote I/O processor and I/O modules.

- A remote subsystem is a rack-type enclosure that holds remote I/O subsystems (racks) for very large PLC systems. Remote racks can be connected to the CPU in either daisy chain, star, or multidrop configurations.

- PLC instructions for discrete I/O devices can be either single bit, which control one field input, or multibit, which control many input connections.

- The types of discrete I/O interfaces include:
  - AC/DC I/O modules
  - DC I/O modules
  - isolated AC/DC I/O modules
  - transistor-transistor logic (TTL) I/O modules
  - register/BCD I/O modules

- AC/DC I/O modules, which contain a power section and a logic section, convert AC and DC voltages. AC/DC input modules convert incoming AC voltages to DC signals, while output modules convert DC signals to AC voltages.

- DC I/O modules interface the processor with field devices that provide a DC output voltage. DC modules can have either *sinking* or *sourcing* configurations.
  - Sinking DC I/O modules receive current from an input or output device.
  - Sourcing DC I/O modules provide current to an input or output device.

- Isolated AC/DC I/O modules operate like standard AC/DC modules except that each input and output has a separate common, or return, line.

- Transistor-transistor logic (TTL) I/O modules allow controllers to accept signals from and send signals to TTL-compatible devices. Like AC/DC modules, TTL modules have an input/output delay filter circuit; however, their delay time is much shorter.

- Register/BCD I/O modules, which allow groups of bits to be input as a unit, use thumbwheel switches to provide parallel communication between field devices and the controller. Some register modules have *multiplexing* capabilities, which allow more than one line to be connected to each terminal in the module.

- Contact output modules are discrete interfaces that allow output devices to be switched by normally open or normally closed relay contacts.

- Some programmable controller use bypass, or manual backup, devices that can override PLC output signals, thus allowing field devices to be operated manually.

- Manufacturers provide electrical, mechanical, and environmental specifications for I/O interfaces. These specifications provide valuable information about the correct and safe application of I/O modules.

REVIEW QUESTIONS

6-1 The I/O system provides the interface between:
a–field equipment and output modules
b–field equipment and the CPU
c–input modules and the CPU
d–input modules and output modules

6-2 What is the most commonly used type of I/O interface?
a–analog
b–special
c–output
d–discrete

6-3 A master rack refers to an enclosure that contains _____.
a–several local racks
b–one local and one remote enclosure
c–the processor
d–input modules

6-4 A local rack houses a _____ that sends information to and from the _____.
a–remote I/O processor
b–local adapter/connector
c–processor
d–total local system
e–local I/O processor

6-5 *True/False.* The rack enclosure has no relationship with a PLC's I/O table.

6-6 Using the input/output specifications in Figure 6-1 and the rack enclosure shown in Figure 6-2, map the respective input/output locations used by each module. For each memory word or byte, indicate whether it is used by inputs or outputs or whether it is empty.

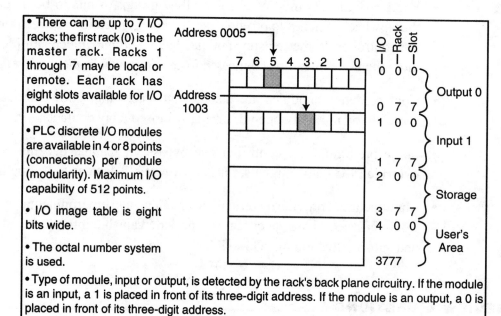

Figure 6-1. Input/output specifications.

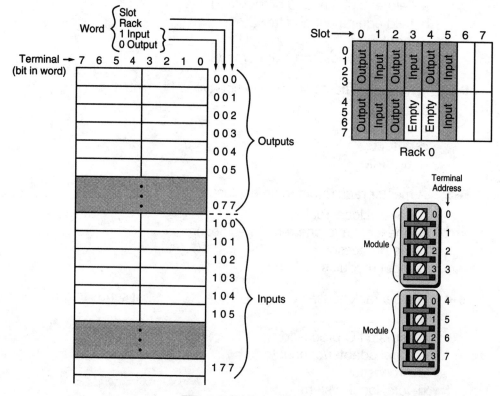

Figure 6-2. I/O rack enclosure.

6-7 *True/False.* The address of an I/O device, which depends on its terminal connection and interface placement in the rack, identifies the device in the control program.

6-8 For the I/O racks shown in Figure 6-3, fill in each blank with the address of the terminal point indicated. Shaded areas indicate input modules; unshaded areas indicate output modules. The modularity of the I/O rack is four points per module.

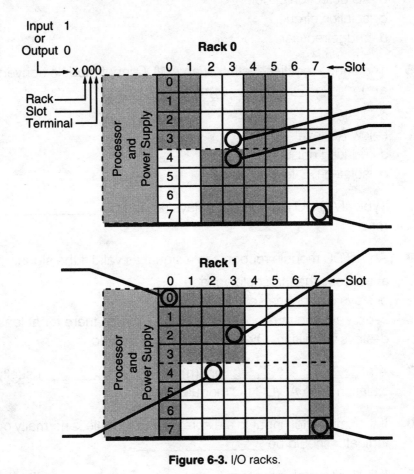

Figure 6-3. I/O racks.

6-9 The characteristics of discrete I/O interfaces limit their use to _____ field devices.
a–ON/OFF
b–OPEN/CLOSED
c–two-state
d–all of the above

6-10 What are the typical configurations for remote I/O subsystems?

6-11 Name an advantage of using remote I/O systems.

6-12 A logic 1 signal indicates that a field device is _____, while a logic 0 signal indicates that a device is _____.

6-13 Name five discrete input devices and list five standard discrete input interface ratings.

6-14 Name the two sections of an AC/DC input module's input circuit.

6-15 After an AC/DC input module detects a valid signal, it passes the signal through a(n) _____.

a–fuse
b–AC detection circuit
c–isolation circuit
d–bridge rectifier

6-16 The bridge rectifier section of an AC/DC input module converts the input signal to a(n) _____ signal.

a–DC-level
b–low AC-level
c–reduced noise level
d–isolated DC-level

6-17 Typical AC/DC input signal delays range from _____ to _____ msec.

6-18 An AC/DC module recognizes a signal as valid if the signal:

a–exceeds the threshold voltage
b–stays ON for one scan
c–exceeds the threshold voltage and remains there for at least the filter delay
d–stays ON within 10% of the voltage threshold

6-19 A(n) _____ or a(n) _____ usually provides electrical isolation in an AC/DC I/O module.

6-20 If the limit switch input to a discrete input module is normally open, then the power indicator should be _____.

6-21 If the limit switch input to a discrete input module is normally closed, then the power indicator should be _____.

6-22 Why are isolated I/O modules used?

6-23 *True/False.* An AC/DC input module can be configured for either a sink or source operation.

6-24 Illustrate how to connect two input devices (115 VAC) to an 8-point input module so that both signals are isolated from each other (two separate L1 lines). The input interface has one common line connection for every four points.

6-25 TTL input modules receive TTL signals from devices such as _____ (name one).

6-26 Are the input delays caused by TTL inputs generally longer or shorter than those caused by AC/DC inputs?

6-27 Complete the isolated AC/DC input diagram in Figure 6-4 by showing the input device module connections.

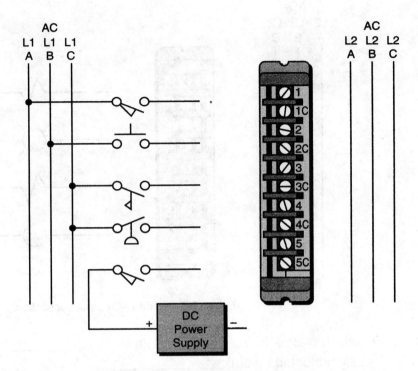

Figure 6-4. Isolated AC/DC input connection.

6-28 Name two typical applications for register/BCD interfaces.

6-29 A thumbwheel switch provides information to the PLC in _____ format.

a–BCD
b–binary
c–serial
d–decimal

6-30 *True/False.* Register interfaces require thumbwheel switches with disable lines.

6-31 Name five discrete output devices and list five standard discrete output interface ratings.

6-32 Draw a diagram illustrating the three sections of an AC output module and the relationship between each section's components. Indicate the signals.

6-33 The switching section of an AC output module generally uses either a(n) _____ or a(n) _____ to switch the power.

6-34 The two most common protection elements in an AC output module are _____ and _____.

6-35 Complete the isolated AC output diagram in Figure 6-5 by showing the output device module connections.

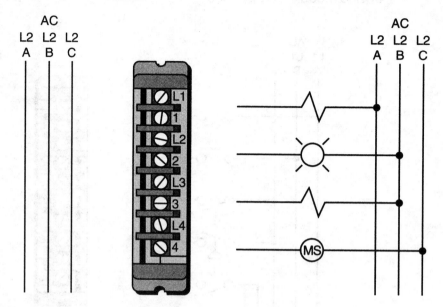

Figure 6-5. Isolated AC output connection.

6-36 To switch a load, a DC output module uses a(n) _____, which is usually protected by a(n) _____.

6-37 For the sink/source configuration in Figure 6-6, indicate how to connect each sourcing or sinking output field device to the module. Also indicate which output channels (terminals) will be operating in a sinking fashion and which will be operating in a sourcing fashion.

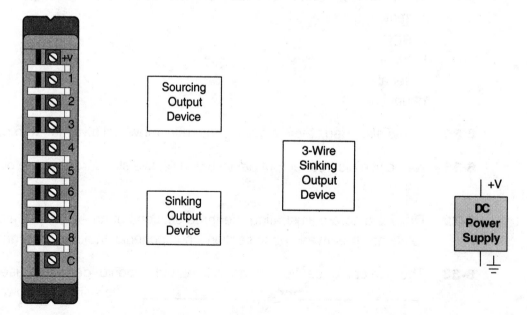

Figure 6-6. Sink/source output device connection.

6-38   DC output modules can be found in:

a–sinking configurations
b–sourcing configurations
c–a and b
d–none of the above

6-39   Name one output device that is generally driven by TTL output modules.

6-40   How many lines will be required at the module to connect two 2-digit TWS to a multiplexing register input module that is capable of interfacing six 4-digit TWS.

6-41   *True/False.* The enable lines of a multiplexing input module allow the module to switch (enable) different inputs so that data can be read.

6-42   Register output modules provide _____ communication between output devices and the processor.

6-43   Register output modules generally provide voltages ranging from _____ to _____ and are grouped in modules containing _____ or _____ output channels.

6-44   Give two examples of output devices that interface with register output modules.

6-45   For the register/BCD module in Figure 6-7, identify the following:

- the least significant bit of the register
- the most significant bit of the register
- the 1s unit
- the 10s unit
- the 100s unit
- the 1000s unit
- the most significant bit of the 100s unit

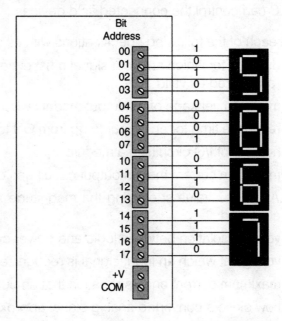

Figure 6-7. Register/BCD module.

6-46   List two applications for contact output modules.

6-47   Identify the type of interface connection shown in Figure 6-8.

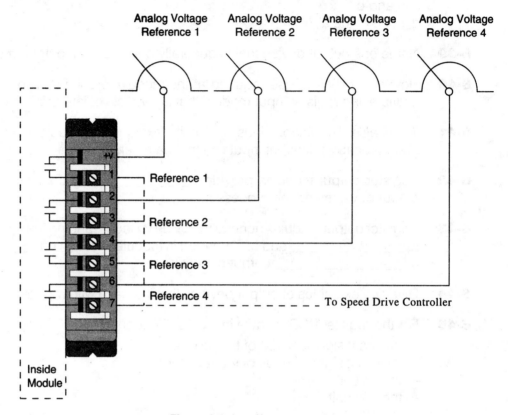

Figure 6-8. Interface connection.

6-48   *True/False*. When a bypass/control station's selector switch is in the OFF position, the PLC can control the connected field devices.

6-49   Match each of the following specifications with its appropriate definition:

_____ duration for which an input signal must exceed the threshold voltage to be recognized as valid

_____ maximum leakage of an output module when it is OFF

_____ response time for an output to go from ON to OFF

_____ number of I/O circuits in a module

_____ maximum current that an output circuit can carry under load

_____ AC or DC value specifying the magnitude and type of signal that will be accepted

_____ voltage isolation between logic and power circuits

_____ voltage at which an input signal is recognized as being ON

_____ maximum current and its duration that an output module can withstand

_____ how close a converted analog signal approximates the actual signal

_____ maximum operating temperature

a–input voltage rating

b–input threshold voltage

c–input delay

d–output current rating

e–surge current

f–OFF-state leakage current

g–output OFF-delay

h–digital resolution

i–points per module

j–ambient temperature setting

k–electrical isolation

THE ANALOG INPUT/OUTPUT SYSTEM

CHAPTER 7 STUDY GUIDE

- Analog signals continuously change between an infinite number of states, unlike discrete signals, which exist in only two states.

- **Analog input modules** translate continuous analog signals into discrete values. This allows PLCs, which can only process discrete signals, to monitor analog field input devices. Typical analog input devices include:
  - temperature transducers
  - pressure transducers
  - load cell transducers
  - humidity transducers
  - flow transducers
  - potentiometers

- Analog input modules use analog-to-digital (A/D) converters to digitize analog signals into proportional discrete values. The processor reads these discrete values and places them in a storage register, where they are represented in either BCD or binary format.

- Transducers convert the process data from an input field device into a very low-level electrical signal that is then amplified and transmitted to the analog input module. The electrical signal may be either *unipolar* (positive voltage only) or *bipolar* (both positive and negative voltages).

- Most analog input modules have multiple channel (signal) capability, so they can use analog input instructions to transfer several input values at a time to the processor's storage register.

- Analog input modules have a high input impedance, allowing them to interface with high source-resistance outputs from input devices.

- Analog input interfaces can receive either *single-ended* or *differential* inputs. In single-ended inputs, the channels are electrically connected to form one common line, whereas in differential inputs, each channel has its own common line.

- **Analog output modules** allow a processor to control output devices that require a continuous analog current or voltage to operate.

- Analog output interfaces use transducers to change their unipolar or bipolar voltage signals into signals that can be read by field devices.

- Analog output modules use digital-to-analog converters (D/A) to transform digital values from the system's memory (word or register) into equivalent analog values that are then output to field devices.

- Analog output interfaces have between two and eight channels per module. They use analog output instructions to transfer data through the channels.

- Analog outputs, like analog inputs, can have either single-ended or differential configurations. Also, analog outputs, as well as inputs, are electrically isolated to protect the system from damage due to overvoltages.

- A PLC system may use a bypass/control station in conjunction with an analog interface to ensure continued production or control in a malfunction situation.

REVIEW QUESTIONS

7-1 *True/False.* Analog interfaces are used in applications requiring measurement and control of continuous signals.

7-2 Draw a block diagram showing the signal transformation that occurs between a process that outputs analog temperature data and an analog input module that accepts a 0 to 10 VDC signal.

7-3 Analog interfaces accept either _____ or _____ types of voltages.

7-4 An analog input module transforms a(n) _____ signal into a(n) _____ value that can be read by the processor.

a–control
b–analog
c–inverse
d–discrete
e–common

7-5 An analog input module _____ an analog signal, which means that it converts the current or voltage into a number.

a–screens
b–inputs
c–digitizes
d–transforms

7-6 An analog input module uses a(n) _____ to convert the input signal into numbers, which are known as _____.

a–active filter
b–performing numbers
c–counts
d–alter circuit
e–A/D converter

7-7 The number of parts that an analog module divides a signal into is called the _____.

7-8   The remaining bits not used by the A/D converter can be used by the manufacturer
to show the _____ of the module.

a–signal direction
b–address
c–status
d–voltage range

7-9   The most common formats used to represent analog values in a PLC are
_____ and _____.

a–Gray code
b–BCD
c–binary
d–octal
e–ASCII

7-10   *True/False.* Modules that provide linearization may allow conversion of the input
signal to engineering units.

7-11   The resolution of a 12-bit A/D converter is _____ the resolution of an
11-bit A/D converter.

a–equal to
b–less than
c–greater than
d–the same as

7-12   An analog input module, which has an A/D with a 12-bit resolution, is connected to
a temperature transducer. The transducer receives a 0 to 200°C signal from a
temperature-sensing device and, in turn, sends a proportional 4 to 20 mA signal to
the analog input module. Find:

(a) the voltage change per one degree temperature change

(b) the voltage change per count

(c) the number of counts per degree temperature change

7-13   Find the solution to problem 7-12 for a module with a 10-bit resolution.

7-14   A temperature transducer provides a voltage signal of –10 to +10 VDC, which is
proportional to the temperature range being measured (0 to 1000°C). The connected analog input module converts the –10 to +10 VDC bipolar signal into a range
of 0 to 4095 counts. The process application that uses the signal specifies that low
and high alarms will occur at 400°C and 500°C, respectively. Find:

(a) the equation that defines the relationship between the input variable signal
(temperature) and the counts being measured by the PLC module

(b) the equivalent number of counts for each of the alarm temperatures specified

7-15 Indicate the order in which a PLC system uses the following devices/areas to read an analog input signal (i.e., place a 1 next to the first step in the process, a 2 next to the second step, etc.):

_____ holding register

_____ transducer

_____ data table

_____ voltage signal

_____ analog input module

_____ analog variable signal

_____ input instruction

_____ A/D converter

7-16 In what register addresses will input data be stored after the execution of the instruction shown in Figure 7-1? The PLC uses the octal number system for addresses.

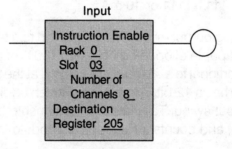

Figure 7-1. Input instruction.

7-17 Analog interfaces can have either _____ or _____ input/output capabilities.

a–single-ended (all commons tied together)
b–differential (all commons tied together)
c–single-ended (all commons separate)
d–differential (all commons separate)
e–all of the above

7-18 True/*False.* Analog interfaces use rotor switches to select single-ended or differential input configurations.

7-19 What type of cable should be used to connect an analog module to the transducer? Why?

7-20 List five standard analog input ratings and five standard analog output ratings.

7-21 *True/False.* The manipulation of analog output data is very similar to the manipulation of input data but in the opposite direction.

7-22 For the following list of field devices, place an *I* beside the input devices and an *O* beside the output devices:

_____ pressure transducer sensor

_____ AC motor drive

_____ chart recorder

_____ control valve

_____ load cell

_____ potentiometer

7-23 Numerical data received at the module from the processor is converted into an analog voltage or current using a(n) _____.

7-24 The halfway point for a 12-bit D/A that converts a 0 to 4095 count range into a proportional 4 to 20 mA current is:

a–0111 1111 1111 or 10 mA

b–0011 1111 1111 or 12 mA

c–0111 1111 1111 or 12 mA

d–0011 1111 1111 or 10 mA

7-25 An analog output module is connected to a transducer that provides a flow control valve capable of opening from 0 to 100% of total flow. The percentage of opening is proportional to a –5 to +5 VDC signal at the transducer's input. The bipolar output module has a 12-bit D/A (binary) with an additional sign bit that provides polarity to the output swing. Tabulate the relationship between percentage opening, output voltage, and counts for the output module in increments of 10% (i.e., 10%, 20%, etc.).

7-26 *True/False.* Some PLCs use arithmetic instructions to access or send data to analog interfaces.

7-27 *True/False.* Analog output modules receive output information updates at a rate of two channels per scan.

7-28 Indicate the order in which a PLC system uses the following devices/areas to output an analog signal (i.e., place a 1 next to the first step in the process, a 2 next to the second step, etc.):

_____ holding register

_____ transducer

_____ data table

_____ voltage signal

_____ analog output module

_____ analog variable signal

_____ output instruction

_____ D/A converter

7-29 A programmable controller system uses a bipolar –5 to +5 VDC signal to control the flow of material being pumped into a reactor vessel. The flow control valve has a range of opening from 0 to 100% to govern the amount of material entering the tank. The processor uses a predefined algorithm to determine the percentage of valve opening for the required flow computation. The computed value for percentage opening is stored in a register and ranges from 0000 to 9999 BCD (0 to 99.99%). The output module has a 12-bit resolution and includes a sign bit.

(a) Find the equation of the line defining the relationship between counts and voltage output.

(b) Find the equation of the line defining the relationship between counts and percentage opening.

(c) Graphically illustrate the relationship between output in counts and the stored register value (0000 to 9999) relating to percentage opening. Also, find the equation of the line that defines this relationship.

7-30 Using the analog output device/transducer diagrams in Figure 7-2, show the analog output module terminations (including return lines) for a:

(a) single-ended configuration

(b) differential configuration

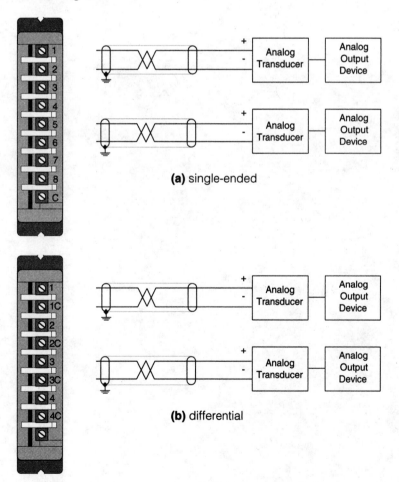

Figure 7-2. Analog output device diagrams for **(a)** single-ended and **(b)** differential configurations.

SPECIAL FUNCTION I/O AND SERIAL COMMUNICATION INTERFACING

CHAPTER 8 STUDY GUIDE

- Special function I/O interfaces provide the connection between PLCs and devices that require or send special types of signals. The categories of special function interfaces include:

  - special discrete
  - special analog
  - positioning
  - computer/network
  - fuzzy logic
  - peripheral

- There are two categories of special I/O interfaces: direct action and intelligent.

  - *Direct action I/O interfaces* preprocess input and output signals and then send them directly to the processor.
  - *Intelligent I/O interfaces* use on-board microprocessors to perform complete processing tasks independently of the CPU. The method of distributing control tasks to independent intelligent modules is known as *distributed I/O processing*.

- **Special discrete I/O interfaces** include:

  - fast-input modules
  - wire input fault modules
  - fast-response modules

- Fast-input modules detect input pulses that are much shorter than the PLC's scan time (i.e., pulses between 50 and 100 microseconds with voltages ranging between 10 and 24 VDC). These modules operate as pulse stretchers, meaning that they enable the input signal to remain valid for one scan.

- Wire input fault modules detect short-circuit and open-circuit conditions in the connections between the module and field devices by sensing changes in the current provided by the module.

- Fast-response modules are an extension of fast-input modules. These modules detect fast inputs and respond with an output. This type of module is used when a system requires a response to an input signal within 1 msec.

- **Special analog interfaces** include:

  - weight input modules
  - thermocouple input modules
  - resistance temperature detector (RTD) input modules
  - proportional-integral-derivative (PID) modules

- Weight input modules read data from load cells by sending an excitation voltage to the load cell and then reading the signal created by the weight force exerted on the cell. The module converts this information into a discrete value and sends it to the PLC.

- Thermocouple input modules are preprocessing modules that accept millivolt signals directly from thermocouple transducers. These modules provide two types of compensation: *cold junction* and *lead resistance*.
    - Cold junction compensation allows the thermocouple to operate as if it had an ice-point reference.
    - Lead resistance compensation compensates for signal loss due to resistance in the connection wires.

- Resistance temperature detector (RTD) modules receive temperature information directly from RTD temperature-sensing devices. RTD devices obtain temperature data through wire-wound elements, typically made of platinum, nickel, or copper, whose resistance changes with temperature.

- Proportional-integral-derivative (PID) modules use a predetermined algorithm to control continuous, closed-loop process applications. A PID module measures the application's process variable to ensure that the variable is at its target set point. If the process variable deviates from its set point, the module initiates a three-step, proportional-integral-derivative algorithm to correct it.

- **Positioning interfaces** are intelligent modules that provide position-related feedback and control output information in machine axis control applications. These interfaces include:
    - encoder/counter modules
    - stepper motor interface modules
    - servo motor interface modules

- Encoder/counter modules interface encoders and high-speed counter devices with PLCs to provide the processor with positioning information. There are two types of encoder/counter interfaces: *absolute* and *incremental*.
    - Absolute interfaces provide information about the angular measurement of the machine's shaft.
    - Incremental encoders provide pulse measurements of shaft rotation over a certain distance.

- Stepper motor interfaces control stepper motors through output pulses. The stepper motor's translator interprets these pulses as distance, rate, and direction commands. The output pulse rate determines the acceleration or deceleration of the motor. Stepper motor interfaces operate in either *single-step profile mode* or *continuous profile mode*.
    - In single-step profile mode, the interface receives a sequence of individual motor control commands from the processor.
    - In continuous profile mode, the interface receives motor control commands from the processor as a single block of instructions.

- Servo motor interfaces control servo motors by sending a signal, which specifies the forward or reverse motion of the motor, to a servo drive controller. These modules are used in applications that require linear or rotational axis motion control.

- **Computer/network interfaces**, which allow PLCs to communicate with the real world, include:
  - ASCII I/O interface modules
  - BASIC modules
  - network interface modules

- ASCII interface modules transmit alphanumeric data between the controller and peripheral equipment, such as printers, video monitors, and displays. Some ASCII modules include on-board microprocessors, which speed up the transmission rate.

- BASIC modules, also referred to as *data-processing modules*, are intelligent, microprocessor-based interfaces that perform data-handling functions typically performed by the processor or a small, dedicated computer.

- Network interface modules allow PLCs and other intelligent devices to communicate through high-speed local area networks.

- **Fuzzy logic interfaces** provide a way to implement "reasoned" closed-loop control of a process. These modules use algorithms consisting of rules and membership functions to determine control outputs based on input data.

- Peripheral interfaces use communication standards to connect peripheral devices with PLCs, so that they can easily communicate with each other.

- Communication standards fall into two major categories: *proclaimed* and *de facto*. Proclaimed standards are officially established standards. De facto standards have no official definition, but have gained popularity through widespread use.

- Serial communication is data transmission that occurs in serial form through twisted-pair cables. RS-232C, RS-422, and RS-485 are popular proclaimed standards for serial communication. The 20 mA current loop is a popular de facto serial communication standard.

REVIEW QUESTIONS

8-1 Special I/O modules that preprocess I/O signals are called _____.

8-2 Some special I/O modules gain added intelligence by using an on-board _____.

8-3 A fast-input module can also be considered a(n) _____, allowing the input signal to remain valid for at least _____.

8-4 Which of the following signals cannot be read by a fast-input module?
a–12 volts DC
b–110 volts AC
c–24 volts DC
d–10 volts DC

8-5 Name two fast-input devices that are typically interfaced with a PLC through a fast-input module.

8-6 Sketch a diagram showing an 85 μsec input pulse signal and the same signal stretched for a PLC with a scan time of 7 msec and a leading-edge trigger.

8-7 A wire input fault module can detect _____ and _____ connections.

   a–peripheral
   b–short-circuit
   c–open-circuit
   d–serial
   e–remote

8-8 *True/False.* A wire input fault module detects circuit wiring conditions by sensing a change in voltage due to changes in wire resistance.

8-9 When is the use of a fast-response module necessary?

8-10 *True/False.* Once a fast-response module receives a signal, it sends an output and remains ON until the processor resets it.

8-11 A weight input module sends an _____ to a load cell and then reads the weight-equivalent response signal.

   a–excitation voltage
   b–output signal
   c–input pulse
   d–excitation current

8-12 A thermocouple input module receives _____ signals from thermocouple devices.

   a–20 mA current
   b–milliamp
   c–4 to 20 mA
   d–millivolt

8-13 *True/False.* A thermocouple sends linear temperature data to a thermocouple input module.

8-14 Cold junction compensation provides:

   a–cold readings
   b–an ice-point reference
   c–compensation for module circuits
   d–all of the above

8-15 Lead resistance compensation deals with:

   a–loss of temperature in the thermocouple wires
   b–wire length
   c–loss of signal due to wire resistance
   d–misreadings of the thermocouple due to resistance changes

8-16 In what format does a thermocouple module report temperature data to the PLC processor?

8-17 *True/False*. It is a good practice to use the same type of lead wire material as is used in the thermocouple.

8-18 A type J thermocouple is connected to a thermocouple module placed in an I/O rack located 750 feet away from the processor. This thermocouple is connected to a heat trace circuit, which measures temperature ranges throughout the length of a process pipe. The thermocouple has 18 AWG lead wires that have a resistance of 0.222 ohms for each foot of double wire (positive and negative wire conductors) at 25°C. The thermocouple module used has a lead resistance compensation of 25 ohms, and the manufacturer has specified a 0.08°C per ohm compensation error factor. Find the following:

(a) the total lead resistance

(b) the necessary compensation in degrees Celsius to be added to the value measured

8-19 *True/False*. RTD devices determine temperature by sensing voltage changes in their wire-wound elements.

8-20 Briefly explain how an RTD module operates.

8-21 Match the following elements with their correct resistance and temperature ratings.

_____ 100 ohms/–200 to 850°C   a–nickel

_____ 120 ohms/–80 to 300°C   b–platinum

_____ 10 ohms/–200 to 260°C   c–copper

8-22 *True/False*. RTD sensing devices are available in 2-, 3-, and 4-wire connection configurations.

8-23 Name the most commonly used RTD configuration and explain why it is used.

8-24 Proportional-integral-derivative control is also referred to as:

a–continuous process control
b–three-mode, closed-loop feedback control
c–ratio control
d–open-loop control

8-25 What is the basic function of a PID control module?

8-26 Name at least three process variables that are typical inputs to a PID module.

8-27 For the following equation, define the terms K_P, K_i, and K_D and explain their main functions.

$$V_{out} = K_P E + K_i \int E\, dt + K_D \frac{dE}{dt}$$

8-28 Match the following terms with their appropriate descriptions.

_____ rate time   a–update time

_____ desired output   b–error dead band

_____ rate or period of update   c–set point

_____ linearized scaled output   d–square root extraction

_____ reset time   e–*Td*

_____ quantity compared to error   f–*Ti*
        signal

8-29 Using the following list of terms, fill in each blank in the PID algorithm block diagram shown in Figure 8-1 with the appropriate signal/device.

- D/A (digital-to-analog converter)
- A/D (analog-to-digital converter)
- SP (set point)
- P (proportional)
- I (integral)
- D (derivative)
- feedforward input
- digital filter
- $E = SP - PV$

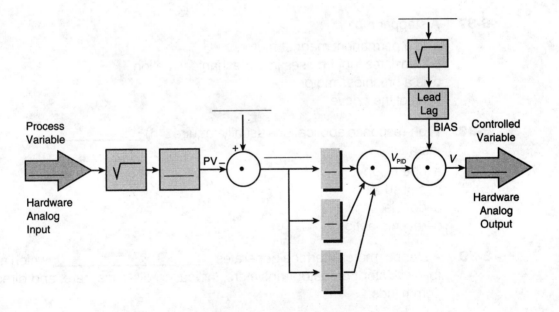

Figure 8-1. PID block diagram.

8-30 *True/False.* The square root function in a PID control module can be useful in flow control applications, where the square root of the pressure differential measurement is required.

8-31 Name two applications for encoder input modules.

8-32 Briefly explain the following:

(a) how an incremental encoder works

(b) how an absolute encoder works

8-33 An encoder input module's operation is _____ the processor and I/O scan.

a–dependent on
b–in series with
c–in parallel to
d–independent of

8-34 When an encoder/counter module is used in a counter configuration, how many input channels are wired to the device?

8-35 An encoder/counter module communicates with the PLC's processor in a(n) _____ manner.

a–bidirectional
b–unidirectional
c–interrupt
d–all of the above

8-36 *True/False.* The maximum length of the cable between an encoder/counter module and the encoder device should not exceed 50 feet.

8-37 A stepper motor:

a–is a permanent magnet motor
b–translates input pulses into mechanical motion
c–is a brushless motor
d–all of the above

8-38 High-response applications usually require a(n) _____ stepper motor interface.

a–open-loop
b–closed-loop
c–double
d–reverse-action

8-39 A stepper motor interface generates _____, which are compatible with stepper motor translators, indicating distance, rate, and direction motor commands.

8-40 The acceleration or deceleration of a stepper motor is determined by the _____ of output pulses.

8-41 Assuming that a 200-step motor is operating at half-stepping conditions (400 steps per revolution) and that the leadscrew has 4 threads per inch, determine:

(a) the linear displacement per step

(b) the step angle

8-42 The _____ portion of a move profile is the time specified to achieve the continuous speed rate of the motor (pulses/sec).

a–ramp
b–acceleration
c–deceleration
d–continuous rate

8-43 In the stepper motor block diagram shown in Figure 8-2, where would you place the element necessary to close the positioning loop and what would that element be?

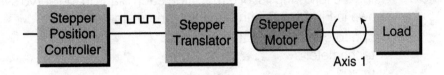

Figure 8-2. Stepper motor block diagram.

8-44 The two kinds of stepper motor profile modes are _____ and _____.

a–single-step (individual mode sequences)
b–single-step (block instructions)
c–continuous (individual mode sequences)
d–continuous (block instructions)
e–none of the above

8-45 *True/False.* Stepper motor loads with high inertia do not require large amounts of power for acceleration and deceleration.

8-46 Describe the difference between independent mode and synchronized mode in stepper motor axis control.

8-47 Sketch diagrams showing movement and speed rate for a two-axis stepper motor system in:

(a) independent mode

(b) synchronous mode

8-48 Briefly describe the operation of a servo interface module.

8-49 Servo interfaces are used in applications requiring:

a–temperature control
b–unidirectional communication
c–axis positioning
d–network interfaces

8-50 List three advantages that servo control has over clutch-gear systems when performing motion control.

8-51 *True/False*. The higher the velocity of the servo system, the lower the feedback positioning resolution.

8-52 Servo positioning controls operate in a(n) _____ system, requiring feedback in the form of velocity or _____.
   a–open-loop
   b–closed-loop
   c–position
   d–power
   e–pulses

8-53 Using the following list of terms, fill in each blank in the servo system block diagram shown in Figure 8-3 with the appropriate signal/device.
   - speed command (±10 VDC)
   - tachometer
   - motor
   - velocity feedback
   - position feedback
   - encoder
   - motor voltage

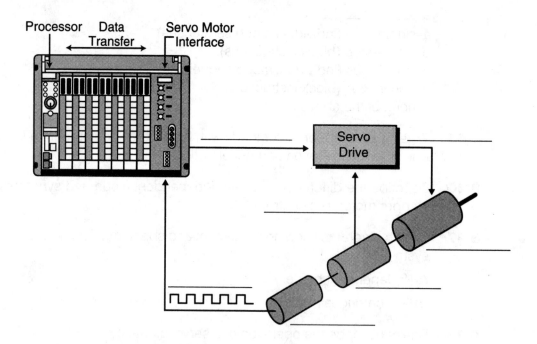

Figure 8-3. Servo system block diagram.

8-54 When implementing linear servo positioning systems, it is important to have a knowledge of:
   a–encoder pulses per revolution
   b–multiplier selection in the module
   c–leadscrew pitch
   d–all of the above

8-55 A servo interface is used in a PLC system to perform a one-axis positioning of metal parts. This part will be machined at a defined profile, which will be stored in the processor's memory. A leadscrew, which allows the axis to travel 3/16 inch per revolution, moves the part along an X-axis. A quadrature incremental encoder, which has a 200 kHz pulse frequency that provides 300 pulses per revolution, provides position feedback. The encoder is connected to an encoder feedback terminal in the servo interface, which provides a software programmable multiplier of ×1, ×2, and ×4 increments per pulse (x = times).

(a) Find the feedback resolution given that the part travels 12.5 inches.

(b) Determine the number of pulses that will be received given that the part travels 12.5 inches.

(c) How could the feedback resolution be doubled without changing the encoder?

8-56 For a leadscrew with a pitch of 1/16 inch, each rotation of the encoder feedback will mean:

a–62,500 pulses of feedback
b–travel of one inch
c–125,000 pulses of feedback
d–travel of 0.0625 inches

8-57 Explain what ASCII modules do and list two devices with which ASCII modules are used.

8-58 Which of the following is not a standard communication link for an ASCII serial communication module?

a–RS-232C
b–RS-422
c–parallel
d–20 mA loop

8-59 An ASCII module containing an on-board microprocessor transmits data _____ an ASCII module without a microprocessor.

a–faster than
b–slower than
c–at the same speed as
d–opposite of

8-60 Which of the following does not describe how nonintelligent ASCII modules transmit data?

a–one byte at a time
b–character by character
c–every two characters
d–on an interrupt basis

8-61 A PLC system, which has a scan time of approximately 8 msec, uses a standard nonintelligent ASCII module. The ASCII interface reads and writes information to and from a remote alphanumeric keyboard/display user interface. What is the maximum baud rate (bits per second) that can be used for proper transmission?

8-62 BASIC modules are also called _____ because they are capable of performing computational tasks without burdening the processor.

8-63 *True/False.* Communication between BASIC modules and the processor generally occurs through transfer instructions.

8-64 Explain the function and operation of network interface modules.

8-65 Fuzzy logic algorithms use rules that are based on _____ and

_____.

    a–IF conditions
    b–IF actions
    c–IF/THEN actions
    d–THEN conditions
    e–THEN actions

8-66 *True/False.* Fuzzy logic modules use fuzzy sets to describe inputs and outputs.

8-67 For the following list of standards, label the ones that are proclaimed with a *P* and the ones that are de facto with a *D*.

    _____ EIA RS-232C

    _____ IEEE 488

    _____ 20 mA current loop

    _____ EIA RS-422

    _____ EIA RS-485

8-68 Serial communication allows peripheral devices to receive _____ information from a PLC.

8-69 _____ is a bidirectional data communication configuration that allows data to be sent in either direction (but in only one direction at a time), while _____ is a bidirectional configuration that allows data to be sent in both directions simultaneously through two lines.

8-70 An RS-232C standard connector has _____ possible signal lines.

8-71 Describe three electrical characteristics of the RS-232C standard.

8-72 Match the following standards with their appropriate descriptions:

    _____ network compatible   a–RS-449

    _____ mechanical specification   b–RS-232C

    _____ TTY serial interface   c–RS-485

    _____ balanced link   d–RS-422

    _____ unbalanced link   e–20 mA current loop

8-73 Using the graph in Figure 8-4, sketch the relationship between distance and data rate for the RS-232C and RS-422 standards (with and without termination).

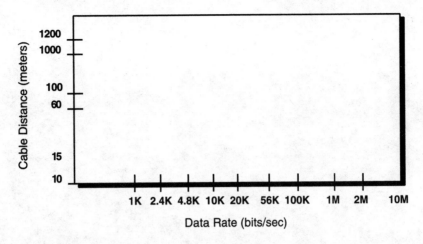

Figure 8-4. Relationship between the RS-232C and RS-422 standards.

8-74 Which of the following wires is <u>not</u> present in a 20 mA current loop?
a–transmit plus
b–receive minus
c–receive plus
d–signal ground

PROGRAMMING
LANGUAGES

CHAPTER 9 STUDY GUIDE

- Programming languages provide PLCs with the instructions necessary for implementing versatile control programs. Three PLC programming languages are:
  - ladder
  - Boolean
  - Grafcet

- Ladder language, which is based on relay ladder symbols, is the most common PLC programming language. The two types of ladder language are *basic ladder language* and *enhanced ladder language*.
  - Basic ladder language includes low-level instructions, such as ladder relay, timing, counting, and some arithmetic and data manipulation instructions.
  - Enhanced ladder language includes high-level instructions and function blocks, such as data transfer, sequencing, and network communication instructions.

- Boolean language uses Boolean logic functions to express the control program. This language, which is displayed on the monitor as ladder language, is primarily a program entry method rather than an instruction-oriented programming language.

- Grafcet is a structural programming method that uses a flowchart-like symbology to express the control program.

- Ladder diagram language expresses the control logic through *rungs*. A rung consists of a set of input conditions (represented by contact instructions) and an output condition (represented by a coil symbol).
  - A ladder rung is TRUE (i.e., energizing an output or functional block instruction) if it has power continuity. It is FALSE (i.e., not energizing an output or functional block instruction) if no power continuity exists.
  - The *ladder rung matrix* defines how many elements, including the output coil, may be programmed in a PLC's rung.

- A ladder diagram may use either individual instructions or functional blocks to implement the control logic.
  - Individual instructions perform each activity in the control logic separately. They can have only one input and one output.
  - Functional blocks, which may have several inputs and outputs, perform several instructions at one time.

- Ladder diagram instructions can be grouped into the following categories:
  - ladder relay
  - timing
  - counting
  - program/flow control
  - arithmetic

- data manipulation
- data transfer
- special function
- network communication

- **Ladder relay instructions** use coil and contact symbols to provide hardwired relay capabilities in a PLC. Ladder relay instructions include:
  - *examine ON/normally open*: tests for an ON condition in a reference address
  - *examine OFF/normally closed*: tests for an OFF condition in a reference address
  - *output coil*: turns a real or internal output ON when logic is 1
  - *NOT output coil*: turns a real or internal output OFF when logic is 1
  - *latch output coil*: keeps an output ON once it is energized
  - *unlatch output coil*: resets a latched output
  - *one-shot output*: energizes an output for one scan or less
  - *transitional contact*: closes for one scan when a trigger contact makes a positive transition

- Ladder scan evaluation refers to the manner in which a PLC solves the control program. The processor solves the control program one rung at a time, starting at the first rung at the top of the program.

- A normally closed input device should be wired as a normally closed device but programmed as a normally open contact. This allows fail-safe operation of the device, even if its wires are cut.

- **Timer instructions** implement hardware timer functions in a PLC. These instructions, which may have one or more selectable time bases that they use to time events, include the following:
  - *ON-delay energize timer*: energizes an output after a set time period when logic 1 exists
  - *ON-delay de-energize timer*: de-energizes an output after a set time period when logic 1 exists
  - *OFF-delay energize timer*: energizes an output after a set time period when logic 0 exists
  - *OFF-delay de-energize timer*: de-energizes an output after a set time period when logic 0 exists
  - *retentive ON-delay timer*: energizes an output after a set time period when logic 1 exists and then retains the accumulated value
  - *retentive timer reset*: resets the accumulated value of a retentive timer

- **Counter instructions** count the number of times an event occurs, storing the target count value in a preset register and the actual count value in an accumulated register. Counter instructions include:
  - *up counter*: increases the accumulated register value every time a referenced event occurs

- *down counter*: decreases the accumulated register value every time a referenced event occurs
- *counter reset*: resets an up or down counter's accumulated value

- **Program/flow control instructions** direct the flow of operations and the execution of instructions within a ladder program. Program/flow control functions include:
  - *master control relay*: activates or deactivates the execution of a group of ladder rungs
  - *zone control last state*: determines whether a group of ladder rungs will be evaluated
  - *jump to*: jumps to a specified rung in the program if certain conditions exist
  - *go to subroutine*: goes to a specified subroutine in the program
  - *label*: identifies the target rung of a jump to or go to subroutine instruction
  - *return*: terminates a ladder subroutine
  - *end*: identifies the last rung of a master control relay or zone control last state instruction

- **Arithmetic instructions** perform individual and function block mathematical operations on PLC data. They can use either *single-precision* or *double-precision* arithmetic.
  - Single-precision arithmetic holds the values of the operands and the result in one register each (sometimes two registers for the result of multiplication and division operations).
  - Double-precision arithmetic instructions use twice the number of registers as single-precision instructions to hold the operand and result values.

- Arithmetic instructions include:
  - *addition*: adds the values stored in two registers
  - *subtraction*: subtracts the values stored in two registers
  - *multiplication*: multiplies the values stored in two registers
  - *division*: finds the quotient of the values in two registers
  - *square root*: finds the square root of a register value

- **Data manipulation instructions** allow multibit operations on data located in one, two, or more registers. The types of data manipulation instructions include:
  - *data comparison*: compares the values stored in two registers
  - *logic matrix*: performs logic operations on two or more registers
  - *data conversion*: changes the contents of a register to another format
  - *set constant parameters*: assigns a fixed value to a register
  - *increment*: increases the contents of a register by one
  - *shift*: moves the bits in a register to the right or left
  - *rotate*: shifts register bits right or left and moves the shifted-out bit to the other end of the register
  - *examine bit*: examines the status of a single bit in a memory location

- **Data transfer instructions**, which move numerical data within a PLC, include:
  - *move*: transfers information from one register to another
  - *move block*: moves data from a group of register locations to another location
  - *table move*: transfers data from a block or table to a register
  - *block transfer*: stores a block of data in specified memory or register locations
  - *ASCII transfer*: transmits ASCII data between a peripheral device and a PLC
  - *FIFO transfer*: constructs a table or queue for storing data
  - *sort*: sorts the data in a block of registers in ascending or descending order

- **Special function instructions** allow specialized operations in a PLC. These special instructions include:
  - *sequencer*: outputs data in a time-driven or event-driven manner
  - *diagnostic*: compares actual input data with reference data
  - *PID*: provides closed-loop control of a process

- **Network communication instructions** facilitate communication among PLCs connected to a local area network. These instructions include:
  - *network output*: passes one-bit status information from a PLC to a network
  - *network contact*: captures status information from a network output
  - *network send*: sends register information to a network
  - *network receive*: captures available register information in a network
  - *send node*: transmits register data to a specific node in a network
  - *get node*: retrieves register data from a specific node in a network

- A complete Boolean instruction set uses Boolean logical operators and other mnemonic instructions to implement basic and enhanced control functions.

REVIEW QUESTIONS

9-1 _____ is a symbolic instruction set that uses basic relay symbols to create a PLC program.

9-2 *True/False.* Functional blocks are a part of basic ladder language.

9-3 Name at least seven categories of instructions that form the PLC ladder programming language.

9-4 For users familiar with relay logic, the PLC language best suited for a relay replacement application is _____.
a–Boolean
b–BASIC
c–ladder diagram
d–Grafcet

9-5 The programming language that uses AND, OR, and NOT logic functions to implement the control program is called _____.

9-6 Fill in the blanks in the Grafcet program shown in Figure 9-1 with the following terms:
- transition
- action
- step

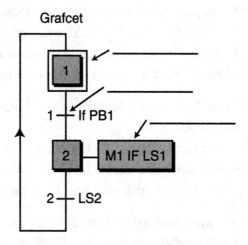

Figure 9-1. Grafcet program.

9-7 *True/False.* The ladder diagram instruction set is often referred to as contact symbology.

9-8 Explain a ladder rung's structure.

9-9 _____ and _____ are the basic symbols of the ladder diagram instruction set.
a–transitions
b–contacts
c–gates
d–steps
e–coils

9-10 *True/False.* The left side of a PLC ladder diagram rung simulates the L1 power line.

9-11 All of the outputs in a ladder diagram control program are represented by

_____.

a–contact symbols
b–coil symbols
c–a or b
d–none of the above

9-12 To provide logic continuity, the power in a ladder rung must flow from

_____.

a–left to right
b–right to left
c–top to bottom
d–top to end of scan

9-13 How would you program a functional block instruction whose execution does not require that any logic conditions be enabled?

9-14 *True/False.* Most PLCs allow reverse power flow.

9-15 For the ladder circuit in Figure 9-2, which of the following sequences of closed contacts would <u>not</u> energize output coil 50?

a–contacts 5, 6, and 7 closed
b–contacts 5, 6, 8, and 9 closed
c–contacts 10, 11, 8, and 7 closed
d–contacts 10, 11, and 9 closed

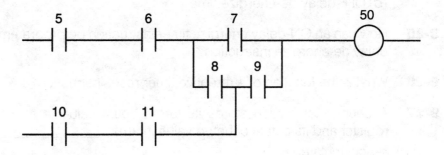

Figure 9-2. Ladder circuit.

9-16 Redraw the ladder circuit shown in Figure 9-2 so that all the contact sequences listed in question 9-15 will energize the output coil.

9-17 For what purpose is an output coil instruction used?

9-18 How is a latched coil condition reset?

9-19 What must occur for a transitional contact instruction to provide a one-shot pulse?

9-20 *True/False.* For an output to control another rung during the same scan, the output must be programmed before that rung.

9-21 Complete the ladder rung shown in Figure 9-3 so that the normally closed push button is wired in a fail-safe manner.

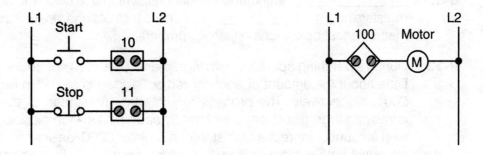

Figure 9-3. Ladder rung with normally closed input device.

9-22 A(n) _____ instruction stops timing when logic continuity is lost; however, it retains the accumulated register value.

9-23 A relay in a PLC's control program requires a delay of 9 cycles at 60 Hz (cycles per second). The PLC's timer instruction has a time base of 0.01 seconds. How many ticks must the timer instruction count to create the delay required by the relay?

9-24 Describe the functions of the following timer instructions:

(a) ON-delay energize timer

(b) ON-delay de-energize timer

(c) OFF-delay energize timer

(d) OFF-delay de-energize timer

9-25 How can an ON-delay energize timer instruction be programmed to act as an ON-delay de-energize instruction?

9-26 What is the function of a retentive timer reset instruction?

9-27 A counter instruction stores its target count value in a(n) _____ register and its actual counted value in a(n) _____ register.

a–accumulated
b–target
c–reference
d–preset
e–cumulative

9-28 An up counter increments its counted value each time its referenced event makes a(n) _____ transition.

a–ON-to-OFF
b–OFF-to-ON
c–left-to-right
d–all of the above

9-29 Describe the function of a master control relay instruction.

9-30 Explain how to create a reserved subroutine area in a PLC.

9-31 A(n) _____ instruction is used to terminate a ladder subroutine.

9-32 _____ arithmetic instructions, which use twice the number of storage registers as _____ arithmetic instructions, are used when performing mathematical operations on large numbers.

9-33 During a batching operation, two ingredients (A and B) are added to a mixing tank. Data about the amount of each ingredient added is stored in registers 2000 and 2001, respectively. The process requires the monitoring of the total amount of combined ingredients once a normally open limit switch closes. The value of the total amount of ingredients is stored in register 3000, and a pilot light is turned on once this data is stored. Draw the ladder diagram for this process using a block format instruction.

9-34 *True/False.* The notation shown in Figure 9-4a is a better way of expressing an arithmetic instruction than the notation in Figure 9-4b.

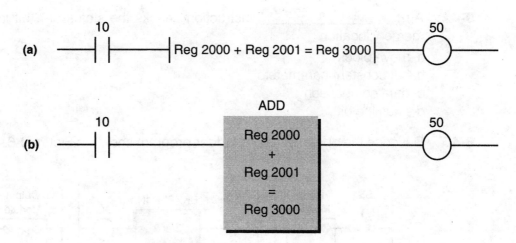

Figure 9-4. Arithmetic instructions: **(a)** contact and **(b)** function block.

9-35 In some controllers, a subtraction instruction can be used to implement a(n) _____ instruction.

a–rotate
b–division
c–data conversion
d–I/O transfer

9-36 Describe the operation of the arithmetic ladder program in Figure 9-5.

```
        100                                              50
  ──┤ ├──┤ ├──┤Reg 2001 MUL Reg 2003 = Reg 3000├──( )──
```

Figure 9-5. Arithmetic ladder program.

9-37 Division block instructions can have up to three possible outputs. Describe what each of these three outputs indicates.

9-38 *True/False.* A compare functional block compares the contents of two or more registers.

9-39 Name at least four conversion operations that are performed with data conversion block instructions.

9-40 Which of the following instructions performs AND, OR, NAND, exclusive-OR, NOR, and NOT operations on two or more registers?

a–data conversion
b–logic matrix
c–set constant parameters
d–logic conversion

9-41 *True/False.* When a rotate-right instruction is executed, the least significant bit of the register is lost.

9-42 A(n) _____ instruction checks the status of a bit in a register or memory location.

a–move block
b–set constant parameters
c–data comparison
d–examine bit

9-43 Describe the operation of the ladder program shown in Figure 9-6.

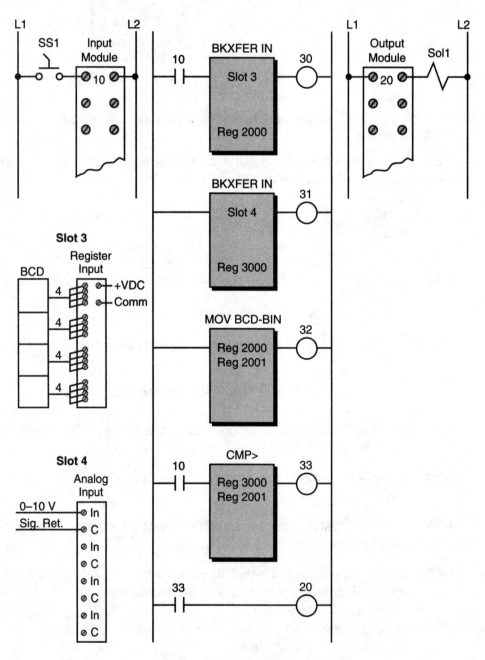

Figure 9-6. Ladder program.

9-44 A(n) _____ instruction copies a group of registers from one location to another.

9-45 Which of the following instructions transmits alphanumeric characters from a PLC to a peripheral device?
a–FIFO transfer
b–block transfer in/out
c–ASCII transfer
d–sequencer

9-46 For the move mask instruction illustrated in Figure 9-7, show the contents of register 1500 after the instruction has been executed.

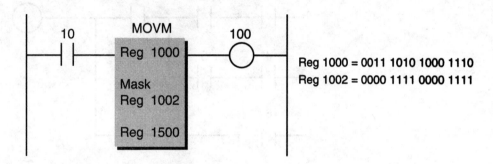

Reg 1000 = 0011 1010 1000 1110
Reg 1002 = 0000 1111 0000 1111

Figure 9-7. Move mask instruction.

9-47 _____ instructions are useful for creating routines that inform the operator of a machine malfunction.
a–sequencer
b–diagnostic
c–PID
d–network

9-48 A(n) _____ functional block provides closed-loop control of a process according to user-defined algorithms based on three control modes.

9-49 *True/False.* A network send instruction sends information to the network, where it is available to anyone.

9-50 Match the following instructions with their appropriate descriptions:

_____ sends data to a specific network node

_____ obtains information from a specific network PLC

_____ captures status data from the network

_____ obtains information from the network

_____ sends one-bit status data to the network

a–network receive

b–network output

c–send node

d–network contact

e–get node

9-51 Using Boolean instructions, write the control sequences for each of the following ladder programs:

(a)

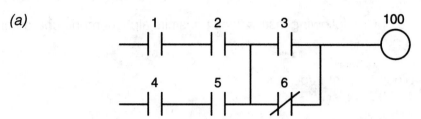

(b)

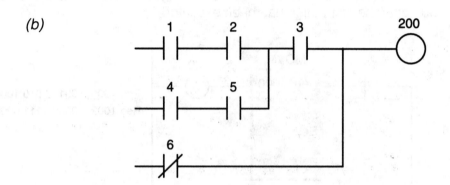

(c)

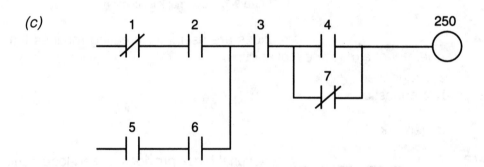

9-52 Draw the ladder diagrams that correspond to the following Boolean programs:

(a) LD 1	*(b)* LD 1	*(c)* LD NOT 1
OR 3	AND 2	AND 2
LD 2	LD 4	LD 4
OR 4	AND 5	OR 7
AND LD	OR LD	AND 5
LD 5	OR 7	OR LD
OR 7	LD 3	LD 3
AND 6	OR NOT 6	OR NOT 6
OR LD	AND LD	AND LD
OUT 300		OR NOT 8
		OUT 450
		AND 9
		OUT 500
		AND NOT 10
		OUT 600

THE IEC 1131 STANDARD AND PROGRAMMING LANGUAGE

CHAPTER 10 STUDY GUIDE

- The IEC 1131 programming standard is an international standard that strives to create a common set of instructions for all PLCs. This standard consists of five sections:
  - general information
  - equipment and test requirements
  - programming languages
  - user guidelines
  - messaging services (communications)

- The IEC 1131 programming language standard is referred to as the IEC 1131-3, since the third section of the IEC 1131 discusses programming languages.

- The IEC 1131-3 standard provides four programming languages, two graphical and two text based, for use in PLC programming.
  - The two graphical languages used with the IEC 1131-3 are *ladder diagrams* (LD) and *function block diagram* (FBD).
  - The two text-based languages are *instruction list* (IL) and *structured text* (ST).

- The IEC 1131-3 includes an object-oriented programming framework—*sequential function charts* (SFC)—with which the other four programming languages are used.

- All variables in an IEC 1131-3 system must be "declared;" that is, the user must specify the data variable type, name, and address. The three types of variables used in PLC programming are Boolean, integer, and real variables.
  - *Boolean variables* are single-bit, discrete variables.
  - *Integer variables* are analog variables containing data in the form of whole numbers.
  - *Real variables* are analog variables containing fractional and floating-point data.

- The ladder diagram language, which is essentially the same language that has always been used to program PLCs, uses a standardized set of ladder programming symbols to implement control functions.

- Function block diagram is a graphical language that uses instruction blocks, which when programmed look like an electrical circuit diagram, to represent the control program. FBD uses both standard and vendor-defined function blocks. It also allows users to create their own blocks.

- Instruction list is a text-based language, similar to assembly language, that is used to create low-level control programs for small or specific applications.

- Structured text is a high-level language that allows complex tasks to be broken down into many smaller tasks, which are then executed as required.

- Sequential function chart is a flowchart-like framework that organizes the subroutines, programmed in LD, FBD, IL, and/or ST, that form the control program.

- SFCs use three main elements to organize the control program: steps, actions, and transitions.
    - A *step* is a stage in the control process.
    - An *action* is a set of instructions prompting the PLC to execute a certain control function during a step.
    - A *transition* moves the PLC from one step to another.

- SFCs also use *macrosteps*, which allow a master sequential function chart to have smaller sequential function charts as its actions. These smaller, embedded SFCs have their own steps, actions, and transitions.

- The programming notation used in each of the four IEC 1131-3 programming languages is very similar. Sometimes, differentiation mnemonics are used to define the beginning and ending of commands programmed in different languages.

- A sequential function chart represents a process's order of events in a sequential manner, using an X*step number* and Y*transition number* notation to distinguish between steps and transitions.

- SFCs are classified by levels, which specify how much detail the charts show.
    - Level 0 charts show only step numbers and transition numbers.
    - Level 1 charts provide labels for the steps and transitions indicating the actions and conditions that occur, respectively, during these process elements.
    - Level 2 charts list the instructions that implement the control actions in the SFC's steps.

- The term *Boolean activity*, or *Boolean attribute*, refers to the ON/OFF status of a step or transition. A dot, or *token*, in a step or transition indicates that it is active.

- SFCs contain two types of transitions: leading edge and trailing edge. Both of these types of transitions can include a timing element that determines how long the associated step will be active.
    - In a *leading-edge transition*, the turning ON of the triggering signal will initiate the transition.
    - In a *trailing-edge transition*, the turning OFF of the triggering signal will initiate the transition.

- As with other programming formats, normally closed devices should be implemented as normally open when using the IEC 1131-3 standard. Moreover, transitions used with these devices should be programmed carefully to obtain the proper device behavior.

- SFCs can have two types of multiple links between their steps and transitions: divergences and convergences.
    - A *divergence* occurs when an SFC element has many links going out of it.
    - A *convergence* occurs when an SFC element has many links coming into it.

- There are two types of divergence and convergence links: OR type and AND type.
  - An *OR divergence*, also called a single divergence, connects one step to many transitions, with only one transition receiving the token from the step.
  - An *OR convergence*, also called a single convergence, links several transitions to the same step, with the step receiving the token from only one of the transitions.
  - An *AND divergence*, or double divergence, links one transition to many steps in parallel form, so that the transition passes control to all of the steps at the same time.
  - An *AND convergence*, or double convergence, links multiple steps to a single transition, meaning that all the steps before the transition must be active before the transition can receive the token.

- Sequential function chart programs can use *subprograms* (smaller, embedded programs) to implement specialized control sequences.
  - Subprograms can be written in any of the IEC 1131-3 languages and can be called directly from an SFC action or transition, again in any of the four languages.
  - Unlike custom blocks and macrosteps, subprograms can pass and receive data to and from the main program.

- A step's action can be either a Boolean action, pulse action, normal action, or SFC action, depending on the desired operation and result. An action can also be a stand-alone action.
  - A *Boolean action* assigns a discrete (ON/OFF) value to a variable during a step's action.
  - A *pulse action* executes one or more instructions in a step's action only once while the step is active.
  - A *normal action*, or nonstored action, executes the instructions in a step continuously while the step is activated.
  - An *SFC action* is a child-type SFC program that can be activated or deactivated when the step is active.
  - A *stand-alone action* acts as an interrupt jump to instruction in the program, specifying which chart program and step to go to.

- Many software manufacturers incorporate IEC 1131 programming standards into their software systems, thus creating "soft PLCs" (i.e., non-PLC devices that operate like PLCs). Moreover, some PLC manufacturers provide their own programmable controller languages that emulate the IEC 1131 standard.

REVIEW QUESTIONS

10-1 Which of the following is <u>not</u> a part of the IEC 1131 programming standard?
a–user guidelines
b–equipment requirements
c–communications
d–application guidelines

10-2 For the following list of IEC 1131-3 programming languages, place a *T* beside the text-based ones, a *G* beside the graphic-oriented ones, and an *F* beside the one that is a programming framework:

_____ structured text

_____ ladder diagrams

_____ sequential function charts

_____ function block diagram

_____ instruction list

10-3 List three types of data variables, three types of data functions, and three types of function blocks.

10-4 _____ variables are discrete variables containing single-bit data, while _____ and _____ variables are continuous variables containing whole number and fractional data, respectively.

10-5 *True/False.* The ladder programming language used in the IEC 1131-3 is similar to the ladder diagrams that have always been used in PLCs.

10-6 The creation of a custom function block that can be used as needed in the control program is known as _____.

a–generation
b–encapsulation
c–composition
d–origination

10-7 In what language is the function block shown in Figure 10-1 programmed?

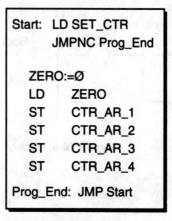

```
Start:   LD SET_CTR
         JMPNC Prog_End

   ZERO:=Ø
   LD      ZERO
   ST      CTR_AR_1
   ST      CTR_AR_2
   ST      CTR_AR_3
   ST      CTR_AR_4

Prog_End:  JMP Start
```

Figure 10-1. IEC 1131-3 function block.

10-8 *True/False.* Structured text language does not support conditional programming statements.

10-9 Draw a simple sequential function chart illustrating a step, a transition, and an action.

10-10 Draw the SFC chart that corresponds to the batching operation timing diagram shown in Figure 10-2.

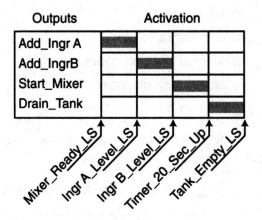

Figure 10-2. Batching operation timing diagram.

10-11 An embedded SFC program that is the action of a larger SFC program's step is called a(n) _____.

10-12 Figure 10-3 shows an electromechanical relay circuit and the variable declaration for its elements. Draw its PLC-equivalent program in:

(a) ladder diagram

(b) function block diagram

(c) structured text

(d) instruction list

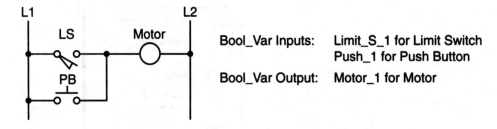

Figure 10-3. Electromechanical relay circuit.

10-13 Match the following types of SFC charts with their appropriate descriptions:

_____ level 0   a–shows action and transition names

_____ level 1   b–shows the action instructions

_____ level 2   c–lists only step and transition numbers

10-14 The ON/OFF status of an SFC element is referred to as its _____.

10-15 *True/False.* The turning OFF of a triggering signal will initiate a leading-edge transition.

10-16 Draw the timing diagrams for the following SFCs given that Push_1 is a normally open push button and Limit_Switch is a normally closed limit switch:

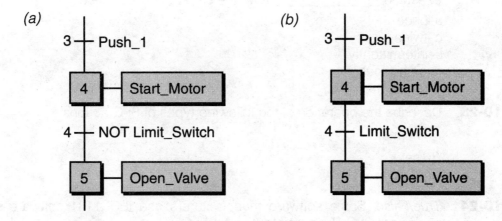

10-17 Match the following types of convergences and divergences with their appropriate definitions:

_____ OR convergence   a–connects one step to many transitions

_____ AND divergence   b–connects one transition to many steps

_____ AND convergence   c–connects many transitions to one step

_____ OR divergence   d–connects many steps to one transition

10-18 Subprograms differ from macrosteps and custom function blocks because they:

a–can be written in any of the IEC 1131-3 programming languages
b–can communicate data with the main program
c–can be initiated from an SFC action
d–initiate a small control program within a larger SFC program

10-19 *True/False*. A subprogram can be called from either an SFC action or transition.

10-20 Using Boolean actions, create a sequential function chart that implements the motor activity shown in Figure 10-4 given that the closing of Limit_S_1 initiates the motor sequence and that the reset push button can stop the sequence at any time.

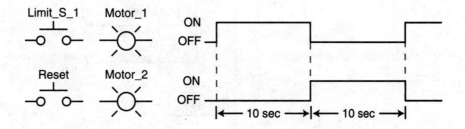

Figure 10-4. Motor sequence.

10-21 Describe how a stand-alone action operates.

10-22 In a pulse action, the instructions in the step's action are executed _____ after the step becomes active; however, in a normal action, the instructions are executed _____ after the step becomes active.

a–once
b–twice
c–intermittently
d–continuously
e–randomly

10-23 Describe the operation of the following types of SFC actions:

(a) normal

(b) set

(c) reset

10-24 *True/False.* Some software manufacturers use IEC 1131 software systems to implement PLC-like control without a PLC.

10-25 Draw the level 1 SFC equivalent of the RLL Plus program shown in Figure 10-5.

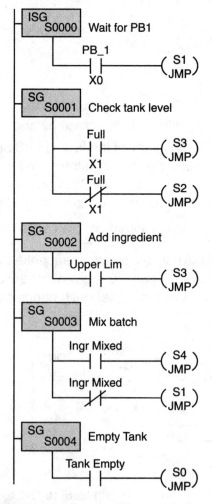

Figure 10-5. RLL Plus program for a batching application.

10-26 List three IEC 1131-3 programming guidelines and two troubleshooting guidelines.

SYSTEM PROGRAMMING AND IMPLEMENTATION

CHAPTER 11 STUDY GUIDE

- The first step in developing a control program is the definition of the *control task*. The control task specifies what needs to be done and is defined by those who are involved in the operation of the machine or process.

- The second step in control program development is to determine a *control strategy*, the sequence of processing steps that must occur within a program to produce the desired output control. This is also known as the development of an algorithm.

- A set of guidelines should be followed during program organization and implementation in order to develop an organized system. Approach guidelines apply to two major types of projects: new applications and modernizations of existing equipment.

- *Flowcharting* can be used to plan a program after a written description has been developed. A flowchart is a pictorial representation of the process that records, analyzes, and communicates information, as well as defines the sequence of the process.

- Logic gates or contact symbology are used to implement the logic sequences in a control program. Inputs and outputs marked with an "X" on a logic gate diagram represent real I/O.

- Three important documents that provide information about the arrangement of the PLC system are the I/O assignment table, the internal address assignment table, and the register address assignment table.
  - The *I/O assignment table* documents the names, locations, and descriptions of the real inputs and outputs.
  - The *internal address assignment table* records the locations and descriptions of internal outputs, registers, timers, counters, and MCRs.
  - The *register address assignment table* lists all of the available PLC registers.

- Certain parts of the system should be left hardwired for safety reasons. Elements such as emergency stops and master start push buttons should be left hardwired so that the system can be disabled without PLC intervention.

- Special cases of input device programming include the program translation of normally closed input devices, fenced MCR circuits, circuits that allow bidirectional power flow, instantaneous timer contacts, and complicated logic rungs.
  - The programming of contacts as normally open or normally closed depends on how they are required to operate in the logic program. In most cases, if a normally closed input device is required to act as a normally closed input, its reference address is programmed as normally open.

- Master control relays turn ON and OFF power to certain logic rungs. In a PLC program, an END MCR instruction must be placed after the last rung an MCR will control.

- PLCs do not allow bidirectional power flow, so all PLC rungs must be programmed to operate only in a forward path.

- PLCs do not provide instantaneous contacts; therefore, an internal output must be used to trap a timer that requires these contacts.

- Complicated logic rungs should be isolated from the other rungs during programming.

• Program coding is the process of translating a logic or relay diagram into PLC ladder program form.

• The benefits of modernizing a relay control system include greater reliability, less energy consumption, less space utilization, and greater flexibility.

REVIEW QUESTIONS

11-1 What is the first step in designing an effective PLC control system?

a–approach the system in a systematic manner
b–flowchart the process
c–define the control task
d–define the control strategy

11-2 A(n) _____ is a procedure that uses a finite number of steps to achieve a desired outcome.

11-3 List four guidelines that are recommended as an approach to modernizing a control system.

11-4 In a modernization project, an existing _____ often defines the sequence of events in the control program.

11-5 System operation for new applications usually begins with:

a–sample diagrams
b–specifications
c–the control strategy
d–logic diagrams

11-6 A(n) _____ is a graphical representation of a solution's algorithm.

11-7 Logic sequences for a control program can be created using:

a–logic gates
b–relay ladder symbology
c–PLC contact symbology
d–all of the above

11-8 Draw the equivalent logic gate diagram for the circuit shown in Figure 11-1.

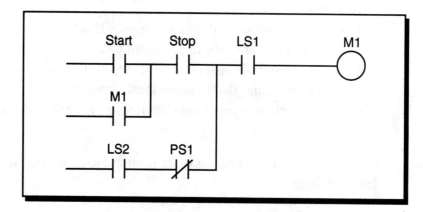

Figure 11-1. Circuit for problem 11-8.

11-9 Draw the equivalent contact symbology diagram for the logic gates shown in Figure 11-2.

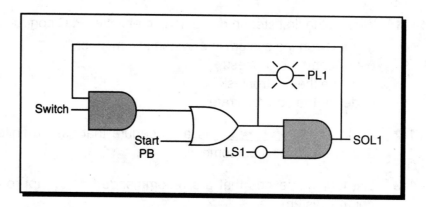

Figure 11-2. Logic gates for problem 11-9.

11-10 *True/False.* Only real inputs and outputs are documented during address assignment.

11-11 I/O address assignments are typically represented in one of three number systems: _____, _____, or _____.

11-12 The I/O address assignment table should closely follow the _____.

11-13 Using the circuit shown in Figure 11-3 and assuming that the PLC has a modularity of 8 points per module, there are eight modules per rack, the master rack is numbered 0, and the number system is octal:

(a) circle all real inputs and outputs

(b) assign the I/O addresses

(c) draw the I/O connection diagram

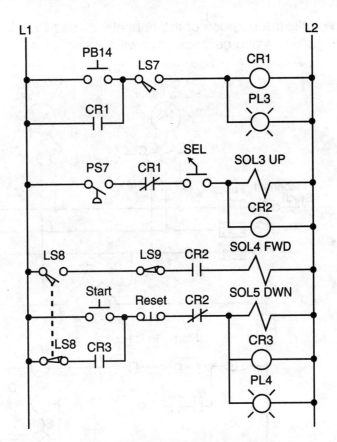

Figure 11-3. Circuit for problem 11-13.

11-14   The principle reason for leaving certain portions of the control circuit hardwired is to:

a–minimize wiring
b–avoid failure of main magnetic elements
c–ensure safety
d–keep some devices running at all times

11-15   The PLC fault contacts are wired to other hardwired emergency circuit elements:

a–in parallel
b–in series
c–normally open
d–normally closed

11-16   The main reason the PLC fault contacts are included in the hardwired circuit is:

a–to prevent system shut down
b–to detect I/O failures
c–to include the PLC as an emergency stop condition
d–to shut down the system if there is a PLC failure

11-17   Describe the purpose and operation of a safety control relay (SCR).

11-18   *True/False*. Normally closed input devices are always programmed normally open.

11-19 What is the purpose of the normally closed PLC fault contacts in the circuit in Figure 11-4 and describe what will happen if the PLC fails?

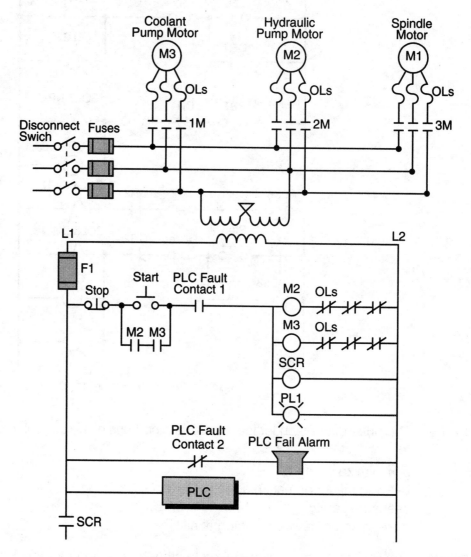

Figure 11-4. Circuit for problem 11-19.

11-20 Using the circuit shown in Figure 11-5 and starting inputs at address 10_8, outputs at address 50_8, and internals at address 100_8:

(a) assign the I/O addresses

(b) draw the equivalent PLC ladder diagram

11-21 *True/False.* In a PLC ladder program, an END MCR instruction must be used to fence the area controlled by a master control relay.

11-22 What element can be used to trap timers in a PLC control program?

a–a reset instruction
b–a start push button
c–a pilot light
d–an internal output

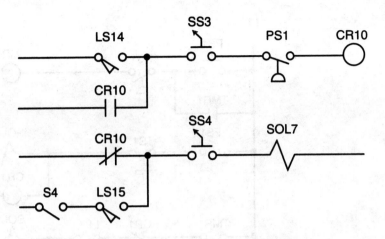

Figure 11-5. Circuit for problem 11-20.

11-23 Explain why the hardwired circuit in Figure 11-6 must be reconfigured when it is translated into a PLC ladder diagram.

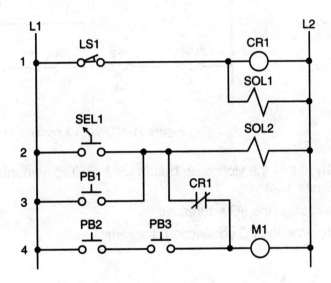

Figure 11-6. Circuit for problem 11-23.

11-24 Program _____ is the process of translating logic or relay contact diagrams into PLC ladder form.

11-25 Assuming that inputs use addresses 000–027, outputs use addresses 030–047, internals start at address 100_8, timers start at address 200_8, and an internal output is used to trap the instantaneous timer contacts, use the circuit shown in Figure 11-7 to:

(a) assign the internal addresses

(b) assign the I/O addresses

(c) draw the I/O connection diagram

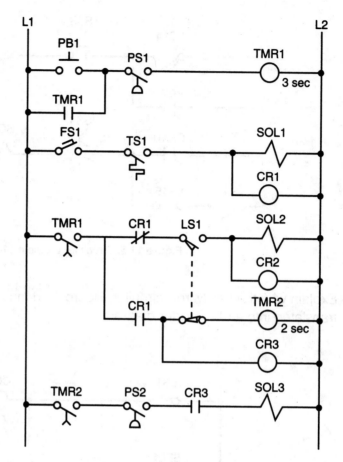

Figure 11-7. Circuit for problem 11-25.

11-26 Given that the stop push button will be wired as normally open, use the circuit in Figure 11-8 to:

(a) assign the I/O addresses

(b) draw the I/O connection diagram

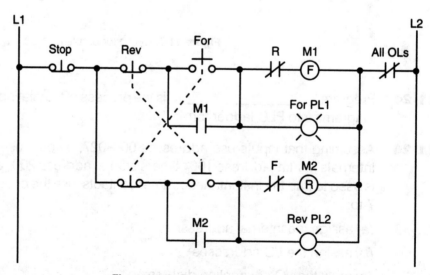

Figure 11-8. Circuit for problem 11-26.

11-27 Circle the locations where timer traps will be used in the PLC implementation of the circuit in Figure 11-9.

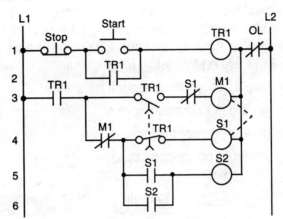

Figure 11-9. Circuit for problem 11-27.

11-28 Figure 11-10 shows a variable speed drive that is manually controlled by an operator station. What input field devices are required for the PLC implementation of this station?

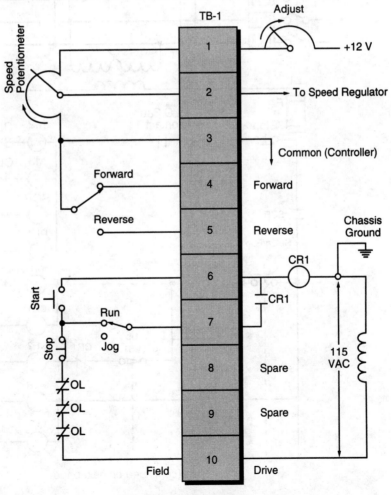

Figure 11-10. Variable speed drive.

11-29 The PLC implementation of the large relay circuit in Figure 11-11 should include a normally open PLC fault contact and use internals to trap the timers. The PLC system has capacity for 512 I/O (000 to 777 octal). Inputs should start at address 000_8 and outputs should start at address 030_8. Internals should have addresses 1000–1777, MCRs should have addresses 2000–2037, and timers should have addresses 2040–2137. Using this large relay circuit:

(a) indicate the portions to be left hardwired

(b) assign the I/O addresses

(c) assign the internal addresses

(d) draw the I/O connection diagram

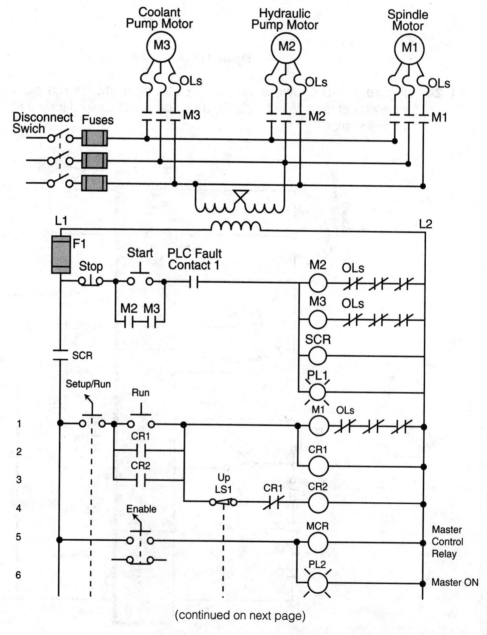

(continued on next page)

Figure 11-11. Large relay circuit.

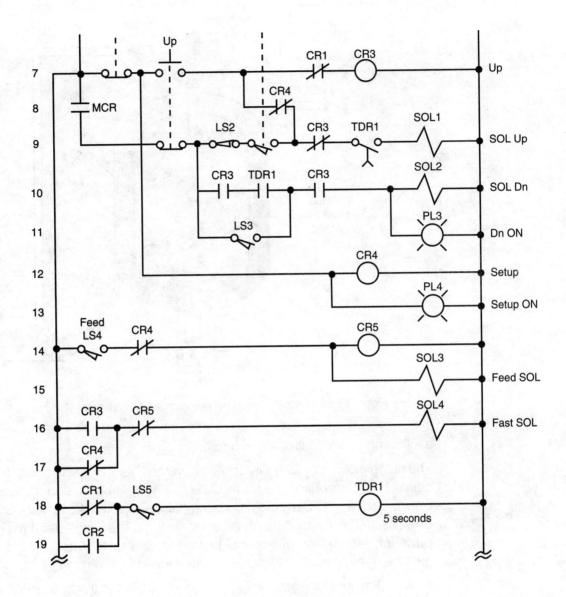

Figure 11-11 continued.

11-30 A look-up table stores _____ for use in the linear interpolation of nonlinear inputs.

11-31 Figure 11-12 illustrates a process flow diagram of a batching application. Two ingredients, A and B, will be mixed in the reactor tank. A cleanser will be used to clean the main line between additions. A pump motor provides the necessary pressure to send the ingredients through the lines. The pump is capable of forward or reverse flow.

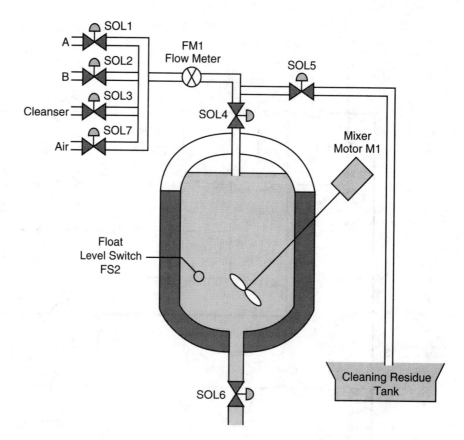

Figure 11-12. Process flow diagram of a batching application.

The following is the control algorithm:

- The pump motor is always ON and is activated by a 115 VAC Forward Pump (FP) signal. First, the controller adds ingredient A by opening solenoid valve 1 (SOL1). Solenoid valve 4 (SOL4) must be open (ON) and solenoid valve 5 (SOL5) must be closed (OFF) for ingredient A to enter the tank. The flow meter (FM1) emits one pulse for each gallon of material that enters the tank. When FM1 detects 500 gallons in the tank, SOL1 and SOL4 are closed.

- After 500 gallons of ingredient A have been added to the tank, the line must be cleaned. However, 83 gallons of ingredient A remain in the line. The controller initiates the Reserve Pump (RP) action to pump the remainder of ingredient A back into tank A. There is a 0.8 second delay when switching from FP to RP actions. The flushing is done when the flow meter does not emit any more pulses after 5 seconds.

- Before the line is cleaned, SOL1 and SOL4 must be OFF, and SOL5 must be open (ON) to dispose of the cleanser. Next, the controller opens SOL3, releasing the cleanser into the line. Once the flow meter detects 90 gallons of cleanser, SOL3 closes, stopping the flow of cleanser. The controller then opens SOL7 to let air flow in for 5 seconds.

- Then, the controller opens SOL2 to add 330 gallons of ingredient B to the tank. The controller follows the same adding procedures for ingredient B as were followed for ingredient A.

- Once the proper amounts of both ingredients are in the tank, the mixer motor (M1) will operate for five minutes (300 seconds). The Reverse Pump will be activated at the same time to flush the line of ingredient B.

- After the mixing is completed, the controller will open SOL6 to release the mixed batch into a finished tank.

For this system, start outputs at address 000_8, inputs at address 020_8, internals at address 1000_8, timers at address 2000_8, and counters at 2300_8. Implement the PLC control program by following these steps:

(a) diagram a flowchart of the process

(b) implement the logic using logic gates, contact symbology, or both

(c) assign the I/O addresses

(d) assign the internal addresses

(e) draw the I/O connection diagram

11-32 The number of parallel branches required in a logic sequence can be _____ by using an internal storage bit.

11-33 *True/False.* An exclusive-OR circuit allows two conditions to activate the same output simultaneously.

11-34 *True/False.* A one-shot output can be ON for less than one scan.

11-35 Draw the timing diagram for the circuit in Figure 11-13 for a preset value of 1 second. Indicate the time between pulses.

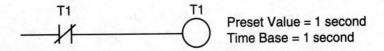

Preset Value = 1 second
Time Base = 1 second

Figure 11-13. Circuit for problem 11-35.

11-36 Implement the PLC program coding for the circuit in Figure 11-14 eliminating any possible bidirectional power flow.

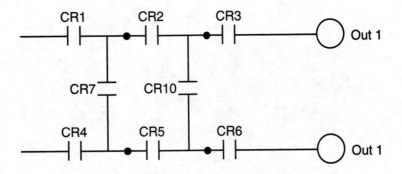

Figure 11-14. Circuit for problem 11-36.

11-37 Counting beyond 9999 BCD, the maximum count a register can hold, can be achieved by:

a–changing number systems

b–cascading two counters

c–adding a zero to the end of the count

d–connecting two registers

PLC SYSTEM DOCUMENTATION

CHAPTER 12 STUDY GUIDE

- Documentation is orderly recorded information about both the operation of a machine or process and the hardware and software components that comprise its control system.

- The components of a good documentation package include:
  - the system abstract
  - the system configuration
  - the I/O wiring connection diagram
  - the I/O address assignment document
  - the internal storage address assignment document
  - the storage register assignment document
  - the variable declaration
  - the control program printout
  - the stored control program

- The system abstract is a statement of the control problem or task that includes a description of the design strategy and a statement of the control objectives.

- The system configuration is a simplified drawing of the hardware elements defined in the system abstract, including their location, connections, and minimum details.

- The I/O wiring connection diagram shows the actual connections of the field input and output devices. This diagram includes the power supplies and subsystem connections to the CPU.

- The I/O address assignment document identifies each field device by address, type of module, type of field device, and the function the device performs in the field.

- The internal storage address assignment document lists the address, type, and function of each internal output in the control program.

- The storage register assignment document describes the contents of each of the storage registers.

- The variable declaration lists the name of each input, output, or internal variable, along with its address and description.

- The control program printout is a hard copy of the control logic program stored in the controller's memory.

- The control program should be stored on a transportable medium, such as a cassette tape or a floppy disk, so that it can be transported easily to the installation site.

- Documentation systems speed up the documentation process and reduce the manpower required to complete the task.

REVIEW QUESTIONS

12-1 The _____ package can be defined as an orderly collection of recorded information that describes not only the software and hardware components of a system, but also the operation of the machine or process control.

12-2 *True/False.* The documentation of a control system should start in the final design stage.

12-3 *True/False.* Proper documentation is part of an ongoing process of recording descriptive details concerning the application software.

12-4 Which of the following is not part of the documentation package?

a–internal I/O address assignment
b–program printout
c–system configuration
d–usage of ladder instructions

12-5 Create the I/O address assignment table for the wiring connection diagram in Figure 12-1.

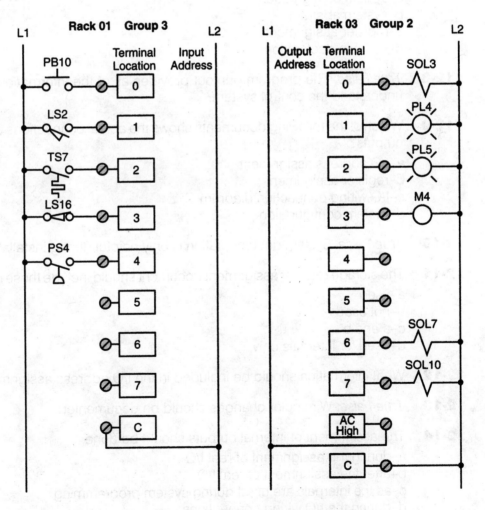

Figure 12-1. I/O wiring connection diagram.

12-6 Draw a system arrangement diagram for a system with the following specifications:

- The PLC system has a main CPU connected to a minicomputer through an RS-232C port. Both are located in the control room. A CRT display and printer are also connected to the main CPU. The main unit has 16 inputs and 16 outputs (115 VAC).

- The main processor communicates with its three subsystem racks, arranged in a star configuration, through a serial interface module located in each subsystem.

- Rack 1 (128 I/O) is located in the warehouse and handles 30 inputs and 58 outputs. The I/O addresses for this rack are 200 through 377.

- Rack 2 (128 I/O) controls a paper machine with 35 inputs and 76 outputs using addresses 400 through 577. It is located on the main plant floor.

- Rack 3 (64 I/O), which is also located on the main plant floor, controls a winding machine. The winding machine has 20 inputs and 30 outputs using addresses 600 through 677.

- The addresses are all octal, and all I/O are 115 VAC. The I/O receiver must be located in the first slot of each remote rack. The modularity is 8 points per module.

12-7 The _____ should included a description of the design strategy.
a–system configuration
b–system abstract
c–register assignment
d–variable declaration

12-8 *True/False.* The program printout provides all of the information required to fully understand the control system.

12-9 Which of the following documents shows the actual connections of field inputs and outputs?
a–I/O address assignment
b–register assignment
c–I/O wiring connection diagram
d–system configuration

12-10 *True/False.* System documentation is only helpful during installation and start-up.

12-11 The storage register assignment document should include those registers that are:
a–used
b–not used
c–a and b
d–used for internals only

12-12 What information should be included in the I/O address assignment document?

12-13 *True/False.* Wire color changes should be documented.

12-14 The assignment of internal outputs should be done:
a–during the assignment of real I/O
b–after the assignment of real I/O
c–as the internals are used during system programming
d–during the I/O wiring connections

12-15 When properly documented, the storage register assignment document will prevent:

a–multiple use of the same registers in the program
b–improper reference to a register
c–register usage cross-references
d–register changes and deletions

12-16 An up-to-date control program printout will <u>not</u> provide:

a–a replica of the PLC's memory
b–a hard copy of the actual control program stored in the PLC
c–the I/O connections for field devices
d–the latest software revision of the program

12-17 *True/False.* The variable declaration lists the names, type, and description of each variable in the control program.

12-18 Name three media that are used to store and transport the control program.

12-19 The safest program backup source is _____.

a–the system abstract
b–the latest ladder program printout
c–the program in the PLC RAM memory
d–the I/O wiring and address assignment document

12-20 Documentation systems generally provide:

a–a reduction in the drafting manpower required to document the system
b–input/output usage reports
c–construction mnemonics documentation
d–all of the above

12-21 Name three features of documentation systems.

DATA MEASUREMENTS
AND TRANSDUCERS

CHAPTER 13 STUDY GUIDE

- Data interpretation is very important when dealing with on-line process control applications. Measurement devices provide valuable information about the inner workings of a process. Therefore, users must understand how to correctly interpret this data to gain knowledge about a process control operation.

- Data-collecting devices use four different methods to interpret data readings:
  - mean
  - median
  - mode
  - standard deviation

- The *mean* is the average value of a set of readings. It is computed by adding the values in a set and dividing their sum by the number of readings in the set. The mean can be used as an estimate of future or expected readings. The formula for computing the mean ($\overline{X}$) is:

$$\overline{X} = \frac{X_1 + X_2 + X_3 + \ldots X_n}{n}$$

or

$$\overline{X} = \frac{\sum_{n=1}^{i} X_n}{n}$$

- The *median* is the middle value of a set of readings arranged in ascending order. The median is not affected by extreme values, as is the case in the mean; therefore, the median is more error tolerant than the mean. The following equations define the median (M):

$$M = X_{\left(\frac{m+1}{2}\right)} \qquad \text{for an odd number of samples}$$

$$M = \frac{X_{\left(\frac{m}{2}\right)} + X_{\left(\frac{m}{2}+1\right)}}{2} \qquad \text{for an even number of samples}$$

where:

$M =$ the median

$m =$ the total number of readings

$X =$ a reading value

- The *mode* is the most frequent value or values in a set of readings. This statistic is primarily used in discrete processes where values are often repeated.

- The *standard deviation* measures the disbursement of all the sample readings in relation to the mean. A small standard deviation indicates that the values are close to the mean, while a large standard deviation indicates that the values are spread out from the mean. Standard deviation (σ) can be expressed as:

$$\sigma = \sqrt{\frac{\sum\limits_{n=1 \text{ to } i}\left(\overline{X} - X_n\right)^2}{n-1}}$$

where:

$\sigma =$ the standard deviation

$\overline{X} =$ the calculated mean

$n =$ the number corresponding to each reading, starting at 1 and ending at the last reading, i

- When the data values are evenly distributed around the mean in a bell form, they are said to have a normal distribution. In a normal distribution, the standard deviation of the values can be anticipated. If a set of values has a normal distribution, then:
  - 68% of all readings will lie within ±1s
  - 95% of all readings will lie within ±2σ
  - 99% of all readings will lie within ±3σ

- Measurement errors are likely to occur in any system that produces a finished good. Errors can be divided into three categories: gross errors, system errors, and random errors.
  - *Gross errors* are the result of human miscalculation.
  - *System errors* are the result of the instrument itself or the environment.
  - *Random errors* are the result of unexpected actions in the process line.

- Errors can be discovered in anticipation of the outcome (error prediction) or after the product is made (error detection). After an error has been detected, it can be interpreted using statistical analysis. By comparing the error data with previous process data stored in a database, the system may later correct or predict errors in the process.

- Two types of errors that occur in PLC systems are propagation errors and guarantee errors.
  - *Propagation errors* are errors caused by the interaction of two or more independent variables, each causing a different problem. These errors can be predicted and corrected using mean and standard deviation calculations.
  - *Guarantee errors* are known values that state that a material's specifications will be within a specified deviation from the mean. To predict the outcome of a process with guarantee error, the arithmetic worst-case scenario must be calculated.

- Two measuring techniques are used to implement transducer circuits. These techniques involve the use of bridge circuits and linear variable differential transformer (LVDT) mechanisms.

  - *Bridge circuits* use resistive elements to sense measurement changes. Depending on how the circuit is configured, the bridge will change the voltage or current of its output in proportion to changes in the resistive element. This voltage or current offset is used to determine the value of the measured variable.

  - *Linear variable differential transformers* (LVDTs) are electromechanical mechanisms that provide a voltage reference proportional to the displacement of the core inside their coil.

- **Thermal transducers** sense and monitor changes in temperature. There are two primary types of thermal transducers: one measures internal resistance changes due to temperature variations, the other measures voltage differentials as a result of a temperature variations. Thermal transducers' outputs are voltage or current signals proportional to the temperature measurement range.

- Thermal transducers include:

  - RTDs
  - thermistors
  - thermocouples

- *RTDs* are temperature transducers made of conductive wire elements. The resistance of the conductive wires in an RTD increases linearly with an increase in temperature; therefore, RTDs are said to have a positive temperature coefficient. RTDs are generally used in a bridge circuit configuration.

- *Thermistors* are temperature transducers made of semiconductor materials. Thermistors have a negative temperature coefficient because their internal resistance decreases as the temperature increases. Thermistors experience large changes in internal resistance in response to small increases in temperature.

- *Thermocouples* are thermal transducers made of two different metals. The two metals are joined together at junctions with different temperatures. This temperature differential creates a voltage across the thermocouple.

  - The temperature being measured is measured at the thermocouple's hot junction and the reference temperature is measured at its cold junction.

  - Several thermocouples can be connected in series, creating a thermopile, to increase thermocouple resolution. Thermocouples may also be configured to measure average temperature and temperature differential.

- **Displacement transducers** measure the movement of objects. Commonly used displacement transducers include:

  - LVDTs
  - potentiometers

- For displacement detection, a rod is attached to an *LVDT*'s movable core. A linear variable differential transformer provides excellent resolution—the most minute movement of the core will produce an output voltage.

- A *potentiometer* is the simplest displacement transducer available. Its measurement is based on resistance changes due to movement of a wiper. A voltage source powers the potentiometer, causing the wiper to produce an output voltage proportional to the movement of the attached element.

- **Pressure transducers** transform the force exerted on their surroundings into a proportional electrical signal through signal conditioning. The three most common pressure transducers are:
  - strain gauges
  - Bourdon tubes
  - load cells

- *Strain gauges* measure body deformation of a rigid body as a result of force applied to it. A strain gauge measures pressure by sensing resistance changes in its wires due to applied force. There are two main types of strain gauges: bonded and unbonded.
  - Bonded strain gauges are set with a thin layer of synthetic thermosetting resin (epoxy) and attached directly to the area of the body where stress is being applied.
  - In unbonded strain gauges, a moving part moves when force is applied.

- Changes in temperature affect strain gauges; therefore, they require temperature compensation. A dummy gauge can be added to a strain gauge to measure resistance change due to temperature only, so that it can be factored out of the reading.

- A *Bourdon tube* is a pressure transducer that converts pressure measurements into displacement. Types of Bourdon tubes include spiral, helical, twisted, and C-tube.

- *Load cells* are force or weight transducers based on a direct application of bonded strain gauges. They measure deformations produced by weight.

- **Flow transducers** measure the flow of materials in a process. The flow material may be in solid, gas, or liquid form.

- Solid flow is measured using strain gauge–based load cell transducers. Solid flow can be calculated using the equation:

$$Q = \frac{WV}{L}$$

where:

$Q =$ the rate of flow

$W =$ the mass/weight of the solid

$V =$ the velocity/speed of the moving transporter

$L =$ the length of the weight transducer (load cell)

- Fluid flow can be obtained by measuring one of two conditions in the process line: pressure differential or fluid motion. The two most common pressure differential transducers are the Venturi tube and the orifice plate. The most common fluid motion transducer is the turbine flow meter. This transducer transforms fluid motion into electrical signals.

- The *Venturi tube* and the *orifice plate* are based on the Bernoulli effect, which relates flow velocity to the pressure differential between two points. These fluid flow meters use pressure transducers to transform pressure into an electrical signal to determine the pressure differential. Fluid velocity is computed using the following equation:

$$V = k\sqrt{\Delta P}$$

where:

$$V = \text{the fluid velocity}$$
$$\Delta P = P_1 - P_2$$
$$k = \text{a constant}$$

The flow rate is then obtained using the equation:

$$Q = VA$$
$$= Ak\sqrt{\Delta P}$$
$$= K\sqrt{\Delta P}$$

where:

$$V = \text{the fluid velocity}$$
$$A = \text{the cross - sectional area of the pipe}$$
$$K = \text{a new constant composed of } k \text{ times the area } A_2$$

- *Turbine flow meters* are commonly used in flow motion detection. Fluid passing through the blades of the motor creates a rotary motion in the turbine generating a magnetic flux that is sensed by a coil inside the flow meter. The coil changes the flux into a small voltage and then amplifies it.

- **Vibration transducers** detect vibration for applications in which vibrations may damage process control equipment or machinery. Some common causes of system vibration are imbalance of a rotating member, misalignment, and defective bearings or belts.

- Vibration is the oscillatory movement of a mass about a reference position characterized by displacement, velocity, and acceleration.
  - *Displacement* is the distance a mass moves from its reference position.
  - *Velocity* is the speed at which a mass moves in meters per second.
  - *Acceleration* is the rate of change of a mass's velocity per second.

- Vibration can be detected by measuring displacement, velocity, or acceleration. One of the most commonly used vibration detectors is the piezoelectric transducer. This transducer produces an electrical output proportional to the acceleration of the vibration.

REVIEW QUESTIONS

13-1 *True/False.* Calculating the mean and the average of a set of readings will produce different values.

13-2 In order to calculate the median of a set of data, the values must be placed in _____ order.

13-3 The _____ is the most frequent value in a set of data.

13-4 *True/False.* The standard deviation of a set of readings measures how the readings are dispersed in relation to the most recent sample value obtained.

13-5 For the following sample readings—19 psi, 10 psi, 14 psi, 15.6 psi, 10 psi, 17 psi, 9 psi, and 8 psi—find:
(a) the mean
(b) the mode
(c) the median
(d) the standard deviation

13-6 For a set of values with a normal distribution, what percent of the values will lie within $\pm 2\sigma$?

13-7 One set of sample data has a standard deviation of 0.9 psi and the other has a standard deviation of 0.04 psi. Which set of values has a distribution that is closer to its mean?

13-8 List the three types of errors and give some examples of how they may be prevented or reduced.

13-9 What can be predicted using a database containing the mean, mode, median, and standard deviations of many sample readings?

13-10 _____ are known values that state that a material's specifications will be within a specified standard deviation from the mean.

13-11 For a cube with the following dimensions:

$$\overline{X} = 10\,\text{cm} \qquad \sigma_x = 0.01\,\text{cm}$$
$$\overline{Y} = 12\,\text{cm} \qquad \sigma_y = 0.02\,\text{cm}$$
$$\overline{Z} = 13\,\text{cm} \qquad \sigma_z = 0.015\,\text{cm}$$
$$\overline{W} = 0.30\,\text{lbs/cm}^3 \qquad \sigma_w = 0.0003\,\text{lbs/cm}^3$$

(a) Find the expected weight in pounds.
(b) Find the standard deviation in pounds.

13-12 Two of the most common transducer techniques used in process measurement involve the use of _____ and _____.

13-13 A _____ occurs when the resistance of one element in a bridge circuit changes.

13-14 A linear variable differential transformer (LVDT) is an electromechanical mechanism that provides a voltage reference that _____ the displacement of its core inside the coil.
a–exceeds
b–is less than
c–is proportional to
d–is inversely proportional to

13-15 Identify which of the following transducers use the LVDT mechanism (circle all that apply):
a–accelerometer
b–piezoelectric transducer
c–load cell
d–Bourdon tube
e–strain gauge

13-16 List the three most common thermal transducers.

13-17 _____ are thermal transducers that exhibit changes in internal wire resistance due to temperature changes.

13-18 Thermistors have a(n) _____ temperature coefficient.

13-19 *True/False.* Thermocouples are not widely used in industry due to their narrow range of temperature tolerance.

13-20 Thermocouple resolution may be increased by connecting several thermocouples connected in series to create a(n) _____.

13-21 LVDTs and potentiometers are _____ transducers.

13-22 A strain gauge is a transducer that measures _____.

13-23 Changes in temperature in strain gauges forming a bridge circuit can be compensated for by adding a(n) _____.

13-24 *True/False.* Load cells are used as pressure transducers because they measure weight.

13-25 *True/False.* A flow transducer can only measure the rate of flow of liquids.

13-26 A conveyor travels at a speed of 22 m/min. It is transporting a material to be weighed on a platform 3 meters in length. The load cell weighs 45 kgs of the material at a time. Find the flow rate of the material in kg/min.

13-27 The Venturi tube and the orifice plate are two flow transducers that base their measurement on _____ differential.

13-28   A turbine flow meter measures flow through _____.

13-29   List at least two common causes of system vibration failures?

13-30   What are the three main vibration motion parameters?

PROCESS RESPONSES
AND TRANSFER FUNCTIONS

CHAPTER 14 STUDY GUIDE

- *Process control* is the regulation of designated process parameters to within a specified target range or to the set point. Process control is commonly used in product manufacturing because many factors must be accurate to maintain a consistent product quality.

- To implement process control, a PLC regulates dynamic variables, variables that vary with time, such as temperature, flow, and pressure, to a desired set point.

- Within a process control system, the dependent, dynamic variable is called the *process variable* (*PV*), the variable that regulates the process variable is called the *control variable* (*CV*), and the device that regulates the control variable is called the *control element*.

- To regulate the system, the controller reads the process variable from the system and compares it with the set point to determine how well the process variable is being regulated. This configuration is known as a closed-loop system, because the controller uses feedback to monitor the system.

- A PLC regulates the process variable by increasing or decreasing the control variable. The PLC receives constant feedback and will raise or lower the control variable accordingly until the process variable is as close as possible to the set point.

- The difference between the process variable and the set point is called the *error*. The error may be positive or negative, depending on whether the process variable is too high or too low. A system with no error is said to be at steady state.

- The adjustment of the control variable according to the data obtained by reading the process variable and analyzing the error between it and the set point is referred to as the *control loop*. Control loops are affected by disturbances, such as lag and dead time, which influence the process and alter the process variable.

- Error (*E*) for a negative feedback system (i.e., a typical process control system) may be calculated using the following equation:

$$E = SP - PV$$

- Error may also be expressed as a percentage of the set point using the following formula:

$$E = \frac{SP - PV}{SP}$$

- A controller can act in two ways in response to a change in the process variable and, thus, the error—that is, in either a direct-acting or a reverse-acting fashion.
  - A *direct-acting* controller increases its output in response to an increase in the process variable.
  - A *reverse-acting* controller increases its output in response to a decrease in the process variable.

- All systems allow a certain amount of fluctuation of error from the set point. This fluctuation allowance is called the *error deadband*. Within this deadband, the controller will treat the error as zero, not making any control variable adjustments.

- A process variable responds to a change in input in a dynamic manner according to the characteristics of the process. These process characteristics, which include factors such as delay time and inherent physical responses of the process, are defined by the process's transfer function (H_T). Every process will have its own unique transfer function, and for most processes, the transfer function is not known.

- Experimentation can be used to approximate the value of H_T. In a step test, a forced change is made in the control variable in order to observe the process variable's response, the step response. The response of a process to a sudden change in input is called its *transient response*. Transient responses provide much information about the dynamics of a process and, accordingly, the process's transfer function.

- A closed-loop controller has two transfer functions, one that defines the controller (Hc) and another that defines the process (Hp).

- *Process gain* (K) defines the ratio between process output and process input. It is calculated by dividing the change in process output over a period of time by the corresponding change in process input.

- The perfect process variable response to a change in input is immediate. However, there is an inherent delay, called the *dead time delay*, in the system's response to an input change. Dead time delay is the time period that occurs between the change in input and the process's initial response to it.

- *Lag time* is the delay between a process variable's initial response to an input and its optimal response to it. A process can have two types of lag time: first order and second order.

  - *First-order lag time* is the lag a process variable exhibits when responding to a rapid change in the control variable.
  - *Second-order lag time* is the oscillating response of a process variable as it settles to its steady-state value after a step change in input.

- A transfer function is defined mathematically as the ratio of output to input. Therefore, a controller's transfer function (Hc) is:

$$Hc = \frac{CV}{E}$$

A process's transfer function (Hp) is:

$$Hp = \frac{PV}{CV}$$

- Transfer functions are expressed through Laplace transforms. Laplace transforms are mathematical functions that are used to solve complex differential equations by converting them into easy-to-manage algebraic equations. They do this by converting differential equations from the time (t) domain—the process response as a function of time—to the frequency (s) domain—the process response as a function of frequency.

  - In the frequency domain, a first-order derivative term becomes an s term times the function in the frequency domain minus a constant, which is the value of the function at $t = 0$ in the time domain.

  - A second-order derivative term becomes an s^2 Laplace term times the Laplace function minus s times the value of the time domain first derivative at $t = 0$ minus the value of the function at $t = 0$ in the time domain.

- An integral transfer function is one of the simplest process responses. An integral process integrates the input with the process over time. Therefore, the rate of change of the process output varies according to the input.

- Dead time in Laplace form involves a shift of the time variable t—the process input occurs at time t, but the output does not occur until time t_d. The dead time factor in a Laplace transform is $e^{-t_d s}$.

- First-order lag is one of the most common processes responses. In this type of system, the process variable response lags behind a step change in the control variable.

- A second-order lag response oscillates while the output signal settles into its final steady-state value. This type of response is caused by a step change in the input or a disturbance to the process.

- A second-order system can exhibit one of three types of responses:

  - overdamped ($\zeta > 1$)
  - critically damped ($\zeta = 1$)
  - underdamped ($\zeta < 1$)

- An *overdamped response* is a second-order response with lag whose damping coefficient is greater than 1. A system with a very large damping coefficient will produce a heavily damped response to a unit step. This sluggish response is similar to a first-order one. Two cascaded first-order systems with different time lags will produce an overdamped second-order response.

- A *critically damped response* is a second-order system response whose damping coefficient is equal to 1. This type of second-order system achieves a steady-state value quicker than the other two types of second-order systems. However, the amplitude of the overshoot of a critically damped response is larger than that of an overdamped response.

- An *underdamped response* is a second-order response whose damping coefficient is less than 1. This type of response exhibits an overshoot and an undershoot of the set point, creating an oscillating response.

REVIEW QUESTIONS

14-1   *True/False.* Process control is the regulation of designated process parameters to a specified set target value called the set point.

14-2   The process variable is also called the _____ because it varies with time.
a–control variable
b–fixed variable
c–dynamic variable
d–set point variable

14-3   The difference between the process variable and the set point is known as the _____.

14-4   Once a process achieves stability and equality (error = 0), the process is said to be _____.
a–accelerated
b–regulated
c–with disturbances
d–looping

14-5   The adjustment of the control variable according to the data obtained by reading the process variable and analyzing the error between it and the set point is referred to as the _____.

14-6   *True/False.* Negative feedback refers to the reading of process variable data and the subtraction of it from the set point to obtain the error.

14-7   *True/False.* Positive feedback can be beneficial for obtaining stability in a process control system.

14-8   Which of the following equations represents a system with negative feedback?
a–$E = PV - SP$
b–$E = SP - PV$
c–$E = PV_{max} - SP$
d–$E = PV_{min} - SP$

14-9   *True/False.* A controller reacts in a direct- or reverse-acting manner due to an increase or decrease in the control variable.

14-10   Using Figure 14-1 as a model, plot the direct-acting and reverse-acting controller curves, showing an increase in error. Indicate the control variable output when the system is at the set point.

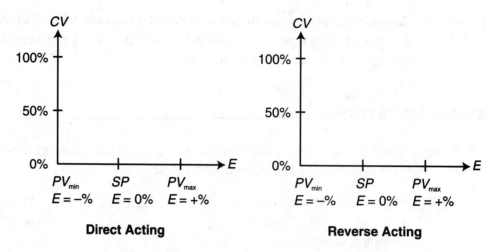

Figure 14-1. Direct- and reverse-acting controller graphs.

14-11 Indicate whether the control variable increases (↑) or decreases (↓) its output in the situations described in Table 14-1.

	Control Variable	
	Direct Acting	Reverse Acting
Error ↑		
Error ↓		

Table 14-1. Control variable–versus–error chart.

14-12 *True/False.* The error deadband (*DB*) allows error fluctuations to occur around the set point without activating the controller.

14-13 Indicate the areas where the controller will take action in Figure 14-3.

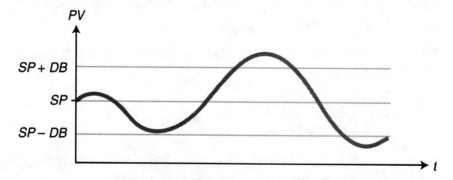

Figure 14-3. Controller with an error deadband.

14-14 *True/False.* When the process variable is constantly changing, the process is said to be at a steady state.

14-15 Process dynamics changes occur due to a change in the set point or the presence of _____ in the process.

a–instability
b–chemical changes
c–error deadband
d–disturbances

14-16 A transfer function can be defined as _____.

a–an equation which describes the input over the output of a process
b–an equation that describes the process in terms of response over time and the outcome of the process variable
c–the relationship of a disturbance in the process to the set point
d–the value of the control variable over the process variable

14-17 *True/False.* A transient response can be defined as the output response of a transfer function (in the time domain) to a change in input over a period of time until a steady-state behavior is achieved.

14-18 For the closed-loop system in Figure 14-3, fill in the system inputs and outputs with the following terms and write the transfer function equations for the process (*Hp*) and the controller (*Hc*):

- *SP*

- *E*

- *CV*

- *PV*

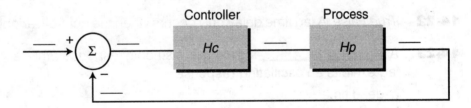

Figure 14-3. Closed-loop system.

14-19 Dead time in a process can be described as _____.

a–the amount of process downtime
b–the time it takes to read 1τ
c–the time it takes for the process variable to start reacting to a change in input
d–the time it takes the control variable to make a 10% change

14-20 For the process shown in Figure 14-4:

(a) calculate the process gain

(b) find the transient response time

(c) explain what each of these terms represents

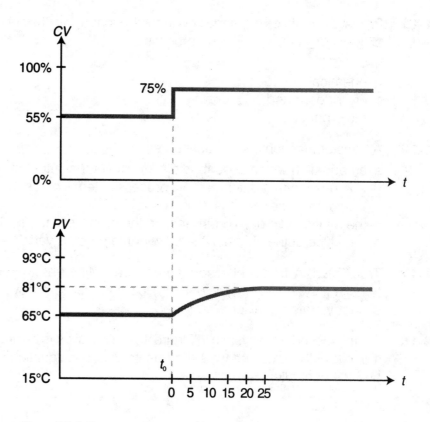

Figure 14-4. Process response and control variable input for problem 14-20.

14-21 *True/False.* Lag time can be defined as the time it takes for a process to achieve its optimum value after it starts reacting to a change.

14-22 *True/False.* A lag time delay only occurs when the control variable input increases.

14-23 A _____ lag exhibits a smooth response, while a _____ lag exhibits an oscillating response.
a–dead time
b–sawtooth
c–first-order
d–second-order
e–step

14-24 *True/False.* Both first-order and second-order responses are referred to as system transient responses.

14-25 _____ are mathematical functions used to solve integro-differential equations by converting them into easy-to-manage algebraic equations.
a–Process functions
b–Laplace transforms
c–Control transforms
d–Error-correcting functions

14-26 Figure 14-5 shows two responses with the same gain. Which has a larger value of τ (time constant)?

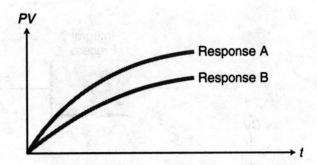

Figure 14-5. Two responses with the same gain.

14-27 Plot a first-order response with a dead time and a gain of A_1. Illustrate the process variable value at time $t = 1\tau$.

14-28 The exponent of a Laplace s term for a second-order lag system is _____.

14-29 Match the following Laplace transforms with their appropriate time domain functions assuming the initial domain value is 0 (i.e., $x_{(t=0)} = 0$):

_____ $sX_{(s)}$	a–$x_{(t)}$
_____ $\dfrac{A}{s}$	b–$\dfrac{d^2x}{dt^2}$
_____ $s^2X_{(s)}$	c–$\dfrac{dx}{dt}$
_____ $X_{(s)}$	d–$\displaystyle\int_0^t Adt$

14-30 Match the following:

_____ $\dfrac{1}{(3s+4)(s+2)}$	a–first-order system
_____ $\dfrac{4}{3s+1}$	b–second-order system
_____ $\dfrac{8}{s^3+s^2+2s+1}$	c–third-order system

14-31 *True/False.* The integral process, represented by an integral transfer function, is the simplest of all process responses.

14-32 The integral response to a step input is _____.
a–sinusoidal
b–decaying
c–decreasing
d–ramping

14-33 Plot the process response for the step input shown in Figure 14-6, indicating the rate of increase.

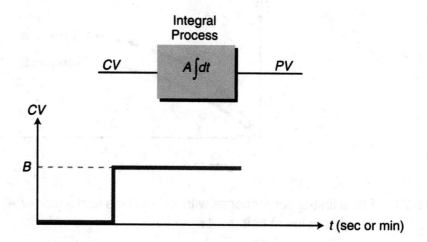

Figure 14-6. Step input.

14-34 Assuming that all initial parameters are 0, find the Laplace representation of a PID controller, which has the error (E) as its input and the control variable (CV) as its output, and that is defined in real time as:

$$CV_{(t)} = K_P E + K_I \int_0^t E\,dt + K_D \frac{dE}{dt} + CV_{(t=0)}$$

14-35 Dead time is represented in Laplace form as _____, where t_d is the dead time.

a– $e^{-\left(\frac{t_d}{s}\right)}$

b– $e^{-t_d s}$

c– $e^{+t_d s}$

d– $e^{-\left(\frac{s}{t_d}\right)}$

14-36 A first-order lag has _____ time constant(s), while a second-order lag has _____ time constant(s).

a–one plus an extra s term
b–one
c–two plus an extra s term
d–two

14-37 One τ is equivalent to _____ of a system's final steady-state value.
a–65%
b–64.7%
c–63.2%
d–53.2%

14-38 At 5τ, a first-order system achieves _____ of its final value.

a–99.3%

b–99%

c–95%

d–86.5%

14-39 If a process achieves 90% of its final value in $t = 11.7$ minutes, how long will it take to achieve 90% with a 3.2-minute dead time?

a–8.5 minutes

b–11.7 minutes

c–14.9 minutes

d–(11.7 x 3.2) minutes

14-40 A system has a first-order response with a time constant of 7.5 minutes. How long will it take for the value of the output V_{out} to be at 50% of the input V_{in}?

14-41 *True/False.* Second-order systems are represented by the following transfer function in Laplace form:

$$Hp_{(s)} = \frac{Out}{In} = \frac{A\omega_n^2}{(s^2 + 2\zeta\omega_n s + \omega_n^2)}$$

14-42 The damping coefficient is represented by the term:

a–ω_n

b–f_n

c–$2\pi f_n$

d–ζ

14-43 In Figure 14-7, label the critically damped, overdamped, and underdamped responses, indicating whether their damping coefficients are equal to, greater than, or less than one.

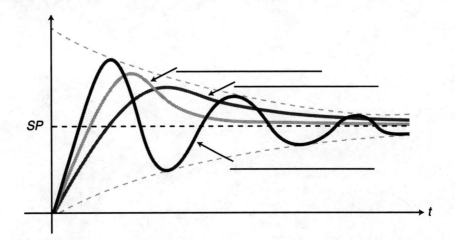

Figure 14-7. Critically damped, overdamped, and underdamped responses.

14-44 *True/False.* If $\tau_1 = \tau_2$ in a second-order system, the system is said to be underdamped.

14-45   *True/False.* If $\zeta = 0$, the response will be very stable.

14-46   If two first-order systems with approximately the same lag time ($\tau_1 = \tau_2$) are cascaded, the result will be _____.

a–a first-order system with $\tau = \tau_1$
b–an unstable system
c–a critically damped second-order system
d–an integral response

14-47   A second-order system with $\tau_1 >> \tau_2$ will have its step response approximate a _____ because of the heavy damping.

a–second-order underdamped lag
b–ramping response
c–first-order lag
d–integral system response

PROCESS CONTROLLERS
AND LOOP TUNING

CHAPTER 15 STUDY GUIDE

- A system controller determines the error in a system by comparing the process variable to the set point. It then uses an algorithm to manipulate the control variable to regulate the process variable. The behavior of a closed-loop control system depends on the type of controller used and its tuning parameters.

- A controller is responsible for the stability of the control system. A process may exhibit three different types of stability responses: stable, conditionally stable, and unstable.
  - *Stable responses* approach a finite value over time.
  - *Conditionally stable responses* have a sinusoidal-type wave shape.
  - *Unstable responses* are unacceptable system responses because they create a runaway condition.

- In a closed-loop system, the error signal is the key variable input to the controller. The controller interprets this signal and then sends commands to the process via the control variable to bring the error to zero.

- Controllers may be either direct or reverse acting. The type of controller used depends on the needs of the application.
  - A *direct-acting controller* increases its control variable input in response to an increase in the process variable. This type of control is commonly used in air-cooling systems.
  - A *reverse-acting controller* decreases its control variable input in response to an increase in the process variable. This behavior is typical of heating systems.

- A controller may also operate in one of two modes:
  - discrete
  - continuous

- A **discrete-mode controller** produces a discontinuous ON/OFF signal, which serves as an input to the process. The two types of discrete-mode controllers are:
  - two position
  - three position

- A *two-position controller* is the most basic type of process controller. It provides an ON/OFF signal to the control element. This type of controller is appropriate for applications where large-scale, sudden changes are uncommon and the process reaction rate is slow.

- A *three-position controller* provides ON/OFF control plus an additional output level corresponding to 50% of the full ON setting. The 50% setting on this controller corresponds to the output level required to keep the process variable at the set point, thus minimizing the cycling behavior of the process variable.

- **Continuous-mode controllers** emit an analog signal as opposed to a discrete one. Continuous controllers can use three different modes to control a process:
  - proportional mode
  - integral mode
  - derivative mode

- A *proportional controller* provides a control variable adjustment that is proportional to the error deviation. This type of control provides a fast response and is easy to implement. However, closed-loop proportional control creates offset error between the desired and actual values of the process variable.

- An *integral controller* provides a control variable output that is based on the time history of the error deviation. Therefore, the larger the error, the faster the controller's output changes and vice versa. Although this control mode does not exhibit the offset error present in a proportional controller, it adversely affects stability. If the integration time is reduced, the response during the slow period of the process will become faster, inducing cycling.

- A *proportional-integral (PI) controller* combines the fast response of proportional action with the offset error elimination of integral action. A PI controller may be configured in two ways: in parallel or in series.
  - In a parallel PI controller, the proportional and integral actions occur independently of each other, making the controller's output equal to the proportional action plus the integral action.
  - In a series PI controller, the integral action occurs after the proportional action. Therefore, the input to the integral action is the proportional action, not the system error.

- A *derivative controller* provides an output proportional to the rate of change of error in the system. Derivative control cannot be used alone in a controller because it will not change its output unless there is a change in the rate of error. It also does not eliminate residual error. There are two types of derivative control: standard and modified.
  - The output of a standard derivative controller is proportional to the rate of change of error in the system.
  - The output of a modified derivative controller is proportional to the rate of change of the process variable over time.

- A *proportional-derivative (PD) controller* combines the actions of proportional and derivative controllers. This controller provides better response stability than a PI controller, but it does not eliminate offset error. The derivative component provides an immediate response to an error change that behaves in ramp form. This ramping action slows down the proportional response as the process variable approaches the set point.

- A *proportional-integral-derivative (PID) controller* combines the increased stability of a PD controller with the eliminated offset feature of a PI controller. A PID controller can be used to control almost any process, including those with long lag and dead times. This controller may be arranged in series or parallel using either a standard or modified derivative action.

- An *integral windup* situation occurs when an integral action saturates a controller's output at 100%. Integral windup usually happens during the start-up of a process and when the error in a slow-responding process is large. This condition can be prevented by disabling the integral action once the controller's output reaches 100%.

- Bumpless transfer refers to a controller's ability to switch from manual to automatic control and vice versa without creating a step change in the input. In a bumpless transfer, the manual controller station tracks the automatic controller's output and vice versa to keep the control variable output constant.

- Cascade control is an advanced control technique where the output of one controller is the set point input to another controller. Cascade control systems respond more quickly than single-controller systems to disturbances that affect the primary loop.

- Controller *loop tuning* is essential for a process control system to operate properly. Loop tuning involves selecting the constants that will be used with the proportional, integral, and derivative actions of a controller. With these constants at the proper levels, the controller can effectively regulate the process variable to the set point.

- The three most common loop tuning methods are:
  - the Ziegler-Nichols open-loop tuning method
  - the integral of time and absolute error (ITAE) open-loop tuning method
  - the Ziegler-Nichols closed-loop tuning method

- The *Ziegler-Nichols open-loop tuning method* is a popular loop tuning technique. This method tests and records the open-loop reaction of a process to a change in control variable output. Once the process response values are obtained, they can be plugged into the Ziegler-Nichols equation to find P, PI, and PID controller gains.

- The *integral of time and absolute error (ITAE) open-loop tuning method* follows the same procedures as the Ziegler-Nichols method, but produces less response oscillation and minimizes the problems associated with it.

- The *Ziegler-Nichols closed-loop tuning method* is used to obtain controller constants in a system with feedback. The main objective of this method is to find the value of the proportional-only gain that causes the control loop to oscillate indefinitely at a constant amplitude. The ultimate proportional gain and the ultimate period are used to find the loop-tuning constants of the controller.

- PID controllers may also be tuned using software tuning systems. These systems reduce the tuning time and optimize control loop performance.

REVIEW QUESTIONS

15-1 Which of the following is <u>not</u> a type of stability response?

a–stable
b–conditionally stable
c–unstable
d–conditionally unstable

15-2 *True/False*. An unstable response can also be referred to as a runaway condition.

15-3 Match the following:

_____ stable response

_____ conditionally stable response

_____ unstable response

a–has a sinusoidal wave shape of low amplitude

b–increases amplitude with response time

c–as time increases the response approaches a finite value

15-4 Find the transfer function for the system in Figure 15-1.

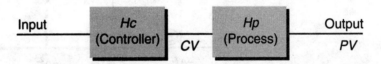

Figure 15-1. System in problem 15-4.

15-5 Reconfigure the system in Figure 15-1 as a closed-loop system that uses negative feedback and has a set point of *SP*. Show the error calculation equation for the system.

15-6 *True/False*. A closed-loop controller can provide only direct action.

15-7 How will a direct-acting controller affect a process?

a–As the control variable decreases, the process variable increases.
b–The control variable creates a null value to hold the process steady.
c–As the control variable increases, the process variable decreases.
d–As the control variable increases, the process variable increases.

15-8 Name the two types of controller modes and the type of output signal each provides.

15-9 A two-position controller is also known as a(n) _____ because it switches its output _____ to control the process variable.

a–from positive to negative
b–ON/OFF controller
c–biposition controller
d–dual voltage controller
e–ON and OFF

15-10 A home air-conditioning and heating system uses a _____ with a _____-acting function.

    a–two-position controller
    b–continuous controller
    c–direct and reverse
    d–direct
    e–reverse

15-11 *True/False.* A two-position controller operates between a deadband of control, producing a conditionally stable response.

15-12 *True/False.* A two-position controller does not have hysteresis.

15-13 Figure 15-2 represents the response of a process (*PV*) to the action of a reverse-acting controller (*CV*). Illustrate the control variable action that a direct-acting controller would take to elicit the same response.

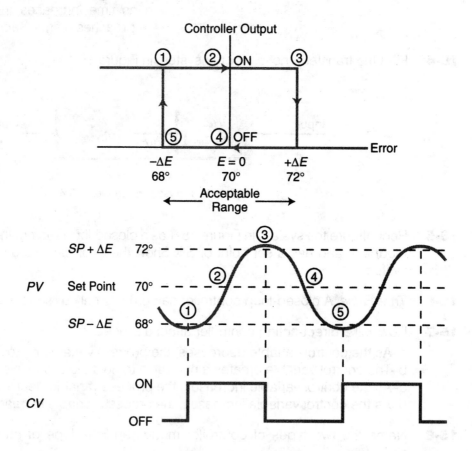

Figure 15-2. Control process for problem 15-13.

15-14 The response's overshoot and undershoot of the deadband in Figure 15–2 is due to:

    a–a partial imbalance in control
    b–the finite warm up and cool off times (lag) of the heater system
    c–the need of more *CV* action
    d–a narrow hysteresis

15-15 Figure 15-3 shows a mixer tank that is heated by an ON/OFF heating control system. The set point temperature is 200°F with a deadband deviation of ±5% from the set point. When the heater is not on, the system linearly loses (cools) 4°F per minute; when the heater is applied, the system gains 8°F per minute. The system's starting point is at the set point temperature with the heater in the OFF mode.

(a) Plot the oscillation response (cycle period) of the system and controller.

(b) Calculate the response in part (a) taking into consideration a heater lag time of 1 minute (60 seconds).

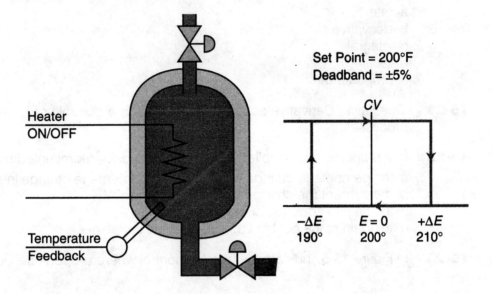

Figure 15-3. Mixer tank with a heating control system.

15-16 Plot the action of a three-position controller for the error values given in Figure 15-4.

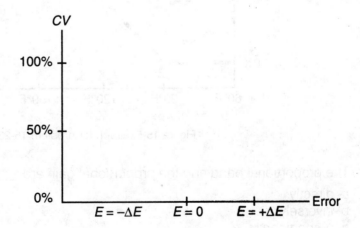

Figure 15-4. Three-position controller graph.

15-17 Illustrate a four-output contact interface being used to implement three-position control of a 0–10V analog valve. Highlight the condition of the output at 50%.

15-18   *True/False.* A continuous controller can be either direct- or reverse-acting.

15-19   Which of the following is not a continuous controller mode?
a–proportional
b–incremental
c–integral
d–derivative

15-20   The _____ mode, which provides a change in the control variable based on the history of the error, is also called the _____ mode.
a–rate
b–derivative
c–integral
d–reset
e–proportional

15-21   *True/False.* Derivative action is used alone in a controller to control problematic processes.

15-22   In a proportional controller, the proportional gain, represented by K_P, indicates:
a–the percentage change in *CV* for each percentage change in error
b–the percentage change in error due to the *CV*
c–the gain needed to correct a set point
d–the gain of the control variable over the set point

15-23   In Figure 15-5, indicate the band of control where proportional output is applied.

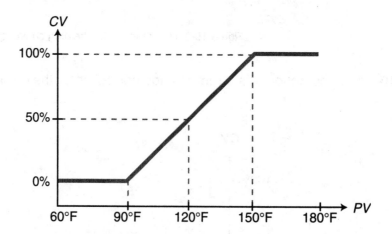

Figure 15-5. Graph for problem 15-23.

15-24   The proportional band and the proportional gain are _____ related.
a–directly
b–inversely
c–proportionally
d–longitudinally

15-25   *True/False.* A proportional controller with a proportional band of 50% has more gain than that of a proportional controller with a 75% proportional band.

15-26 Write the equation for the proportional controller's output ($CV_{(t)}$) for the controller shown in Figure 15-6, taking into consideration the previous value of CV (CV_{old}).

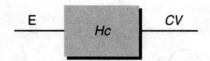

Figure 15-6. Controller for problem 15-26.

15-27 *True/False.* A proportional controller has a Laplace *s* term in its Laplace transfer function.

15-28 Compute the closed-loop transfer function equation of the process for the system shown in Figure 15-7.

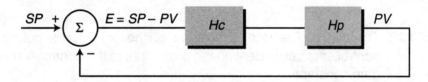

Figure 15-7. Control system for problem 15-28.

15-29 A drawback of using proportional control alone is that:

a–a load disturbance may cause a permanent change in the control variable
b–it always creates an offset error
c–it does not eliminate the error
d–all of the above

15-30 *True/False.* A step change in set point is used to simulate a load disturbance when evaluating the response of a closed-loop system that uses a proportional controller.

15-31 For the closed-loop system shown in Figure 15-8:

(a) find the closed-loop transfer function

(b) calculate the response to a unit step

(c) find the steady-state value of the process variable

(d) find the system time constant

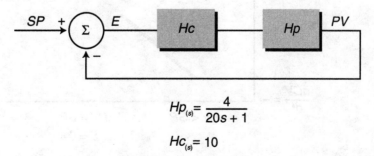

$$Hp_{(s)} = \frac{4}{20s + 1}$$

$$Hc_{(s)} = 10$$

Figure 15-8. Closed-loop control system for problem 15-31.

15-32 For the closed-loop second-order system shown in Figure 15-9, use the final value theorem to find the final value of the process variable given a controller with a gain of $K_P = 3$.

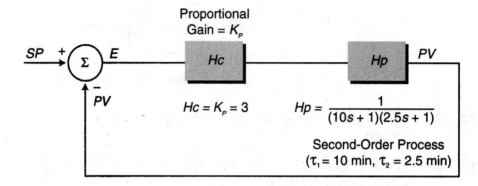

Figure 15-9. Control system for problem 15-32.

In the figure: $Hc = K_P = 3$, $Hp = \dfrac{1}{(10s + 1)(2.5s + 1)}$

Second-Order Process ($\tau_1 = 10$ min, $\tau_2 = 2.5$ min)

15-33 *True/False.* The rate of change of the controller's output (*CV*) in an integral controller is dependent on the error input to the controller multiplied by an integral gain constant.

15-34 If a constant error exists in an integral controller, its output will:

a–stop ramping
b–no longer be able to continue controlling the process
c–continue to ramp due to the integration of the error
d–ramp for a preset time value equal to 10% of the error in seconds

15-35 Determine which integral curve in Figure 15-10 has more gain and state whether these curves belong to a direct- or reverse-acting integral controller?

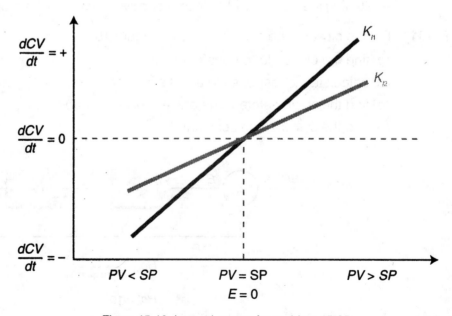

Figure 15-10. Integral curves for problem 15-35.

15-36 The gain of an integral controller (K_I) is expressed as:

$$a-K_I = \frac{\% \text{ change in } PV}{\% \text{ change in error}}$$

$$b-K_I = \frac{\% \text{ change in } CV}{\% \text{ change in error}}$$

$$c-K_I = \frac{\% \text{ error over full range}}{\% \text{ change in } \frac{dCV}{dt}}$$

$$d-K_I = \frac{\% \text{ change in } \frac{dCV}{dt}}{\% \text{ error over full range}}$$

15-37 An integral controller has a gain of $K_I = 0.6$ sec^{-1} and its output is at the set point (50%). A constant error of 5% occurs, lasting 4 seconds. What is the controller's output after the error?

15-38 *True/False.* Integral control can eliminate system error completely.

15-39 A proportional-integral (PI) controller has a(n) _____ and it _____.

a–fast response
b–slow response
c–does not eliminate error because of the proportional action
d–eliminates offset error
e–null response

15-40 For the response in Figure 15-11, fill in the blanks with the following terms:

- integral action
- proportional action
- proportional and integral action
- pure integral action
- pure proportional action

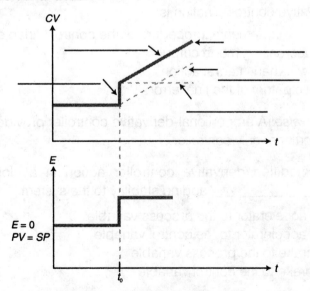

Figure 15-11. Response for problem 15-40.

15-41 *True/False.* There are two types of integral controllers—series and parallel.

15-42 Why does a proportional-integral controller respond faster than an integral-only controller?

15-43 A series integral controller is said to repeat its action when:

a–it repeats the integral action for the same error

b–it executes an integral gain

c–the integral gain is equal to the amount of proportional gain after the integral time period

d–it repeats its value equivalent to two times the proportional gain

15-44 *True/False.* An integral windup situation occurs when the output of a controller containing integral action saturates at 100% of the control variable output.

15-45 A derivative controller changes its control variable output in:

a–proportion to the magnitude of the error

b–proportion to the rate of change of the error

c–inverse proportion to the rate of change of the error

d–proportion to the rate of change of the set point

15-46 *True/False.* The derivative gain is also called rate time and can be expressed in seconds or minutes.

15-47 Match the following controller types with their proper equations:

_____ modified derivative controller $\quad$ a–$CV_{new} = K_D \dfrac{dE}{dt} + CV_{old}$

_____ standard derivative controller

$\quad$ b–$CV_{new} = -K_D \dfrac{dPV}{dt} + CV_{old}$

15-48 Derivative controller action is:

a–a slow incremental procedure of the control variable

b–a decreasing mode output

c–slower than integral action

d–anticipatory of the final error

15-49 *True/False.* A proportional-derivative controller provides a faster response than a proportional-only controller.

15-50 The modified derivative controller action in a closed-loop system acts as _____, adding stability to the system.

a–an accelerator to the process variable

b–an accelerator to the control variable

c–a brake to the process variable

d–a brake to the control variable

15-51 A proportional-integral-derivative controller is also called a _____ controller.

a–modified integral
b–modified derivative
c–process
d–three-mode

15-52 *True/False.* A PID controller can be used to control virtually any process that involves lag and dead times.

15-53 A PID controller can be arranged in:

a–parallel with standard derivative action
b–parallel with modified derivative action
c–series with standard derivative action
d–series with modified derivative action
e–a and d
f–b and c
g–all of the above

15-54 Loop sampling time is:

a–the time it takes to complete the control loop
b–the frequency of how often a PLC reads and executes the integral and derivative terms in a PID algorithm
c–the time it takes to integrate the error in a PID controller
d–a sample of how long it takes to update the process variable

15-55 *True/False.* Bumpless transfer eliminates error in an open-loop process.

15-56 In cascade control, the _____ of the _____ loop is the _____ of the _____ loop.

a–output
b–input
c–throughput
d–primary
e–secondary
f–tertiary

15-57 Quarter-amplitude responses are characterized by:

a–a reduction in the response every 1/4 cycle
b–an update of the process variable every 1/4 cycle
c–a reduction of their overshoots by 1/4 of the previous one
d–an amplification of their overshoots by 1/4 of the previous one

15-58 *True/False.* The integral of time and absolute error (ITAE) tuning method is performed in a closed-loop configuration.

15-59   In the Ziegler–Nichols open-loop tuning method, the process is:

a–repeated until the correct tuning constants are obtained

b–observed for long periods of time to obtain the constants

c–tested for a non-oscillating response

d–stepped by 10% of the *CV* and the results are charted to determine several parameters used to calculate the tuning constants

15-60   The reaction rate parameter (*N*) in a Ziegler-Nichols open-loop method is calculated by:

a–dividing the lag time by the rise time

b–dividing the change in process variable by the time as calculated by the tangent of the steepest point in the reaction curve

c–calculating the process gain over the percentage of control variable change

d–obtaining the reaction value of the change in the process variable over the dead time of the process

15-61   The ITAE tuning method uses a(n) _____ configuration to determine the _____ to obtain the tuning constants.

a–open-loop

b–closed-loop

c–lag time and dead time

d–rise time and lag time

e–rise time and dead time

15-62   *True/False.* The Ziegler-Nichols closed-loop tuning method obtains the value of the proportional-only gain, which creates an oscillating response with constant amplitude.

15-63   If a Ziegler-Nichols closed-loop method test shows an increasing amplitude oscillation, then:

a–the proportional gain should be increased

b–the time of response should be increased

c–the proportional gain should be reduced

d–the integral gain should be reduced

15-64   *True/False.* Software tuning methods provide hard-to-find data, such as the process transfer function in Laplace form.

ARTIFICIAL INTELLIGENCE
AND PLC SYSTEMS

CHAPTER 16 STUDY GUIDE

- Artificial intelligence is a branch of computer science that encompasses the creation of intelligent computer programs to solve tasks that require extensive knowledge.

- There are three types of artificial intelligence systems: diagnostic, knowledge, and expert.

  - *Diagnostic AI systems* are the lowest level of artificial intelligence systems. They primarily detect faults in an application, but do not try to solve them.

  - *Knowledge AI systems* are enhanced diagnostic systems that not only detect faults, but also makes decisions about their probable causes.

  - *Expert AI systems* are advanced artificial intelligence systems that provide all of the capabilities of a knowledge system, but also examine process data to predict outcomes based on the current process assessment.

- The three primary components of an AI system are the global database, the knowledge database, and the inference engine.

  - The *global database* contains all of the available information about the process being controlled. This database usually resides in the memory of the control system implementing the artificial intelligence.

  - The *knowledge database* stores process information extracted from the expert, as well as information about faults and their possible causes and solutions. The knowledge database also stores the rules used to make process decisions.

  - The *inference engine* uses the information stored in the knowledge database to arrive at a decision about the process and then executes all applicable rules. The inference engine usually resides in the AI system's main CPU.

- *Knowledge representation* deals with the way the complete AI system strategy is organized. Rule-based knowledge representation uses IF...THEN statements to use the expert's knowledge to make decisions. The IF part of the statement defines the decision's antecedents, while the THEN part of the statement defines its consequences.

- *Knowledge inference* is the process used to gather and analyze data to draw conclusions. This process occurs in the inference engine during the execution of the main control program, as well as in the knowledge database during the comparison and computation of rule solutions.

- *Blackboard architecture* refers to a type of large AI system containing several subsystems with local global and knowledge databases. In this type of architecture, knowledge inferencing is distributed throughout the system.

- Artificial intelligence systems use two methods of rule evaluation during their knowledge inferencing. These two methods are forward chaining and backward chaining.

- *Forward chaining* determines the possible outcomes of an input.
- *Backward chaining* determines the possible causes of an output.

• Both the forward chaining and the backward chaining rule evaluation methods can employ either a breadth-first or a depth-first searching technique.
  - A *breadth-first search* evaluates every rule at the same level of the decision tree before proceeding to the next level.
  - A *depth-first search* evaluates every rule in one branch of the decision tree before proceeding to the next branch.

• AI systems use statistical probability analysis to make process decisions. One commonly used probability method is Baye's theorem, which defines the probability that an event will occur based on the fact that another event has already occurred. This theorem is defined by the equation:

$$P(X/Y) = \frac{[P(Y/X)][P(X)]}{[P(Y/X)][P(X)] + [P(Y/\overline{X})][P(\overline{X})]}$$

where:

$P(Y/X) = $ the probability that Y occurs when X has occurred

$P(X) = $ the prior probability that X has occurred

$P(Y/\overline{X}) = $ the conditional probability that Y occurs if X does not occur

$P(\overline{X}) = $ the prior probability that X has not occurred

• AI systems use conflict resolution to determine which rule to execute when several rules are triggered at the same time. This decision is based on the rule's priority, which is determined by the expert.

REVIEW QUESTIONS

16-1 _____ is a subfield of computer science that encompasses the creation of intelligent computer programs to solve tasks that require extensive knowledge.

16-2 *True/False.* The concept of AI was first introduced in the early 1970s.

16-3 _____, _____, and _____ are three types of AI systems, which differ from each other in their degree of sophistication.

16-4 *True/False.* The most sophisticated AI-based system is the expert system.

16-5 Describe the features of the following types of AI systems:
(a) diagnostic
(b) knowledge
(c) expert

16-6 The _____, the _____, and the _____ are the three primary elements in the architecture of an artificial intelligence system.

16-7 *True/False.* The knowledge engineer is the person responsible for developing the AI information into a form ready for system implementation and execution.

16-8 Draw a schematic of the architecture of an artificial intelligence system.

16-9 Define the following terms:

(a) global database

(b) knowledge database

(c) inference engine

16-10 *True/False.* Feedback information is sent directly to the global database so that new knowledge information can be accessed immediately to draw statistical predictions.

16-11 The global database in a diagnostic system is most likely to be located in the PLC's _____.

16-12 *True/False.* The knowledge database is where most of an AI system's decisions are made.

16-13 *True/False.* Knowledge representation relates to how the complete artificial intelligence process is organized and presented.

16-14 _____ knowledge representation is used in PLC-based systems to define the outcomes of system inputs.

16-15 A rule consists of an IF part, called the _____, and a THEN part, called the _____.

a–consequent

b–precedent

c–intercedent

d–extracedent

e–antecedent

16-16 *True/False.* In a rule-based system, knowledge is not represented in a hierarchical structure.

16-17 _____ defines how conclusions are drawn from system data that has been gathered and analyzed.

a–Chaining

b–Annunciation

c–Inferencing

d–Implementation

16-18 *True/False.* Knowledge inference is executed in an AI system's global database.

16-19 _____ is the term used to describe large AI systems whose subsystems contain local global and knowledge databases.

16-20   *True/False.* In a network that utilizes a blackboard architecture, all decisions take place at the main controller.

16-21   _____ is the method used to arrive at expected outcomes from existing data.

16-22   *True/False.* It is possible to have a local inference engine, local global database, and a local knowledge database in a blackboard architecture.

16-23   _____ deals with finding the cause of an outcome.

16-24   A(n) _____ searches a decision tree in a vertical sequence.

16-25   *True/False.* A breadth-first search uses a horizontal sequence to evaluate the rules in an AI system.

16-26   Using the diagrams provided, indicate the sequence of evaluation for each of the following backward chaining methods:

(a) breadth-first

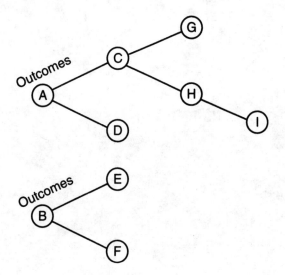

(b) depth-first

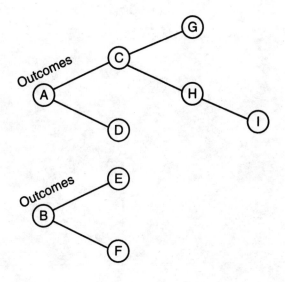

16-27 *True/False.* Most AI systems use random data analysis to anticipate the outcomes of a process.

16-28 _____ is a statistical probability method that determines the probability of an event occurring given that another event has already occurred.

16-29 Determine the probability that a temperature regulator is faulty even though the batch it is regulating is at the right temperature given the following information:

- The probability that the regulator is faulty is 30%.

- The probability that the batch will be at the right temperature when the regulator is faulty is 50%.

- The probability that the batch will be at the right temperature when the regulator is working properly is 80%.

16-30 *True/False.* Conflict resolution takes place when a controller executes a rule based on its priority.

FUZZY LOGIC

CHAPTER 17 STUDY GUIDE

- Fuzzy logic is the branch of artificial intelligence that deals with reasoning algorithms used to emulate human thinking and decision making in machines.

- Fuzzy logic was developed to overcome the limitations of binary logic, in which an input can only be ON or OFF. Fuzzy logic uses *grades* to allow an input or output to belong to more than one set; for example, an input can be 25% ON and 75% OFF.

- Fuzzy logic operation consists of three steps:
  - fuzzification
  - fuzzy logic processing
  - defuzzification

- **Fuzzification** is the translation of inputs into fuzzy form. This process consists of two main components:
  - membership functions
  - labels

- *Membership functions* are user-defined charts that group the input data into sets. Each input receives a grade that specifies how well it fits into the membership function.
  - Membership functions can have either an S, Z, Λ, or Π shape.
  - A membership function can have up to three line segments and four end points, which must occur at a grade of 1 or 0.
  - A fuzzy system can have up to seven membership functions.

- *Labels* are names associated with each membership function. The generic membership labels are as follows:
  - NL (negative large)
  - NM (negative medium)
  - NS (negative small)
  - ZR (zero)
  - PS (positive small)
  - PM (positive medium)
  - PL (positive large)

- **Fuzzy processing** involves the analysis of input data to arrive at an outcome conclusion. The two actions that occur during this stage are:
  - rule evaluation
  - fuzzy outcome calculation

- *Rule evaluation* is the analysis of the fuzzy inputs according to user-defined IF…THEN rules. If an input condition satisfies the IF part of a rule, then it will trigger the outcome associated with the THEN part of the rule. If two inputs are logically ANDed or ORed in several rules, they can produce several outcomes.

- If two inputs are ANDed, then the controller will choose the triggered outcome with the lowest grade.
- If two inputs are ORed, then the controller will choose the triggered outcome with the highest grade.

• *Fuzzy outcome calculation* is the determination of the final output outcome, given the outputs triggered by the inputs. To arrive at a final outcome value, the controller logically adds the triggered fuzzy outcomes to produce an aggregate outcome curve.

- Some controllers represent their outcomes as continuous curves mapping the grade of the outcome over the output range.
- Other controllers represent their outcomes as noncontinuous spikes, with each spike corresponding to a particular output value.

• **Defuzzification** is the process of translating the fuzzy outcome into a real-world data value that will be sent to the output module. The two most common defuzzification methods are:

- maximum value
- center of gravity

• The *maximum value* defuzzification method selects the final output value based on the rule output with the highest membership function grade. In the event that two outcomes have the same maximum value, then the controller will select either the right-most or left-most output based on the programmed criteria.

- The right-most criteria selects the maximum output with the highest output value (counts).
- The left-most criteria selects the maximum output with the lowest output value (counts).

• The *center of gravity* defuzzification method determines the final output value by calculating the center of the mass of the triggered output membership functions. The formula for obtaining the center of gravity is:

$$\text{Output data} = \frac{\sum_{n=A}^{n=G}\left[(FO_n)(FGrade_n)\right]}{\sum_{n=A}^{n=G}FGrade_n}$$

where:

Output data = the number of counts to be used for the output

FO = the fuzzy output in counts for labels n = A through G

$FGrade$ = the fuzzy grade level for levels n = A through G

• Theoretically, fuzzy logic can be used in any type of control system, but it should only be used for applications that cannot be implemented using a more standard control method. Otherwise, the system outcome may become confusing.

- Fuzzy logic can be used alone, or it can be used to complement more conventional control methods.

- Input selection should be done with the process in mind. Inputs should be related to each other. Inputs that are not related to the same process element will not produce as valuable of outcomes as those that are related to the same element.

REVIEW QUESTIONS

17–1 Fuzzy logic is the branch of artificial intelligence that deals with _____.
a–logical processes involving technical computations
b–complex solutions to process with long dead times
c–reasoning algorithms used to emulate human thinking and decision making in machines
d–combinational logic structures that describe a process in man-machine interfaces without any decision making

17–2 *True/False.* Fuzzy logic assigns a grade, or level, to an in-between logic value defined by a variable.

17–3 Using the membership function shown in Figure 17–1, the fuzzy logic controller will input the temperature of 65°F as _____.
a–50% cool, 50% hot
b–50% cool, 50% cold
c–cool
d–cold

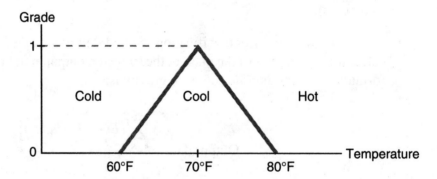

Figure 17-1. Temperature membership function.

17–4 *True/False.* The term "a little bit to the left" cannot be interpreted using fuzzy logic.

17–5 Illustrate a fuzzy logic system with four membership functions corresponding to the following age ranges:

- young (to 35 years)

- middle age (35–55 years)

- mature (45–65 years)

- old (more than 65 years)

17–6 The _____ to a fuzzy logic system is the _____ of the process.

a–logic
b–input
c–grade
d–output
e–membership function

17-7 *True/False.* A fuzzy logic system can have an input, through an analog input interface, that ranges from 0 to 4095 counts.

17–8 _____ are used in fuzzy logic computations to determine an outcome result.

a–conditional inputs
b–variables
c–IF…THEN rules
d–integro-differential process equations

17–9 In the fuzzy logic system chart in Figure 17–2, what IF conditions will be selected if the input temperature to the fuzzy logic system is 137°F?

a–no condition will be selected
b–IF too hot, THEN more speed
c–IF normal, THEN normal speed and IF too cool, THEN less speed
d–IF too cool, THEN less speed

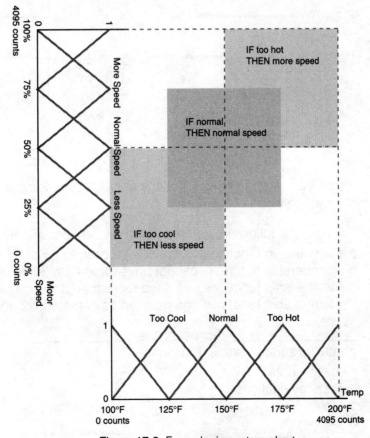

Figure 17-2. Fuzzy logic system chart.

17–10 What are the three major components of the fuzzy logic process that deal with the inputs, processing, and outputs of a control decision?

17–11 Match the following:

_____ evaluation of user-supplied information

_____ conversion of a fuzzy outcome into a real output value

_____ translation of an input variable into fuzzy form

_____ fuzzy input

a–fuzzification

b–fuzzy processing

c–defuzzifucation

d–fuzzy variable

17–12 *True/False.* Membership functions and labels are components of the fuzzification process.

17–13 Label the following four membership function representations according to their shape—S, Z, Λ, or Π:

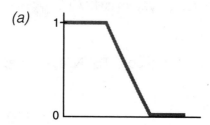

(a)

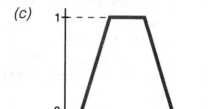

(c)

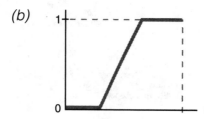

(b)

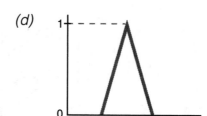

(d)

17–14 *True/False.* Membership functions must be symmetrical to maintain a proper ratio of grade to input.

17–15 Which of the following statements about membership functions is <u>not</u> true?
a–Membership functions must end at a grade of 1 or 0.
b–Membership functions cannot have more than 3 line segments.
c–Membership functions can have more than 3 line segments.
d–Membership functions can have an asymmetrical Z shape.

17–16 _____ represent the _____ of the inputs to a fuzzy controller's membership functions.
a–fuzzy inputs
b–fuzzy evaluations
c–labels
d–conditions
e–outcomes

17–17   Fill in the blanks in the fuzzification diagram in Figure 17-3 with the following terms:

- label

- membership function

- fuzzy variable

- fuzzy set

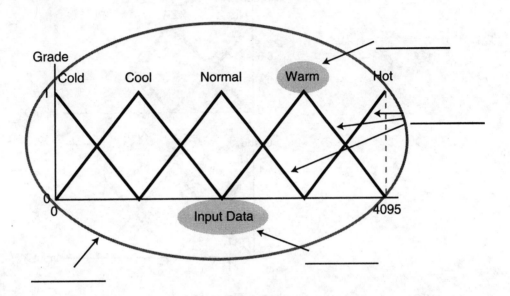

Figure 17-3. Fuzzification diagram.

17–18   *True/False.* Fuzzy labels are generally described from negative large to positive large by the labels NL, NM, NS, ZR, PS, PM, and PL.

17–19   Fuzzy processing involves the evaluation of _____ to determine the fuzzy outcome.

a–membership function grades
b–logic inputs
c–IF...THEN rules
d–logic outputs

17–20   When a fuzzy logic controller evaluates a(n) _____ condition and finds it to be satisfied, it _____ an outcome.

a–triggers
b–deactivates
c–THEN
d–IF
e–validates

17–21   *True/False.* IF conditions can have either one fuzzy input or two fuzzy inputs linked with a logical AND function.

17–22 The two fuzzy sets with three membership functions each shown in Figure 17–4 will trigger a maximum of _____ possible rules based on the inputs indicated and linked by logical ANDs.

a–two
b–four
c–six
d–nine

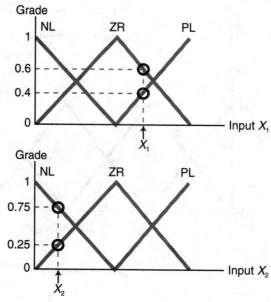

Figure 17-4. Two fuzzy input sets.

17–23 If a rule contains two inputs linked by an AND function, the selected outcome will be the one with the _____ grade; however, if the inputs are linked by an OR function, the selected outcome will be the one with the _____ grade.

a–second
b–lowest
c–highest
d–first
e–best

17–24 Referring to Figure 17–4, what will be the selected outcome for Y_1 given the rule IF X_1 = ZR AND X_2 = ZR, THEN Y_1 = ZR?
a–0.6
b–0.75
c–0.25
d–0.4

17–25 Referring to Figure 17-4, _____ is the maximum number of rules that can be obtained from the two fuzzy inputs using the membership functions.
a–four
b–six
c–nine
d–twelve

17-26 If several rules are triggered resulting in several selected outcomes, the fuzzy controller must logically _____ the outcomes before the defuzzification process can begin.

a–multiply
b–subtract
c–add
d–divide

17-27 Some fuzzy controllers use _____ to represent the output membership functions.

a–logical curves
b–centroids
c–computational centers
d–noncontinuous functions

17-28 Plot the result of the logical sum of the two triggered outputs at 0.25ZR in the output curve shown in Figure 17–5.

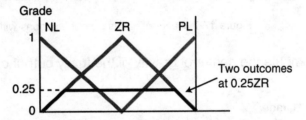

Figure 17-5. Two triggered 0.25ZR outputs.

17-29 Which of the following is <u>not</u> a defuzzification method?

a–maximum value left-most criteria
b–maximum value right-most criteria
c–center of gravity
d–sum of the averages

17-30 *True/False*. The centroid of an apple can be said to be the point where the apple can be cut into two exact weight masses.

17-31 Using the maximum value method, what is the selected count output for the three triggered noncontinuous output membership functions shown in Figure 17–6?

a–1755 counts
b–2340 counts
c–3510 counts
d–2535 counts

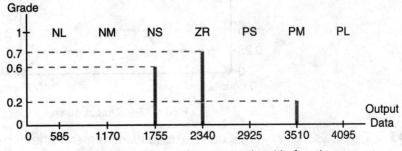

Figure 17-6. Noncontinuous membership functions.

17-32 Referencing the output functions shown in Figure 17–7, the left-most maximum value defuzzification method will specify an output of _____, while the right-most maximum value method will specify an output of _____.

a–1170

b–1755

c–3510

d–2145 (average of all three)

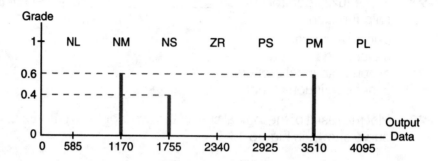

Figure 17-7. Noncontinuous output functions with two maximum values.

17-33 Compute the center of gravity of the fuzzy output curve shown in Figure 17–8.

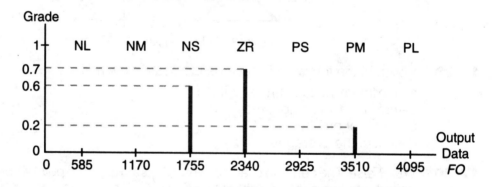

Figure 17-8. Noncontinuous fuzzy output curve.

17-34 Approximate the centroid of the outcomes whose logical sum is shown in the output curve in Figure 17–9.

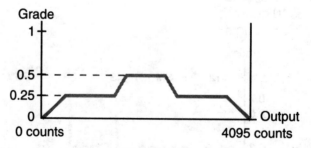

Figure 17-9. Output curve.

17-35 *True/False*. Fuzzy logic can be used to implement other types of systems, such as cascaded control.

17–36 Referencing Figure 17–10, the area between the labels NL and NS has
_____ sensitivity than the area between labels NS and PS.

a–more
b–the same
c–less
d–average

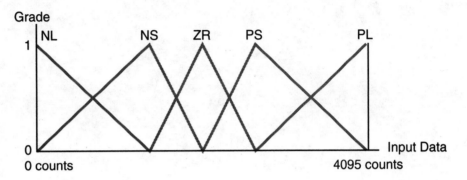

Figure 17-10. Asymmetrical fuzzy input curves.

17–37 *True/False.* A fuzzy set can only have an odd number of membership functions.

17–38 The membership functions shown in Figure 17–11 illustrate a case where
_____.

a–there are flat areas
b–all labels are very sensitive
c–there are points where no sensitivity exists between labels
d–there is no sensitivity around a grade level of 0.5 for all labels

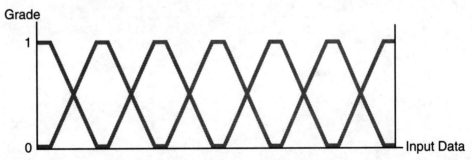

Figure 17-11. Fuzzy input set.

17–39 *True/False.* When developing rules, the user must be certain to include all possible fuzzy input combinations to avoid an error output.

17–40 If an input received by a fuzzy controller falls into a gap that is not defined by a membership function, the controller will generate _____.

a–an output proportional to the gap
b–the previous output selected
c–a reference command to the gap location
d–an error condition

LOCAL AREA
NETWORKS

CHAPTER 18 STUDY GUIDE

- Local area networks (LANs) are high-speed, medium-distance communication systems that connect computers located at distances of up to one mile, allowing them to exchange information with each other. Devices connected to a LAN are referred to as *nodes*, and different types of LANs can support different numbers of nodes.

- One type of local area network, the industrial networks, must meet the following criteria:
  - capable of supporting real-time control
  - high data integrity
  - high noise immunity
  - high reliability in harsh environments
  - suitable for large installations

- The main differences between business networks and industrial networks are that business networks do not require as much noise immunity and they can tolerate longer access times.

- Local area networks greatly reduce the wiring costs associated with connecting dispersed PLCs and provide an efficient way of transmitting data among them.

- The topology of a network describes the way in which the individual nodes are connected to it. The four topologies used in local area networks are:
  - star
  - common bus
  - ring
  - star-shaped ring

- The *star topology* consists a multiport host computer to which all of the nodes are connected. The main advantage of this topology is that it can be easily implemented with a simple point-to-point protocol. However, a major disadvantage is that if the central node fails, the whole network communication scheme fails.

- The *common bus topology* is characterized by a main trunkline to which the individual nodes are connected in a multidrop fashion.
  - Common bus topology is very applicable to distributed systems, since each station has equal independent control capabilities and can exchange information at any time.
  - In a master/slave common bus topology, communication is governed by a master controller that polls each slave controller to determine whether it has any information to send.

- In *ring topology*, the nodes are connected to each other in a circular fashion. This topology is not used in industrial environments because the failure of one node will cause the entire network to crash.

- *Star-shaped ring topology*, a modification of the ring topology, uses a wire center to bypass failed nodes. This topology eliminates the problem of failed rings breaking the network, but requires twice as much wire as a standard ring network.

- Several data transmission techniques, such as Manchester encoding, frequency shift keying, and nonreturn to zero invert on ones, are used to code data for transmission through a network. Different networks use different data transmission techniques.

- Network access methods determine the manner in which a PLC accesses the network to transmit information. The three most common network access methods are:
  - polling
  - collision detection
  - token passing

- In the *polling* access method, a master controller questions each slave station in sequence to determine whether it has data to transmit. If a slave does not respond in a set period of time, the master proceeds to the next slave.

- *Collision detection*, also referred to as CSMA/CD, is an access method in which each node with a message to transmit waits until there is no traffic on the network and then sends its message.
  - If two nodes try to transmit at the same time, a collision occurs; at which point, each nose will wait a variable amount of time before trying to retransmit its message.
  - Each collision and retry decreases data throughput time. Also, access time increases as traffic increases. Thus, collision detection is not a popular access method for control networks.

- In the *token passing* access technique, the PLCs pass a token giving the station with the token the exclusive right to transmit on the network. This access method eliminates contention among PLC stations trying to gain access to the networks.

- The most common transmission media used for PLC networks are:
  - twisted-pair conductors
  - coaxial cables
  - fiber-optic cables

- A *twisted-pair conductor* is a relatively inexpensive medium that is used extensively in industry for point-to-point applications at distances of up to 4000 feet and at transmission rates as high as 250 kilobaud. However, it is characterized by performance limitations over great distances due to its nonuniform impedance.

- Coaxial cables have extremely uniform cable impedancesallowing them to transmit data for greater distances at very high transmission speeds. The two types of coaxial cable used in networks is baseband and broadband.
  - *Baseband coaxial cable* can send one signal at a time at its original frequency. It can transmit data at speeds of up to 2 megabaud at distances of up to 18,000 feet.

- *Broadband coaxial cable* uses frequency division multiplexing to provide many simultaneous transmission channels, each with a different frequency. Broadband cable can support a transmission rate of up to 150 megabaud.

- *Fiber-optic cable*, which consists of glass or plastic fibers enclosed in a material with low refraction, transmits data through pulses of reflected light. Fiber-optic cable is immune to all kinds of electrical interference and can transmit data at high speeds for long distances; however, a low-loss tap has yet to be perfected and it is expensive to use.

- When selecting a network, a designer must determine how many nodes are required and what type of devices will be connected to it to ensure that the network can support the application's requirements.

- Each network has a maximum specified transmission distance. This maximum distance consists of two parts: the maximum length of the main cable and the maximum length of the drop cable used between a node and the main cable. These lengths affect the distance at which individual nodes can be placed, as well as the type of cable required for the network.

- Response time is the sum of the time required to detect an input transition, transmit the information to the output node, and operate the output. The system designer should determine the response time for the worst-case network scenario to determine the maximum network response time.

- A LAN's throughput specification specifies the number of I/O points that can be updated per second through the network.

- The designer should determine what types of devices the network will support as well as what is involved in connecting the devices to the network. Some devices require gateways, specialized connection devices with network- and device-compatible ports, to interface with the network.

- A protocol is a set of rules that two or more devices must follow to communicate with each other. Protocols define how a network will handle problems like data translation, flow control, access by multiple devices, and communication line errors.

- Three common protocol standards are:
  - the OSI reference model
  - the IEEE standards
  - the TCP/IP protocol

- The ISO's OSI reference model divides the various functions that protocols must perform into seven hierarchical layers. These layers are defined as follows:
  - layer 1: physical (electrical characteristics)
  - layer 2: data link (error detection, framing)
  - layer 3: network (routing)

- layer 4: transport (end-to-end service)
- layer 5: session (establishment and disconnection)
- layer 6: presentation (data conversion)
- layer 7: application (user interface)

- The IEEE provides three network protocol standards that apply to different types of network access methods and different network speeds. Three of these standards that apply to local area networks are the IEEE 802.3, the IEEE 802.4, and the IEEE 802.5.

  - The IEEE 802.3 provides specifications for networks that operate at speeds of 1 to 20 Mbaud (baseband) or 10 Mbaud (broadband) using the collision detection access method.

  - The IEEE 802.4 provides specifications for token bus LANs operating at 1 to 20 Mbit/second data rates.

  - The IEEE 802.5 specifies a token ring network at a transmission rate of 1.4 Mbaud for baseband cables.

- The TCP/IP protocol guarantees control of end-to-end connections, protection against loss of sequence, and connection time control, among other services. It also performs functions such as addressing network data, distributing data packages, and routing data in multinetwork systems.

- Before a local area network is installed, the designer should test it to ensure that it performs the desired functions and provides the required response time.

- The biggest differences among the various types of local area networks are their transmission media and their network access methods. These factors should be evaluated when selecting the appropriate network for an application. Other factors that should be considered include speed and capacity, reliability, flexibility, and cost.

REVIEW QUESTIONS

18-1   Local area networks _____ computing tasks by allowing computers to exchange information among themselves, without having to go through a central location.

18-2   A device connected to a network or data highway is referred to as a _____.

18-3   List five criteria of an industrial network.

18-4   What are the main differences between industrial and business networks?

18-5   Describe two methods that were used to communicate between PLCs before local area networks came into use?

18-6   The two most common applications of local area networks are _____ and _____.

18-7 List three disadvantages of large applications that use a single PLC system for data collection and control?

18-8 *True/False*. Performance and reliability are usually improved in distributed control applications when control functions are spread among several controllers.

18-9 *True/False*. The topology of a local area network defines how individual nodes are connected to the network.

18-10 Which of the following factors is/are influenced by a network's topology?
a–throughput
b–implementation cost
c–reliability
d–all of the above

18-11 Which of the following topologies is not commonly used in PLC networks?
a–star
b–common bus
c–tree
d–ring

18-12 *True/False*. A disadvantage of the star topology is that it does not allow easy implementation of point-to-point protocol

18-13 Which of the following factors is the greatest disadvantage of using the star topology in an industrial environment?

a–dependence on central node speed
b–high wiring cost
c–failure of the central node will bring down the system
d–all messages must pass through the central node resulting in low throughput

18-14 Sketch the star topology showing the multiports in the main controller.

18-15 The common bus topology is characterized by a main trunkline in which individual nodes are connected to a PLC in a _____ fashion.

18-16 Which of the following factors is <u>not</u> an advantage of the common bus topology?
a–high-speed throughput
b–each station has equal independent control
c–reconfiguration of the network is easy
d–stations can exchange information at any time

18-17 *True/False*. A break in a common bus network's trunkline would affect at least one node, but it would not hamper total network communications.

18-18 *True/False*. It is possible for a common bus topology to have a master/slave configuration.

18-19 How does a master controller communicate with a slave controller?

18-20 What is the major disadvantage of the ring topology?

a–It does not require multidropping.
b–Failure of a node brings down the system.
c–It cannot use fiber-optic links.
d–Collision detection cannot be avoided.

18-21 *True/False.* In a star-shaped ring, the use of a wire center allows failed nodes to be automatically bypassed.

18-22 The major disadvantage of a star-shaped ring network using a wire center is that:

a–a modem cannot be interfaced with the wire center
b–a failed node will still bring down the network
c–it requires twice as much wiring as ring networks
d–it is too complicated for practical applications

18-23 The _____ defines the manner in which a PLC gains access to a network's data highway.

a–token pass
b–access method
c–polling scheme
d–introductory method

18-24 The network access method most often used in a master/slave configuration is _____.

18-25 Communication in the polling access method is initiated by the _____ controller.

18-26 The collision detection method is sometimes referred to as CSMA/CD which stands for:

a–collision sense maximum access with collision detection
b–collision sense multiple access with carrier detection
c–carrier sense multiple access with collision detection
d–carrier sense maximum access with collision detection

18-27 Explain how the collision detection access method functions and what happens when a collision occurs.

18-28 The CSMA/CD method works well as long as:

a–the distance between nodes is not too long
b–the data transmission rate is fast
c–there are not many nodes in the network
d–none of the above

18-29 In the CSMA/CD method, many nodes in constant communication will cause:

a–network throughput to increase and access time to decrease
b–network throughput to drop off and access time to increase
c–network throughput to drop off and access time to decrease
d–network throughput to increase and access time to increases

18-30   *True/False.* Collision detection is one of the most popular access methods for PLC networks.

18-31   Token passing is an access technique used to eliminate:

a–master/slave communication problems
b–collision problems in the CSMA/CD method
c–contention among stations trying to gain access to the network
d–the station that is trying to transmit

18-32   A(n) _____ is a message granting a polled station the exclusive but temporary right to control the network.

18-33   In the token passing method, after a station (or node) finishes transmitting a message, it must _____ the right to network transmission to the _____ node.

a–keep
b–next available
c–next designated
d–previously designated
e–relinquish

18-34   *True/False.* In token passing, the token is passed from one station to the next in a random manner.

18-35   How are the stations identified in a common bus network that uses the token passing technique?

18-36   The token passing technique is preferred in applications requiring distributed control with:

a–few stations
b–many nodes
c–many nodes and/or stringent response time
d–fast responses

18-37   *True/False.* A star topology can use fiber-optic links as its transmission medium.

18-38   Twisted-pair conductors are generally used as the transmission medium in:

a–applications with fast baud rates
b–point-to-point applications
c–applications that span long distances
d–places with high noise

18-39   Twisted-pair conductor performance is limited primarily due to:

a–reflection in the transmission media
b–nonuniformity of the cable impedance
c–problems with distance
d–all of the above

18-40   Which type of coaxial cable is used as the medium for regular cable television signal transmission?

18-41   True/False. Baseband coaxial cable is thicker than broadband coaxial cable.

18-42   True/False. Broadband networks use division multiplexing to provide many simultaneous channels.

18-43   The characteristics of fiber-optic cable include:

a–high cost
b–small and light weight
c–totally immune to electrical interference
d–all of the above

18-44   True/False. The types of devices that can be supported by a network may include intelligent devices other than PLCs.

18-45   What are the two span lengths that must be evaluated in local area networks?

18-46   True/False. The required transmission distance does not affect the type of coaxial cable selected for a local area network.

18-47   An important parameter to consider when evaluating the speed of a local area network is:

a–the minimum response time
b–the maximum response time
c–the average response time
d–the throughput of the network

18-48   A(n) _____ may be required to facilitate communication between two different networks or between a network and a foreign device.

18-49   Information typically exchanged on a network does not include:

a–information stored in the executive memory
b–I/O point status
c–register contents
d–PLC status

18-50   What is a protocol?

18-51   What kind of network problems does a protocol usually address?

18-52   Match each of the following layers with its function as specified by the OSI model:

_____ layer 7: application   a–data conversion

_____ layer 6: presentation   b–error detection

_____ layer 5: session   c–end-to-end service

_____ layer 4: transport   d–routing

_____ layer 3: network   e–user interface

_____ layer 2: data link   f–electrical characteristics

_____ layer 1: physical   g–establishment and disconnections

18-53   True/False. The IEEE 802 protocols are based on the OSI model.

18-54 The _____ part of the TCP/IP protocol governs the control of end-to-end connections, while the _____ part performs complementary addressing and routing functions.

18-55 PLC manufacturers, for the most part, lean toward the use of a _____ topology using the _____ access method.
a–ring
b–common bus
c–CSMA/CD
d–polling
e–token passing

18-56 Match the following terms with the most appropriate answer:

_____ broadband   a–a device in a network

_____ baseband   b–interrogation

_____ local area networks   c–immune to noise

_____ polling   d–unstable line impedance

_____ twisted pair cable   e–interface for a network

_____ OSI   f–single signal transmission

_____ coaxial cable   g–sequential network communication

_____ gateway   h–seven-layer model

_____ node   i–high-speed, medium-distance
                                  communication method

_____ token passing   j–two channels

_____ fiber optics   k–uniform impedance

I/O BUS
NETWORKS

CHAPTER 19 STUDY GUIDE

- I/O bus networks allow PLCs to communicate directly with I/O devices through digital communication. The basic function of an I/O bus network is to communicate information with, as well as supply power to, the field devices that are connected to the bus.

- An I/O bus scanner reads and writes information to each of the field device addresses in an I/O bus network, as well as decodes the information contained in the network information packet.

- The two major types of I/O bus networks are device bus networks and process bus networks.
  - *Device bus networks* interface with low-level information devices that primarily transmit data relating to the state of the device and its operational status. These devices include discrete and simple analog devices.
  - *Process bus networks* interface with high-level information devices (i.e., analog devices) that transmit large amounts of data about not only their own operation, but the operation of the process as well.

- Neither device bus nor process bus networks have set protocol standards; however, several companies and organizations are working towards developing I/O bus network specifications.

- The digital communication scheme used by I/O bus networks offers a great advantage over other field device communication schemes because it eliminates the errors associated with analog-to-digital conversions, allows more than one device to be connected to a wire, provides a signal less susceptible to interference, and eliminates the need to scale process data. Another advantage of I/O bus networks is that they reduce the amount of wiring required to connect the field devices with the PLC.

- **Device bus networks** can only transmit small amounts of information, but they do so at a high transmission speed. Device bus networks can either be bit wide or byte wide.
  - *Byte-wide device bus networks* interface with discrete and small analog devices that transmit only a few bytes of data. These networks can transfer between 1 and 50 or more bytes of data at a time.
  - *Bit-wide device bus networks* interface with simple discrete devices only. They can transfer less than 8 bits of data over relatively short distances.

- The two most common types of byte-wide device bus networks are:
  - InterBus-S
  - CANbus (DeviceNet and SDS)

- The *InterBus-S byte-wide device bus network* connects discrete and small analog field devices to a PLC or computer via a ring network configuration. A PLC in this network communicates with the field devices in a master/slave method.

- An InterBus-S network can handle up to 4096 field I/O devices at a speed of 500 Kbaud with cyclic redundancy check error detection.

- I/O device addresses in an InterBus-S network are automatically determined by the devices' physical locations. Also, this network transmits data in frames, simultaneously updating information to all connected devices.

• *CANbus byte-wide device bus networks* use an open protocol system featuring nondestructive arbitration, variable length messages, and advanced error management. A four-wire cable—two wires for power, two for signal transmission, and a "fifth" shield wire—provides the connection to field devices. Two common types of CANbus networks are the DeviceNet and the SDS networks.

- DeviceNet networks can support 64 field devices and a maximum of 2048 field devices. The PLC connects to the field devices in a trunkline configuration.

- SDS networks also support 64 nodes; however, this increases to 126 addressable locations when the nodes are multiplexed.

• The CANbus network uses three OSI protocol layers and defines both the medium access control method and the physical signaling for the network. A CANbus scanner or an I/O processor provides the interface between a PLC and a CANbus network.

• The three most common types of bit-wide device bus networks are:

- ASI
- InterBus Loop
- Seriplex

• The *ASI bit-wide device bus network* is appropriate for simple, discrete applications requiring no more than 124 I/O field devices. These field devices can be connected to up to 31 nodes in either a tree, star, or ring topology. ASI networks require a 24-VDC power supply connected through a two-wire, unshielded, untwisted cable.

• The *InterBus Loop bit-wide device bus network* is used to interface a PLC with simple sensor and actuator devices. This network uses the same protocol as the InterBus-S byte-wide network, thus these networks can communicate with each other through an InterBus Loop terminal module.

• The *Seriplex bit-wide device bus network* can connect up to 510 field devices to a PLC in either a master/slave or peer-to-peer communication scheme. This network can span distances of up to 5000 feet in a star, loop, tree, or multidrop configuration. A Seriplex network can connect with simple analog devices.

• **Process bus networks** are high-level, open, digital communication networks that are used to connect analog devices to a control system. These networks are capable of transmitting the enormous amounts of information associated with a process control application. The two most commonly used process bus protocols are:

- Fieldbus
- Profibus

- The *Fieldbus process bus network* is a digital, serial, multiport, two-way communication system that provides the desirable features associated with 4–20 mA analog systems, but also provides the advantages of reduced wiring, compatibility among Fieldbus devices, smaller space requirements, and reliability.

- The Fieldbus protocol is based on three layers of the OSI protocol—the physical layer (layer 1), the data link layer (layer 2), and the application layer (layer 7).
  - The physical layer of the Fieldbus protocol, corresponding to layer 1 of the OSI model, provides physical specifications for the network.
  - The communication stack portion of the Fieldbus network, corresponding to layers 2 and 7 of the OSI model, controls the transmission of messages through the network, as well as the coding and decoding of messages.

- The Fieldbus also provides another layer, the user layer, which implements the network's distributed control strategy and defines the software model for user interaction. This layer has three key elements: function blocks, device description services, and system management.
  - The function block capabilities allow connected field devices to be programmed through function blocks containing any instruction available in the system.
  - Device description services act as drivers, allowing the host computer in the network obtain message information.
  - The system management portion of the user layer schedules the execution of function blocks at precisely defined intervals.

- The *Profibus process bus network* is capable of communicating information between a master controller and an intelligent slave field device, as well as between hosts in the network. The three types of Profibus networks are Profibus-FMS, Profibus-DP, and Profibus-PA.
  - The Profibus-FMS network allows communication between the upper level, cell level, and device level of the Profibus hierarchy.
  - The Profibus-DP is a performance-optimized version of the Profibus-DP designed to handle time-critical communications.
  - The Profibus-PA is the process automation version of the Profibus network, providing bus-powered stations and intrinsic safety according to the transmission specifications of the IEC 1158-2 standard.

- The Profibus network follows the OSI model; however, each type of Profibus network contains slight variations of the model's layers.

- The most important aspects of I/O bus network installation are the use of the correct type of cable, number of conductors, and type of connectors. I/O bus networks can also have either open or enclosed ports.

- A typical device bus network wiring scheme includes two trunk connections with five wires each providing the signal, power, and shielding. Most device bus networks require a terminator resistor at the end of the main trunkline. Similar cabling criteria apply to process bus networks.

• The addressing of devices in an I/O bus network occurs during the programming of devices in the system. This can be done either on the network using a PC connected directly to the network or connected to it through a gateway, or it can be done through the PLC's RS-232 port.

REVIEW QUESTIONS

19-1 An I/O bus network can be defined as a _____.

a–network that communicates I/O operating status

b–local area network that connects with an Internet router

c–network that allows direct communication between a PLC and intelligent I/O field devices

d–communication scheme used to establish peer-to-peer data exchange

19-2 I/O bus networks require the use of an _____ to communicate with the host controller.

a–I/O connector

b–I/O RS-232 compatible cable

c–I/O network sequencer

d–I/O bus scanner

19-3 Match the following terms with their appropriate descriptions:

_____ I/O field devices   a–interfaces with low-level devices

_____ device bus network   b–interfaces with high-level devices

_____ process bus network   c–uses built-in intelligence to communicate with the network

19-4 Device bus networks transmit _____ information, while process bus networks transfer _____ information.

a–reversible

b–large amounts of

c–small amounts of

d–medium amounts of

e–direct

19-5 The two types of device bus networks are _____ and _____.

a–table wide

b–bit wide

c–byte wide

d–register wide

e–baud wide

19-6 *True/False.* The digital transmission of data in an I/O bus network is one of its greatest advantages.

19-7 *True/False.* The process bus is an attempt to eliminate the need to transmit 4–20mA analog signals to host controllers.

19–8 Match the following types of networks with their appropriate descriptions:

_____ Profibus   a–CANbus

_____ DeviceNet   b–byte wide

_____ Fieldbus Foundation   c–bit wide

_____ Seriplex   d–process bus network

_____ InterBus-S   e–Fieldbus protocol

19–9 The InterBus-S from _____ can support _____ through the use of smart I/O modules.

a–Square D
b–Phoenix Contact
c–RS-232 devices
d–nonintelligent field devices
e–intelligent devices

19–10 There are _____ wires in a CANbus network, including _____ power wires, _____ signal wires, and _____ shield wire.

19–11 _____ and _____ are both CANbus networks.

a–SDS
b–InterBus-S
c–Profibus
d–Fieldbus
e–DeviceNet

19–12 *True/False.* The InterBus-S uses only two layers of the ISO model.

19–13 The number of field devices connected to an SDS device network can be expanded using _____.

a–additional connector expanders
b–smart single-point I/O field devices
c–a high-density I/O concentrator
d–standard PLC remote subsystems

19–14 CANbus stands for _____ and its technology was originally developed by _____.

a–several companies
b–the automotive industry
c–control area network bus
d–control actuator network bus
e–the computer industry

19–15 *True/False.* ASI is a bit-wide process bus network.

19-16 *True/False.* The InterBus Loop bit-wide device network cannot communicate with the byte-wide InterBus-S.

19–17   Seriplex utilizes the _____ chip, which is also used by the intelligent field devices in the bus's interfaces.
a–ASI
b–asynchronus communicator
c–ASIC
d–proprietary

19–18   *True/False.* A Seriplex network can be configured without a host controller.

19–19   *True/False.* The Fieldbus and Profibus are the two most common process bus network protocols.

19–20   *True/False.* Process bus networks transfer data at a very slow rate because of the nature of the analog signals they transmit.

19–21   Layers 2 and 7 of the Fieldbus protocol compose the protocol's _____.
a–Fieldbus transport layers
b–Fieldbus application transport
c–communication stack
d–data link stack

19–22   The Fieldbus protocol is characterized by a(n) _____, which contains capabilities for function block programming, device description services, and network system management.
a–extended application layer
b–user layer
c–network layer
d–function layer

19–23   *True/False.* The Fieldbus process bus network from the Fieldbus Foundation can support intrinsically safe devices and installations.

19–24   The Fieldbus network can operate at two speeds, _____ and
_____.
a–H1 (low speed of 15 Kbaud)
b–H1 (low speed of 31.25 Kbaud)
c–H1 (low speed of 30 Kbaud)
d–H2 (high speed of 1 Mbaud or 2.5 Mbaud)
e–H2 (high speed of 7 Mbaud)

19–25   *True/False.* In a Fieldbus network, it is not possible to connect networks at both speeds to only one host.

19–26   The Fieldbus protocol uses two types of message transmissions, _____ and _____, which relate to _____ and _____ transmissions, respectively.
a–cyclic
b–acyclic
c–unscheduled
d–rescheduled
e–scheduled

19–27 _____ are encapsulated control functions that allow the performance of I/O operations, such as PID control and the reading of analog I/O.

a–User instructions
b–Data instructions
c–Ladder instructions
d–Function blocks

19-28 *True/False.* All devices connected to a Fieldbus network must have a device description.

19–29 *True/False.* The system manager in a Fieldbus network schedules the execution of function blocks at precisely defined intervals and automatically assigns field device addresses.

19–30 Match the following types of Profibus networks with their descriptions:

_____ process automation version   a–Profibus-FMS

_____ performance-optimized version   b–Profibus-DP

_____ communicates between upper-   c–Profibus-PA
level, cell-level, and field-level
devices

19–31 *True/False.* The Fieldbus message specification (FMS) and the lower layer interface (LLI) used in the Profibus-FMS are implemented in layer 7 of the ISO model.

19–32 *True/False.* The Profibus-DP network does not implement layer 7 of the ISO model so that it can achieve the high operational speed required for its application.

19–33 The Profibus-DP uses a _____ to provide the mapping between the user interface and layer 2 of the network.

a–direct access mapper (DAM)
b–data mapping manager (DMM)
c–direct data link mapper (DDLM)
d–direct Profibus mapper (DPM)

19–34 *True/False.* The Profibus-PA protocol implements function blocks in layer 7 of the ISO model.

19–35 A Profibus network can support _____ communication.

a–master-master
b–master-slave
c–a combination of master-master and master-slave
d–none of the above

19–36 The Profibus network adheres to the _____ standard.

a–EIA RS-429
b–EIA RS-232
c–EIA RS-422
d–EIA RS-485

19–37   *True/False.* All device bus network cables are the same.

19–38   *True/False.* When computing network distances, the user must take into consideration the maximum drop length in addition to the trunk length.

19–39   In general, _____ field devices are more expensive than _____ field devices because their components are more expensive.
a–I/O bus–compatible
b–process bus–compatible
c–program bus–compatible
d–device bus–compatible
e–LAN-compatible

CHAPTER TWENTY

Study Guide and Review Questions

PLC START-UP AND MAINTENANCE

CHAPTER 20 STUDY GUIDE

- The system layout is the conscientious approach to placing and interconnecting the system components not only to satisfy the application, but also to ensure that the controller will operate trouble free in its environment.

- The system layout takes into consideration not only the PLC components as well as other equipment, such as isolation transformers, auxiliary power supplies, safety control relays, and incoming line noise suppressors.

- PLC system layout includes the consideration of many factors. Some guidelines for system layout, wiring, and component placement are as follows:
  - The best location for the PLC enclosure is near the machine or process that it will be controlling. The enclosure should conform to NEMA standards for the operating environment.
  - The temperature inside the enclosure should not exceed the controller's maximum operating temperature, which is typically 60°C.
  - A fan or blower should be installed if "hot spots" develop inside the enclosure. If condensation occurs, a thermostat-controlled heater should be installed.
  - The system enclosure (with the PLC) should not be placed close to equipment generating high noise, such as welding machines.
  - To allow for maximum convection cooling, all controller components should be mounted in a vertical (upright) position.
  - Grouping of common I/O modules is a good practice. All AC wiring should be kept away from low-level DC wiring to avoid crosstalk interference. If I/O wiring must cross AC power lines, it should do so at right angles.
  - The duct and wiring layout defines the physical location of wireways and the routing of field I/O signals, power, and controller connections within the enclosure.
  - Proper grounding techniques specify that the grounding path must be permanent, continuous, and able to safely conduct the ground-fault current in the system with minimal impedance.

- PLC system power requirements include the following:
  - The system power supply and I/O devices should have a common AC source to minimize line interference and prevent faulty input signals.
  - The use of an isolation transformer is recommended if noise is likely to be introduced into the power lines by noise-generating equipment. A constant voltage transformer should be used in the event of soft AC lines.

- The PLC system should contain enough emergency circuits to either partially or totally stop controller and machine operation in the event of an emergency. Emergency devices include emergency stops, master and safety control relays, and emergency power disconnects.

- Excessive noise, heat, and line voltage variations can all have a detrimental effect on the PLC system. Thus, the components should be placed away from high noise-generating devices, temperature levels should be kept within specifications, and the incoming voltage should be kept to within acceptable parameters. Typical PLC conditions include:
    - 60% of the inputs are ON at any one time
    - 30% of the outputs are ON at any one time
    - the currents supplied by all modules average a certain value
    - the ambient temperature is around 40°C

- When installing the I/O devices, the user should make sure that the modules are installed in the correct locations, the correct size wire is used, the wires and terminals are labeled, and the wires to each module are bundled together.

- Certain field device wiring connections require special attention. These connections include leaky inputs, inductive loads, output fusing, and shielded cables.
    - A bleeding resistor may be used in cases where a field device exhibits an output current leakage that could cause the input circuitry to turn ON.
    - Inductive loads should be suppressed using RC snubbers and/or MOVs.
    - If fuses are not incorporated into an output module, they should be installed externally at the terminal block.
    - Shielded cables should be grounded at one end only, preferably at the chassis rack.

- The system start-up includes prestart-up procedures, the static input wiring check, the static output wiring check, the control program review, and the dynamic system checkout.
    - The prestart-up procedure involves several inspections of the hardware components before power is applied to the system.
    - The static input wiring check should be performed with power applied to the controller and input devices. This check verifies that each input device is connected to the correct terminal and that the input modules are functioning properly.
    - The static output wiring check should be performed with power applied to the controller and output devices. All the devices that will cause mechanical motion should be locally disconnected.
    - The control program review consists of a final review of the complete documentation package of the control program.
    - The dynamic system checkout involves bringing the entire system under PLC control to verify correct operation of the outputs according to the logic program.

- Even though a PLC system requires minimal maintenance, certain maintenance measures should be performed periodically to reduce the chance of system malfunction. These preventative maintenance procedures should be scheduled during regular machine maintenance to minimize downtime.

- As a rule of thumb, 10% of each part used in the PLC system, as well as one of each main board, should be kept as spare parts.

- Ground loops can occur in a PLC system when two or more electrical paths exist in a ground line. To avoid this problem, shielded cable should only be connected to ground at only one end.

- When diagnosing I/O malfunctions, the first check should be the LED power and/or logic indicators in the module. After that, the key to finding the problem, whether it is an input or output problem, is to isolate the problem to either the module, the field device, or the wiring.

REVIEW QUESTIONS

20-1 Briefly define the term *system layout*.

20-2 *True/False.* In a proper system layout, the components can be easily maintained, but components may not be easily accessible.

20-3 Name three types of equipment other than the PLC that can form part of the system layout.

20-4 The best location for the PLC enclosure is:
a–close to the incoming power
b–in the control room
c–close to the machine or process
d–far away from the machine or process

20-5 Placing a remote I/O panel close to the controlled machine will generally:
a–simplify start-up
b–minimize wire runs
c–simplify maintenance and troubleshooting
d–all of the above

20-6 A NEMA panel enclosure can provide protection from all of the following conditions except:
a–atmospheric contaminants
b–vibration
c–conductive dust
d–moisture

20-7 Name four guidelines concerning the placement of components inside the enclosure, the wiring of I/O, and the location of the enclosure.

20-8 *True/False.* Placing AC power outlets inside the enclosure should be avoided when possible.

20-9 Typically, programmable controller systems installed inside an enclosure can withstand a maximum temperature of:
a–60°C outside the enclosure
b–50°C outside the enclosure
c–60°C inside the enclosure
d–50°C inside the enclosure

20-10 If "hot spots" are generated inside the enclosure, a(n) _____ should be installed to help dissipate the heat.

20-11 A thermostat-controlled heater should be used in a panel enclosure if _____ is anticipated.

20-12 *True/False.* A PLC can operate trouble free near an arc welding machine if it is installed in an enclosure.

20-13 Most controllers should be mounted in a(n) _____ position to allow maximum convection cooling.

a–horizontal
b–vertical
c–sideways
d–inverted

20-14 The _____ dissipates more heat than any other system component.

20-15 Input/output racks are not typically placed:

a–adjacent to the CPU
b–beside the power supply
c–directly above the CPU
d–in a remote enclosure

20-16 Other equipment inside the enclosure should be placed away from the controller components so that:

a–power is independent
b–space is maximized
c–the effects of noise are minimized
d–none of the above

20-17 *True/False.* Fans or blowers should be placed at the top of the panel enclosure.

20-18 One good reason for grouping common I/O modules is to minimize _____ interference.

a–crisscross
b–crosswave
c–crosscorner
d–crosstalk

20-19 What does the duct and wiring layout define?

20-20 *True/False.* The enclosure's duct and wiring layout depends on the placement of I/O modules within each I/O rack.

20-21 Incoming AC power lines should be kept _____ low-level DC lines.

a–separate from
b–together with
c–adjacent to
d–level with

20-22   If the I/O wiring must cross the AC power lines, it should do so at _____.

20-23   The National Electric Code (NEC) article 250 provides data such as size, type of conductors, colors, and connections necessary for safe _____ of electrical components.

20-24   Proper grounding procedures specify that the ground termination must be a(n) _____ connection.

20-25   *True/False.* All electrical racks should be grounded to a central ground bus.

20-26   What precaution should be taken when grounding a chassis or rack to the enclosure?

20-27   *True/False.* It is a good practice to use a common AC source for the system power supply and I/O devices.

20-28   When is the use of an isolation transformer required?

20-29   *True/False.* To avoid uncontrollable conditions, emergency stop switches should be wired to the programmable controller.

20-30   *True/False.* To minimize wiring, a system should have as few emergency stops as possible.

20-31   _____ can be used as a convenient way to remove power to the I/O system in an emergency situation.
a–Electromechanical MCRs
b–Software MCRs
c–Software routines
d–Bleeding resistors

20-32   Briefly describe outrush, what causes it to occur, and how it can be avoided.

20-33   Temperature specifications for PLCs consider typical conditions to exist when:
a–60% of the inputs are ON at one time
b–60% of the outputs are ON at one time
c–60% of the inputs and 30% of the outputs are ON at one time
d–40% of the inputs and 60% of the outputs are ON at one time

20-34   A(n) _____ transformer can be used in an installation that is subject to soft AC lines.

20-35   The I/O placement and wiring documents should be updated:
a–during maintenance
b–every time there is a change
c–at the end of the project
d–during the documentation

20-36   *True/False.* All wires can be bundled together as long as the bundles are kept neat.

20-37 Which of the following is not a common method for terminal and wire labeling?

a–color coding
b–the use of wire numbers
c–the use of address numbers
d–size matching

20-38 When placing I/O modules in the I/O racks, the following should be checked:

a–type of module
b–slot address
c–I/O address assignment
d–all of the above

20-39 *True/False.* If two or more modules share the same power source, the power wiring can be jumpered from one module to the next.

20-40 Identify three types of devices that may require special wiring considerations.

20-41 Some input devices may have a small leakage current when they are in the _____ state.

20-42 *True/False.* Transistors exhibit more current leakage than triacs.

20-43 A leakage problem can occur when connecting an output module to an input module of another PLC; this problem can be corrected by using a(n) _____ across the input.

20-44 *True/False.* Snubber circuits are used for the suppression of inductive loads.

20-45 Label the following drawings according to the type of suppression they provide:

(a)

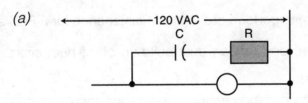

(b)

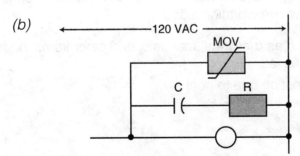

(c)

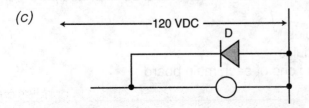

20-46 *True/False.* If fuses are not provided as part of the PLC's output modules, they should be installed at the terminal blocks, especially when the output is driving an inductive load.

20-47 *True/False.* The static input wiring check should be performed with power applied to the controller and input devices.

20-48 *True/False.* The static output wiring check is performed with power applied to the controller but not to the output modules.

20-49 When testing output wiring, all outputs that create mechanical motion should be

_____.

a–at half-stepping speed
b–connected
c–disconnected
d–at normal speed

20-50 Output devices can be tested by using a forcing function or by programming a(n)

_____.

20-51 Dynamic system checkout assumes that:

a–the static checks have been completed
b–the wiring is correct
c–the software has been reviewed
d–all of the above

20-52 When should changes to the control logic be documented and stored on a permanent storage device?

20-53 When is it appropriate to perform preventive maintenance for a PLC system?

20-54 Why is it a good practice to clean dust build-up off of heat sinks and electric circuitry?

20-55 *True/False.* Plugs, sockets, and terminal connections should be checked periodically in environments where vibration exists.

20-56 Leaving materials, such as drawings, manuals, and other items, on top of a CPU rack or I/O rack can cause:

a–the system to malfunction due to heat
b–obstruction of air flow
c–hot spots
d–all of the above

20-57 As a rule of thumb, the following items should be kept as spare parts for a PLC system:

a–10% of input modules
b–10% of output modules
c–a power supply and one of each main board
d–all of the above

20-58   If a module's fuse blows repeatedly, the probable cause may be that:

a–the module's output current is being exceeded
b–the output device is shorted
c–the fuse rating is incorrect
d–all of the above

20-59   Explain a ground loop condition.

20-60   Input modules generally have a power indicator to show that power is present at the module; however, some input modules also have a logic indicator whose function is to:

a–show that the isolation circuit works
b–show that the logic side is ON
c–indicate that the PLC should read a logic 1
d–all of the above

20-61   What is the first step to perform when troubleshooting a PLC malfunction?

20-62   Indicate the order in which the following steps should occur when troubleshooting a PLC input:

_____ check the wiring connection to the module

_____ close the field device and measure the voltage to the input module

_____ place the PLC in standby mode

_____ evaluate the PLC's reading of the module

_____ check for voltage at the field device

20-63   The key in diagnosing I/O malfunctions is to:

a–observe the LEDs
b–check the I/O wiring
c–isolate the problem to the module, the field device, or the field wiring
d–measure the input or output voltage

SYSTEM SELECTION
GUIDELINES

CHAPTER 21 STUDY GUIDE

- Programmable controllers are divided into five major categories: micro, small, medium, large, and very large. These areas of segmentation are based primarily on the I/O count capacity of the system. As the I/O count increases, so does the cost and complexity of the system.

  - The first category, micro PLCs, contains controllers that have 32 I/O or less. These PLCs are used in small ON/OFF control applications.
  - The second segment, small PLCs, have less than 128 I/O and are generally used in ON/OFF control.
  - The third segment, medium PLCs, consists of PLCs with between 128 and 1024 I/O that provide analog control, data manipulation, and arithmetic capabilities.
  - The fourth segment, large PLCs, includes systems ranging from 512 to 4096 I/O. These PLCs are used in applications requiring extensive data manipulation, acquisition, and reporting. Products in this segment are capable of higher arithmetic operations.
  - The fifth category, very large PLCs, includes systems that can handle from 2048 to 8192 I/O. These larger systems are used in large applications that require centralized control or a supervisory PLC. This segment is characterized by PLCs with large memory systems and host computer communication capability.

- Within the five PLC categories, three overlapping areas, areas A, B, and C, include products of one section that have features associated with the products of the next range category.

- During the definition of the control system, the following items must be considered and evaluated:
  - inputs and outputs
  - type of control
  - memory
  - software
  - peripherals
  - physical and environmental specifications

- The amount of I/O required is typically the first factor addressed during the selection of a controller. The type of I/O required—discrete, analog, and/or special—must also be investigated, along with whether remote I/O subsystems are needed.

- Three control schemes are used in PLC systems: individual control, centralized control, and distributed control.
  - *Individual control* consists of one PLC controlling a single machine.
  - *Centralized control* consists of several machines or processes controlled by one central PLC.
  - *Distributed control* involves two or more PLCs controlling several stations and communicating information through a local area network.

- The two most important considerations concerning the system memory are the type and amount of memory required. The total number of inputs and outputs to be controlled along with the complexity of the system determines the amount of PLC memory required.

- Software considerations include the type of instructions needed to accomplish the control program. The programming instruction set included in the software will directly affect the time required to implement and execute the control program.

- Peripheral devices should be evaluated to determine what type will be required for what functions. The first peripheral to be evaluated should be the programming device.

- Physical and environmental characteristics of various controllers should be evaluated to ensure that the system work properly in the environment in which it will be placed.

- Product reliability plays an important role in the overall system performance. Two criteria, mean-time-between-failures studies and burn-in procedures, can provide important product reliability data.
    - A *mean-time-between-failures study* provides information about the average time between equipment malfunctions, so that the operator knows how long the equipment should operate without failure.
    - *Burn-in procedures* operate a product at an elevated temperature to determine which parts will fail first.

- Plant standardization should be considered during the selection of a controller. If future applications will be done at the same location, standardization to one or two products will mean fewer spare parts in inventory and less retraining on equipment.

- The following is a list of the steps required in selecting a PLC:
    - Step 1: Know the process to be controlled.
    - Step 2: Determine the type of control.
    - Step 3: Determine the I/O interface requirements.
    - Step 4: Determine the required software languages and functions.
    - Step 5: Consider the type of memory.
    - Step 6: Consider memory capacity.
    - Step 7: Evaluate processor scan time requirements.
    - Step 8: Define programming and storage device requirements.
    - Step 9: Define peripheral requirements.
    - Step 10: Determine any physical and environmental constraints.
    - Step 11: Evaluate other factors that can affect selection.

REVIEW QUESTIONS

21-1 Small-size programmable controllers are low-end PLCs that are designed to be used as _____.

21-2 Which of the following PLC categories is most appropriate for supervisory control and hierarchical systems?

a–micro PLCs
b–small PLCs
c–medium PLCs
d–large PLCs

21-3 What is the primary specification for categorizing programmable controllers?

21-4 *True/False.* As the I/O count increases in a system, so does the cost but not the memory capacity.

21-5 *True/False.* Area A, B, and C controllers have feature enhancements over the standard products in categories 2, 3, and 4, respectively.

21-6 Micro PLCs generally have _____ I/O.

a–64 or less
b–128
c–32 or more
d–32 or less

21-7 *True/False.* A micro PLC is likely to be an area A controller.

21-8 Products in area B include:

a–enhancements of the standard features of segment 1 controllers
b–enhancements of the standard features of segment 2 controllers
c–features of area C controllers
d–enhancements of area A controllers

21-9 Which of the following is not a feature of medium PLCs?

a–128 I/O
b–analog control
c–32K of memory
d–data manipulation

21-10 Name five features that are generally available in large PLCs.

21-11 Very large controllers are used:

a–in distributed control applications
b–in centralized control applications
c–as a host
d–all of the above

21-12 *True/False.* When selecting a PLC, only the current application requirements should be considered.

21-13 Which of the following does not need to be evaluated and defined during the selection of a PLC?

a–inputs/outputs
b–type of control
c–documentation
d–peripherals

21-14 Name at least three factors that must be considered when evaluating discrete outputs.

21-15 When a digital output module has fuses incorporated in the module, attention should also be placed on their _____.
a–current requirements
b–accessibility
c–indicators
d–none of the above

21-16 If an application calls for different power sources for output devices, then the output modules should have:
a–proper ratings
b–fuses
c–isolated commons
d–common returns

21-17 Match the following terms with the appropriate description:

_____ bipolar	a–fast input, positioning
_____ special analog input	b–current output
_____ 4 to 20 mA	c–±10 VAC
_____ special I/O	d–RTD
_____ PID module	e–measurement of flow, temperature
_____ analog I/O	f–processing in module

21-18 Remote inputs and outputs should be considered to _____ the wiring in the system when the distance between the processor and the field devices is very long.
a–double
b–change
c–lengthen
d–reduce

21-19 Sketch each of the following control system configurations:

(a) individual

(b) centralized

(c) distributed

21-20 *True/False.* Individual control is the same as segregated control.

21-21 Which of the following statements does not apply to individual control:
a–It is used to control a single machine.
b–It is used to control more than one machine.
c–It can have a few remote I/O.
d–It can be applied to an injection molding machine.

21-22 *True/False.* Centralized control should be used when several machines or processes must be controlled by one programmable controller.

21-23 An advantage of centralized control is that:

a–it has short control programs
b–it can control one large process or several smaller processes
c–it minimizes wiring
d–it has expansion capability

21-24 A(n) _____ system can be used in centralized control applications that require a backup.

21-25 A distributed control configuration involves at least:

a–one large PLC
b–one mile communication distance
c–two PLCs that communicate with each other
d–special I/O modules

21-26 Distributed control systems use a(n) _____ to implement communication between PLCs.

21-27 *True/False.* It is easy to communicate between different manufacturers' PLCs.

21-28 The two most important considerations when evaluating the system memory are the _____ and _____ of memory.

21-29 *True/False.* In general, small PLCs have a fixed amount of memory.

21-30 A PLC system's memory requirements are a function of _____ and _____.

a–the number of inputs
b–the number of outputs
c–the number of inputs and outputs
d–the complexity of the control program
e–the size of the controller

21-31 *True/False.* The instruction set selected in a programmable controller will affect the degree of difficulty in implementing the software program.

21-32 What is the first peripheral that should be considered when selecting a PLC system?

21-33 Why should peripheral requirements be evaluated along with the CPU?

21-34 *True/False.* The physical and environmental characteristics of a system have little impact on the total system reliability.

21-35 Which of the following should be taken into consideration when specifying the controller and the I/O system?

a–labeling requirements
b–operating parameters
c–wiring gauge
d–all of the above

21-36 *True/False.* The controller's reliability plays an important role in the overall performance of the control system.

21-37   Describe a typical burn-in procedure for PLCs and its purpose.

21-38   The _____ of a product line should be considered when possible as part of the PLC selection process.
a–looks
b–manufacturing process
c–standardization
d–salesman

21-39   Programmable controller families generally share the same:
a–I/O structure
b–programming device
c–elementary instruction set
d–all of the above

21-40   Indicate the order in which the following items should be considered when selecting a PLC:

_____ the process to be controlled

_____ memory type

_____ type of control

_____ memory capacity

_____ I/O interface requirements

_____ scan requirements

_____ software language and functions

_____ physical and environmental constraints

_____ programming and storage devices

_____ peripheral requirements

_____ other PLC factors

SECTION TWO

ANSWERS

CHAPTER 1 ANSWERS

1-1   A PLC (programmable logic controller) is a solid-state device that can be programmed to control process or machine operations. A programmable controller consists of five basic components: the processor, memory, input/output, power supply, and programming device. PLCs are designed to be industrial control systems.

1-2

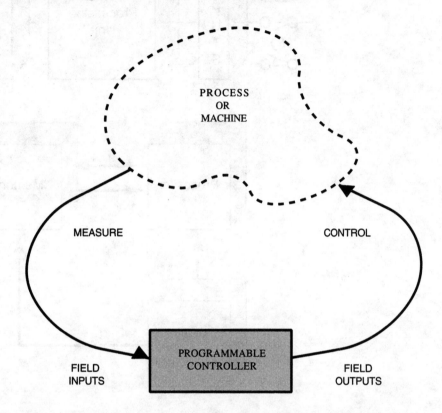

1-3   The Hydramatic Division of General Motors Corporation defined and specified the design criteria for the first programmable controller in 1968.

1-4   The initial specifications for the first PLC design were as follows:
-    PLCs had to be price competitive with the use of relay systems.
-    The system had to be capable of sustaining an industrial environment.
-    The input and output interfaces had to be easily replaceable.
-    The controller had to have modular architecture so that subassemblies could be easily removed for replacement or repair.
-    PLC systems had to be capable of passing data collection to a central system.
-    The method used to program the controller had to be simple, so that it could be easily used and understood by plant personnel.

1-5   a–ON/OFF control

1-6   ___S___ machine diagnostics
       ___H___ fast scan time
       ___H___ intelligent I/O
       ___S___ functional block instructions
       ___H___ peripheral equipment
       ___S___ floating-point math
       ___H___ small, low-cost PLCs

1-7   central processing unit (CPU), input/output (I/O) interface

1-8

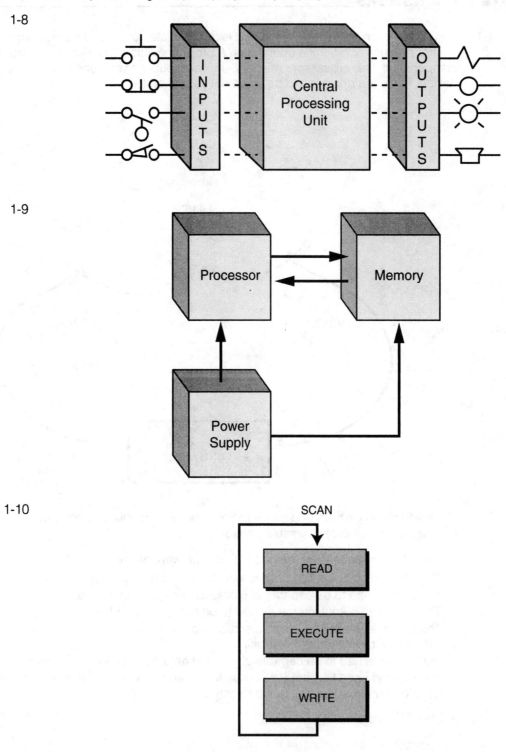

1-9

1-10

1-11   true

1-12   true

1-13   programming

1-14   personal computer, miniprogrammer

1-15   PLCs are designed to survive the industrial environment, which includes electrical noise, electromagnetic interference, mechanical vibration, extreme temperatures, and noncondensing humidity. PLCs are also designed to be software-friendly to engineers and designers, as well as technical electricians.

1-16   false; PLCs are much easier and cheaper to modify than relay controls

1-17   International Electrotechnical Commission (IEC) 1131-3

1-18   b–I/O interfaces

1-19   true

1-20   small PLCs

1-21   true

1-22   true

1-23   d–softwired

1-24   false; PLCs require less than half the space of relay control panels

1-25   The use of remote input and output subsystems greatly reduces the amount of wiring required. Many parts of remote subsystems can be prewired by the OEM or PLC vendor. This translates into material and labor cost savings.

1-26   true

1-27   __d__ solid-state components
       __a__ small size
       __e__ software timers/counters
       __f__ microprocessor-based
       __c__ modular architecture
       __b__ diagnostic indicators

1-28   programmable

1-29   true

1-30   graphic user interfaces (GUIs)

1-31   PLC applications in the metals industry include:
       - steelmaking
       - loading and unloading of alloys
       - continuous casting
       - cold rolling
       - aluminum making
       - blast furnace control
       - soaking pits

1-32   PLC applications in the automotive industry include:
       - internal combustion engine monitoring
       - carburetor production testing
       - automotive production machine monitoring
       - power steering valve assembly and testing

CHAPTER 2 ANSWERS

2-1 d–Every system has the same number of symbols.

2-2 true

2-3 the base minus one

2-4   _c_ hexadecimal
     _d_ binary
     _b_ octal
     _a_ decimal

2-5 (a) 9
     (b) 7
     (c) 1
     (d) 10
     (e) 15
     (f) 2

2-6 true

2-7 b–14 in decimal

2-8 The binary system is used in PLCs and digital computers because it is easier to design digital systems that can only distinguish between two states as possible values, rather than ten as decimal. Most discrete devices have two states, ON (1) or OFF (0).

2-9 The decimal equivalent of 72351_8 is $29{,}929_{10}$:

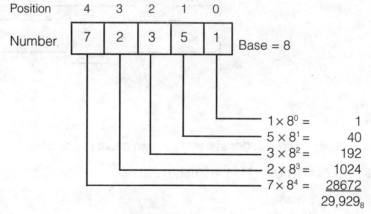

2-10 (a)

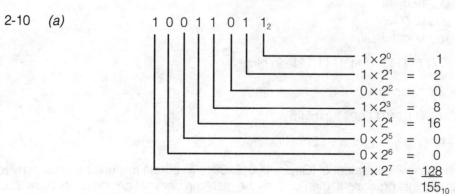

(b)

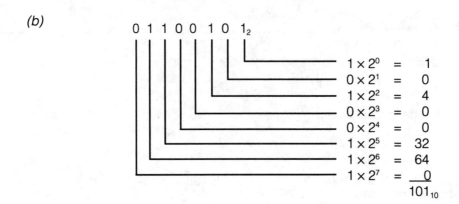

$$0\ 1\ 1\ 0\ 0\ 1\ 0\ 1_2$$

$$1 \times 2^0 = 1$$
$$0 \times 2^1 = 0$$
$$1 \times 2^2 = 4$$
$$0 \times 2^3 = 0$$
$$0 \times 2^4 = 0$$
$$1 \times 2^5 = 32$$
$$1 \times 2^6 = 64$$
$$1 \times 2^7 = \underline{\ \ 0}$$
$$101_{10}$$

2-11   c–one-zero (10)

2-12   *(a)* A bit is one digit in the binary number system.

(b) A nibble is a group of four bits.

(c) A byte is a group of eight bits.

(d) A word is a group of one or more bytes.

2-13

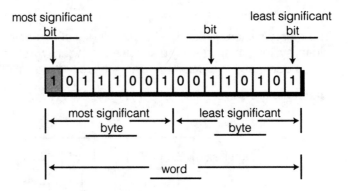

2-14   true

2-15   false; in any number system, you can count to any decimal equivalent

2-16   377 octal (1111 1111 in binary)

2-17   __c__ 5 octal
__d__ 10 octal
__a__ 12 octal
__b__ 17 octal

2-18   177777 (1111 1111 1111 1111 in binary)

2-19   10 hexadecimal

2-20   10 bits (10 1011 1001 in binary)

2-21   FFFF (1111 1111 1111 1111 in binary)

2-22   The base 3 equivalent of $IG4_{27}$ is 200121001_3. To obtain this number, first convert $IG4_{27}$ to its decimal equivalent, then convert the resulting decimal number to its base 3 equivalent.

The decimal equivalent of IG4$_{27}$ is 13553$_{10}$:

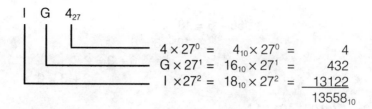

$$4 \times 27^0 = 4_{10} \times 27^0 = 4$$
$$G \times 27^1 = 16_{10} \times 27^1 = 432$$
$$I \times 27^2 = 18_{10} \times 27^2 = \underline{13122}$$
$$13558_{10}$$

The base 3 equivalent of this number is then 200121011$_3$:

Divisions	Remainders
13558 ÷ 3 = 4519	1
4519 ÷ 3 = 1506	1
1506 ÷ 3 = 502	0
502 ÷ 3 = 167	1
167 ÷ 3 = 55	2
55 ÷ 3 = 18	1
18 ÷ 3 = 6	0
6 ÷ 3 = 2	0
2 ÷ 3 = 0	2

2-23   Using the same procedure as in the previous problem, A3$_{16}$ is 163$_{10}$ and 2203$_4$.

$$A \quad 3_{16}$$
$$3 \times 16^0 = 3_{10} \times 16^0 = 3$$
$$A \times 16^1 = 10_{10} \times 16^1 = \underline{160}$$
$$163_{10}$$

Divisions	Remainders
163 ÷ 4 = 40	3
40 ÷ 4 = 10	0
10 ÷ 4 = 2	2
2 ÷ 4 = 0	2

2-24   AA$_{16}$ must first be converted to decimal and then to base 3 to obtain the answer, 20022$_3$.

$$A \quad A_{16}$$
$$A \times 16^0 = 10_{10} \times 16^0 = 10$$
$$A \times 16^1 = 10_{10} \times 16^1 = \underline{160}$$
$$170_{10}$$

Divisions	Remainders
170 ÷ 3 = 56	2
56 ÷ 3 = 18	2
18 ÷ 3 = 6	0
6 ÷ 3 = 2	0
2 ÷ 3 = 0	2

2-25   *(a)* $001\ 101\ 011_2$

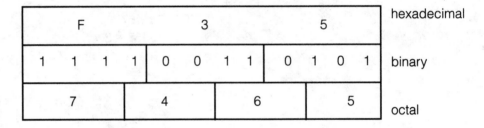

1		5		3		octal
0	0	1	1	0	1	0	1	1	binary

(b) 7465_8

F			3			5			hexadecimal
1	1	1	1	0	0	1	1	0	1	0	1	binary
7		4		6		5		octal

(c) 11100_2

Divisions	Remainders
28 ÷ 2 = 14	0
14 ÷ 2 = 7	0
7 ÷ 2 = 3	1
3 ÷ 2 = 1	1
1 ÷ 2 = 0	1

(d) 43_8

Divisions	Remainders
35 ÷ 8 = 4	3
4 ÷ 8 = 0	4

(e) 45_{10}

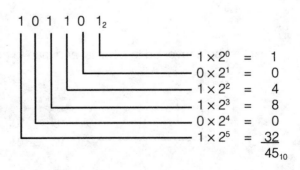

$$
\begin{array}{lcr}
1 \times 2^0 &=& 1 \\
0 \times 2^1 &=& 0 \\
1 \times 2^2 &=& 4 \\
1 \times 2^3 &=& 8 \\
0 \times 2^4 &=& 0 \\
1 \times 2^5 &=& \underline{32} \\
& & 45_{10}
\end{array}
$$

(f) 38_{10}

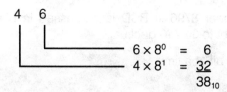

$$6 \times 8^0 = 6$$
$$4 \times 8^1 = \underline{32}$$
$$38_{10}$$

(g) $2F_{16}$

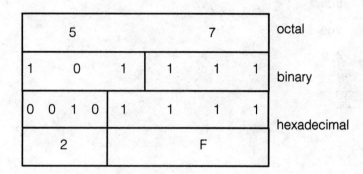

octal					
5			7		

binary					
1	0	1	1	1	1

hexadecimal					
0	0	1	0	1	1	1	1
2			F		

2-26 true

2-27 addition

2-28 false; the number 20 in binary requires five bits (10100); however, a sixth bit would be required to represent the sign

2-29 The binary equivalent of $+24_{10}$ is 11000_2. Therefore:

   (a) its one's complement is 100111_2

   (b) its two's complement is $1\ 01000_2$

2-30 true

2-31 c–7-bit, d–8-bit

2-32 American Standard Code for Information Interchange

2-33

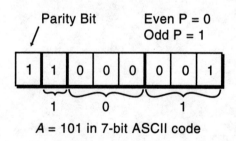

Parity Bit   Even P = 0
               Odd P = 1

1	1	0	0	0	0	0	1

   1   0   1

A = 101 in 7-bit ASCII code

2-34

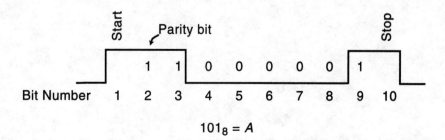

Start   Parity bit   Stop

        1   1   0   0   0   0   0   1

Bit Number   1   2   3   4   5   6   7   8   9   10

$101_8 = A$

2-35   4

2-36   The number 8796 in BCD is expressed in binary as 1000 0111 1001 0110, which is equivalent to 34,710 decimal.

2-37   only one bit at a time

2-38   encoders

2-39   true

2-40   true

2-41   4, 9

CHAPTER 3 ANSWERS

3-1   binary

3-2   a–positive logic

3-3   d–all of the above

3-4   true

3-5   at least one

3-6   Either PB1 or PB2 must be ON or pressed (TRUE) in order to complete the circuit, causing the alarm horn to sound.

3-7   b–in series

3-8   c–inverter

3-9   b–deactivate

3-10   c–NOR

3-11   false; Boolean algebra is a simple way to analyze and express logic functions

3-12   d–Y equals A ANDed with B

3-13   _2_ AND
       _1_ NOT
       _3_ OR

3-14   true

3-15   _I_ timer contact
       _I_ push button
       _O_ pilot light
       _O_ control relay
       _O_ timer
       _I_ limit switch

3-16   Rung is a ladder program term referring to the programmed instructions that drive one output.

3-17   false; most PLCs allow only one output per rung

3-18   d–all of the above

3-19

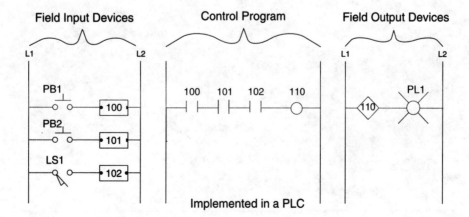

3-20 b–at the far right

3-21 false; a PLC can have as many normally open and normally closed contacts as needed

3-22 a–normally closed contact

3-23 parallel

3-24 NOT

3-25 true

3-26 *(a)* S
(b) P
(c) S/P
(d) S/P
(e) P/S
(f) P/S
(g) S

3-27

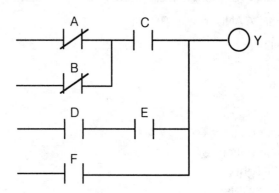

3-28 Using Boolean algebra, the equation can be minimized to $Y = A$.

$$Y = [(A + AB) + (\overline{\overline{A} + \overline{B}})][\overline{B} + (A + \overline{A}B)]$$
$$= (A + \overline{\overline{AB}})(\overline{B} + A + B)$$
$$= (A + AB)(\overline{B} + A + B)$$
$$= (A)(\overline{B} + A + B)$$
$$= A\overline{B} + A + AB$$
$$= A\overline{B} + A$$
$$= A$$

CHAPTER 4 ANSWERS

4-1   processor, memory system, power supply

4-2   processor

4-3   true

4-4   d–microprocessor

4-5   executive

4-6   multiprocessing

4-7   intelligent I/O interfaces

4-8   true

4-9   program, I/O update

4-10   a–increases

4-11   c–twice in 5 msec

4-12   true

4-13   a–immediate instructions

4-14   pulse stretcher

4-15   true

4-16   error-checking

4-17   vertical redundancy check (VRC)

4-18   even, odd

4-19   parity bit

4-20   ASCII $E = 1000101_2$

(a) 0

(b) 1

4-21   a–single errors

4-22   false; the ASCII characters A and B both contain an even number of ones, so the parity check will not detect an error

4-23   true

4-24   c–block check character

4-25   b–horizontal redundancy check

4-26   true

4-27   false; only one input can be ON (1) for the output to be 1

4-28   Hamming code

4-29   *(a)* The BCC is 101001.

Word 1	1 1 1 0 0 1
⊕	⊕
Word 2	1 0 1 0 1 1
Result	0 1 0 0 1 0
⊕	⊕
Word 3	0 1 1 0 1 0
Result	0 0 1 0 0 0
⊕	⊕
Word 4	1 0 0 0 0 1
Result	1 0 1 0 0 1 (BCC)

(b) The BCC is 101001.

Start	0 0 0 0 0 0
⊕	⊕
Word 1	1 1 1 0 0 1
Result	1 1 1 0 0 1
Rotate	1 1 0 0 1 1
⊕	⊕
Word 2	1 0 1 0 1 1
Result	0 1 1 0 0 0
Rotate	1 1 0 0 0 0
⊕	⊕
Word 3	0 1 1 0 1 0
Result	1 0 1 0 1 0
Rotate	0 1 0 1 0 1
⊕	⊕
Word 4	1 0 0 0 0 1
Result	1 1 0 1 0 0
Rotate	1 0 1 0 0 1 (BCC)

4-30   b–two or more, c–one

4-31   CPU diagnostics include:
   -   memory OK
   -   processor OK
   -   battery OK
   -   power supply OK

4-32   c–watchdog

4-33   false; although PLCs usually require an AC power source, some can accept a DC power supply

4-34   b–10–15%

4-35   shutdown

4-36   c–primary, a–secondary

4-37   b–worst-case power requirements

4-38   Isolation transformers are required when a PLC is installed in an environment where surrounding equipment introduces considerable amounts of electromagnetic interference (EMI) into the power lines.

4-39 false; the cause of an overload is often difficult to find because overloads can occur intermittently

4-40 When current requirements exceed the power supply's capabilities, a second power supply should be added or a power supply with greater current capability should be used.

4-41 The power supply must be able to supply at least 3525 mA of current.

Module Type	I/O Devices Connected	Connections per Module	Modules Required	Modules' Current @ 5 V	Total Current Required
Discrete in	40	8	5	280 mA	1400 mA
Discrete out	28	8	4	250 mA	1000 mA
				Total (I/O current)	2400 mA
				Processor's current	1125 mA
					3525 mA

4-42 miniprogrammers and personal computers (PCs)

4-43 a–small

4-44 Miniprogrammer programming functions include:
- editing and inputting the control program
- starting up, changing, and monitoring the control logic
- performing diagnostic routines
- displaying English messages to the user

4-45 d–memory cards

4-46 PC programming functions include:
- ladder program entry and editing
- documentation
- real-time monitoring of the PLC's control program

CHAPTER 5 ANSWERS

5-1   executive, application

5-2   application memory

5-3   false; the executive software is normally stored in nonvolatile memory, which does not require a battery backup

5-4   lose

5-5   false; the contents of nonvolatile memory cannot be easily altered

5-6   __N__ electrically alterable read-only memory (EAROM)

        __V__ random-access memory (RAM)

        __N__ programmable read-only memory (PROM)

        __N__ erasable programmable read-only memory (EPROM)

5-7   random-access memory (RAM) (or read/write memory)

5-8   erasable programmable read-only memory (EPROM)

5-9   true

5-10   electrically erasable programmable read-only memory

5-11   1s, 0s

5-12   false; a bit is the smallest unit of memory

5-13   b–bit status

5-14   false; memory capacity is fixed in small PLCs and expandable in larger ones

5-15   1024 (or 2^{10})

5-16   4095

5-17   c–65,536 bits

5-18   d–memory utilization

5-19

total contact elements	(8×10)	80
total outputs	(2×10)	20
		100
total contact elements	(6×20)	120
total timers	(3×20)	60
		180
total contact elements	(1×30)	30
total counters	(3×30)	90
		120

The total words of memory required to store these instructions is 400 words (100 + 180 + 120). Therefore, the total amount of memory required by the controller to satisfy its 30% future expansion requirement is 520 words (400 × 1.3 = 520).

5-20   true

5-21   memory map

5-22   _c_ executive

        _d_ scratch pad

        _a_ application memory

        _b_ data table

5-23   a–system memory

5-24   user program

5-25   data table

5-26

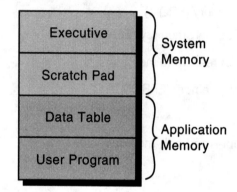

5-27   true

5-28   true

5-29   a–128 bits

5-30   c–16 bytes (16 bytes × 8 bits = 128 bits)

5-31   processor

5-32   d–program scan, a–I/O update scan

5-33   internal bit storage, register/word storage

5-34   false; they control internal outputs, which are used for interlocking purposes

5-35   binary, BCD, and ASCII

5-36   _C_ timer preset values

        _V_ analog input values

        _V_ BCD outputs

        _C_ set points

        _V_ counter accumulated values

        _C_ ASCII messages

        _C_ decimal tables

5-37   control logic

5-38   executive

5-39

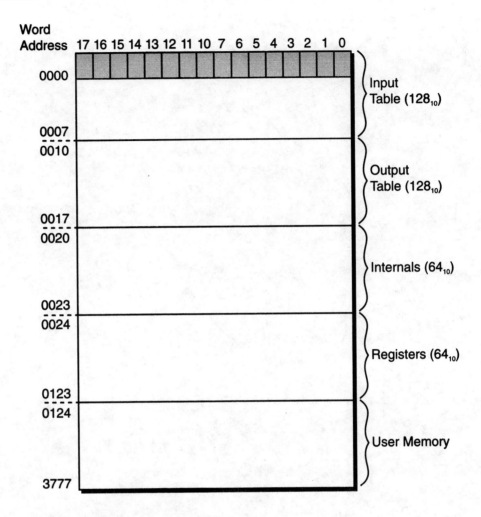

5-40   1964 words decimal (or 3654 words octal)

5-41   b–ON for one scan

5-42   true

CHAPTER 6 ANSWERS

6-1 b–field equipment and the CPU

6-2 d–discrete

6-3 c–the processor

6-4 e–local I/O processor, c–processor

6-5 false; a module's rack location defines its address, which is mapped to the I/O table

6-6

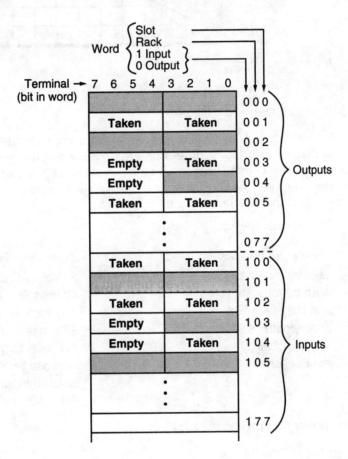

6-7 true

6-8

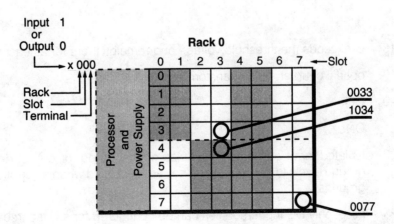

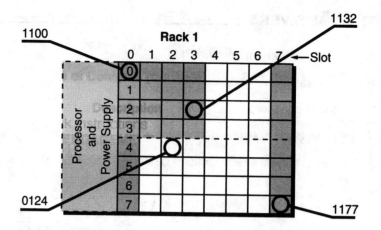

6-9   d–all of the above

6-10   daisy chain, star, and multidrop

6-11   The advantages of remote I/O systems include savings on materials and labor costs for large systems in which the field devices are at various spread-out locations. The only cable necessary for communication with the remote units is a pair of twisted or coaxial cables running between the subsystem and the main CPU, instead of hundreds of cables running to the CPU from the field devices.

6-12   ON (or CLOSED), OFF (or OPEN)

6-13   *Discrete input devices:*
- selector switches
- push buttons
- proximity switches
- photoelectric switches
- limit switches
- level switches

Discrete input interface ratings:
- 24 volts AC/DC
- 48 volts AC/DC
- 120 volts AC/DC
- 230 volts AC/DC
- TTL level (5 VDC)
- nonvoltage
- isolated input
- 5–50 VDC (sink/source)

6-14   the power section and the logic section

6-15   c–isolation circuit

6-16   a–DC-level

6-17   9, 25

6-18   c–exceeds the threshold voltage and remains there for at least the filter delay

6-19   optical coupler, pulse transformer

6-20   OFF

6-21   ON

6-22   Isolated input and output modules connect input or output devices that have different ground levels to the controller. They are also used when an application requires isolation of grounds.

6-23   false; only DC input modules can be configured for sink/source operation

6-24

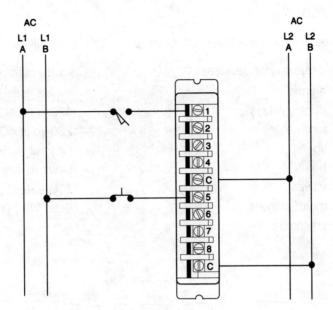

6-25 Devices that send TTL signals include:
- solid-state controls with TTL levels
- sensing instruments with TTL voltages
- some 5 VDC-level control devices
- several types of photoelectric sensors

6-26 shorter

6-27

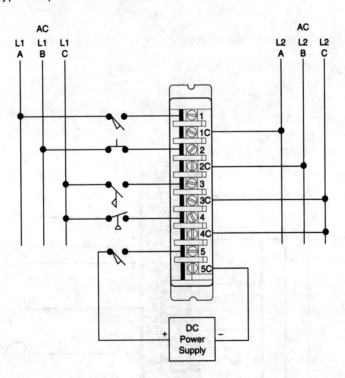

6-28 Register/BCD interface applications include:
- entering or modifying preset values for timers, counters, and shift registers
- entering and modifying other values, such as high and low set point limits

6-29   a–BCD

6-30   false; they require thumbwheel switches with enable lines

6-31   *Discrete output devices:*

- alarms
- control relays
- fans
- lights
- horns
- valves
- motor starters
- solenoids

Discrete output interface ratings:

- 12–48 volts AC/DC
- 120 volts AC/DC
- 230 volts AC/DC
- contact (relay)
- isolated output
- TTL level (5 VDC)
- 5–50 VDC (sink/source)

6-32

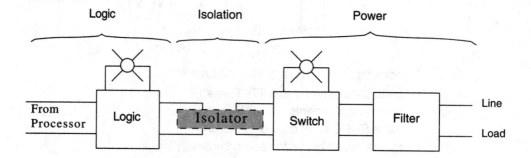

6-33   triac, silicon controlled rectifier (SCR)

6-34   metal oxide varistors (MOVs), RC snubbers

6-35

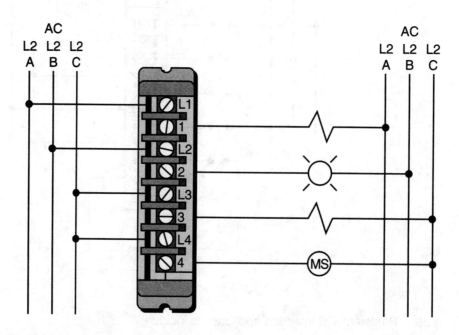

6-36   power transistor, freewheeling diode

6-37

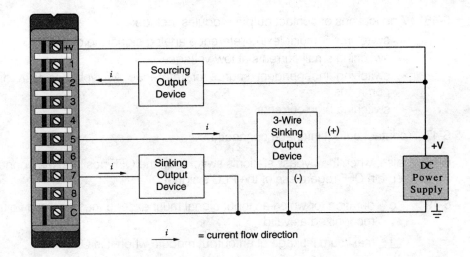

i = current flow direction

6-38 c–a and b

6-39 TTL output modules drive:
- seven-segment LEDs
- integrated circuits
- various 5-VDC devices

6-40 eight single lines connecting each set of TWS plus two enable lines (one for each TWS set)

6-41 true

6-42 parallel

6-43 5 VDC, 24 VDC, 16, 32

6-44 Devices that interface with register output modules include:
- seven-segment displays
- BCD alphanumeric displays
- small DC loads

6-45

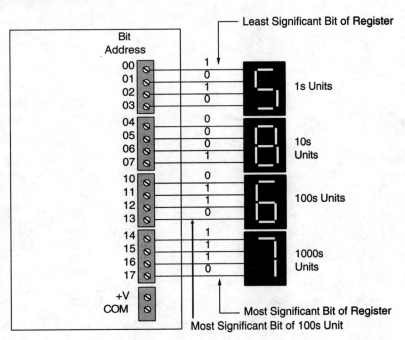

6-46　Applications of contact output modules include:
- switching or multiplexing reference analog signals to drives
- switching small currents at low voltages
- switching independent source or reference AC voltages with different or internal commons
- switching high currents

6-47　contact output interface connection

6-48　false; when the bypass station's switch is in the OFF position, the connected field devices remain OFF regardless of the PLC's signal

6-49　_c_ duration for which an input signal must exceed the threshold voltage to be recognized as valid

_f_ maximum leakage of an output module when it is OFF

_g_ response time for an output to go from ON to OFF

_i_ number of I/O circuits in a module

_d_ maximum current that an output circuit can carry under load

_a_ AC or DC value specifying the magnitude and type of signal that will be accepted

_k_ voltage isolation between logic and power circuits

_b_ voltage at which an input signal is recognized as being ON

_e_ maximum current and its duration that an output module can withstand

_h_ how close a converted analog signal approximates the actual signal

_j_ maximum operating temperature

CHAPTER 7 ANSWERS _____

7-1   true

7-2

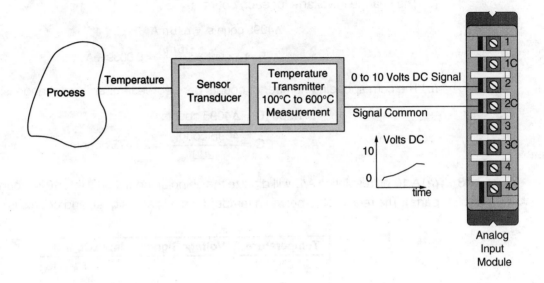

7-3   unipolar, bipolar

7-4   b–analog, d–discrete

7-5   c–digitizes

7-6   e–A/D converter, c–counts

7-7   resolution

7-8   c–status

7-9   b–BCD, c–binary

7-10   true

7-11   c–greater than

7-12   *(a)* The relationship between temperature, voltage signal, and module counts is as follows:

Temperature	Voltage Signal	Input Counts
0°C	4 mA	0
•	•	•
•	•	•
•	•	•
200°C	20 mA	4095

The changes (Δ) in temperature, voltage, and input counts are 200°C, 16 mA, and 4095 counts, respectively. Therefore, the voltage change per one degree temperature change is:

$$\Delta 200°C = \Delta 16\,mA$$

$$1°C = \frac{16\,mA}{200} = 0.08\,mA$$

(b) The change in voltage for each count is:

$$\Delta 4095\ counts = \Delta 16\,mA$$

$$1\ count = \frac{16\,mA}{4095} = 0.0039\,mA$$

(c) The corresponding number of counts per degree temperature change is:

$$\Delta 200°C = \Delta 4095\ counts$$

$$1°C = \frac{4095\ counts}{200} = 20.475\ counts$$

7-13 *(a)* A 10-bit resolution A/D will digitize the unipolar input signal into 1024 counts (one in 2^{10} parts). The relationship between temperature, voltage signal, and counts is:

Temperature	Voltage Signal	Input Counts
0°C	4 mA	0
•	•	•
•	•	•
•	•	•
200°C	20 mA	1023

The changes (Δ) in temperature, voltage, and input counts are 200°C, 16 mA, and 1023 counts, respectively. Therefore, the voltage change per one degree temperature change is:

$$\Delta 200°C = \Delta 16\,mA$$

$$1°C = \frac{16\,mA}{200} = 0.08\,mA$$

(b) The change in voltage for each count is:

$$\Delta 1023\ counts = \Delta 16\,mA$$

$$1\ count = \frac{16\,mA}{1023} = 0.015640\,mA$$

(c) The corresponding number of counts per degree temperature change is:

$$\Delta 200°C = \Delta 1023\ counts$$

$$1°C = \frac{1023\ counts}{200} = 5.115\ counts$$

7-14 *(a)* The following illustration shows the relationship between counts, the input signal in volts, and degrees Celsius. Line *Y* describes the relationship between the input signal and the number of counts (assuming a linear relationship).

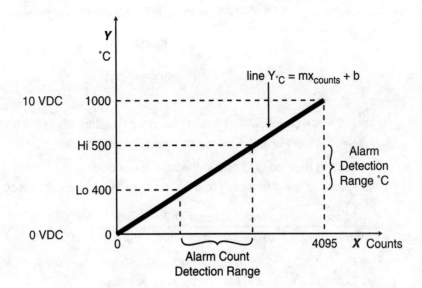

The numerical representation of the equation for line *Y* takes the form $Y = mX + b$, where *m* is the slope of the line described by:

$$m = \frac{\Delta Y}{\Delta X} = \frac{°C_2 - °C_1}{\text{count } 2 - \text{count } 1}$$

$$= \frac{1000 - 0}{4095 - 0}$$

$$= \frac{1000}{4095}$$

and Y_2, Y_1, and X_1 are known points. The term *b* is described as the intersection of *Y* (or °C) when *X* (or counts) equals 0. This value can be computed as:

$$b = Y_{°C} - mX_{counts}$$

where *Y* and *X* are values at known points (i.e., at 0°C and 0 counts). When *X* is at 0 counts, *Y* is at 0°C; therefore:

$$b = 0 - \left(\frac{1000}{4095}\right)0$$

$$= 0$$

Thus, the equation of line $Y_{°C}$ is:

$$Y_{°C} = \frac{1000}{4095} X_{counts}$$

Substituting 4095 counts for *X* and 1000°C for *Y* would have yielded the same equation.

(b) There are two ways to determine the equivalent number of counts for the alarm temperatures. The first method is to use the previous equation to derive the equation defining the number of counts for each temperature:

$$Y_{°C} = \frac{1000}{4095} X_{counts}$$

$$X_{counts} = \frac{4095 \, Y_{°C}}{1000}$$

So, for the $Y_{°C}$ values of 400°C and 500°C , the count values are:

$$X_{counts\ @\ 400\ °C} = \frac{(4095)(400)}{1000} = 1638\ counts$$

$$X_{counts\ @\ 500\ °C} = \frac{(4095)(500)}{1000} = 2047.5\ counts$$

Therefore, at a count of 1638, the low-level temperature alarm will be enabled; and at a count of 2048, the high-level temperature alarm will be enabled.

The second method is to obtain the number of counts equivalent to 1°C. The temperature changes 1000 degrees per 4095 counts, which can be expressed as:

$$\frac{\Delta counts}{\Delta temperature} = \frac{max\ counts - min\ counts}{max\ degrees - min\ degrees} = \frac{4095 - 0}{1000 - 0} = 4.095\ counts\ /\ degree$$

Therefore, each degree is equivalent to 4.095 counts. So the count values for 400°C and 500°C are 1638 and 2047.5 counts, respectively:

$$(400)(4.095) = 1638\ counts$$

$$(500)(4.095) = 2047.5\ counts$$

7-15 __6__ holding register

__2__ transducer

__8__ data table

__3__ voltage signal

__4__ analog input module

__1__ analog variable signal

__7__ input instruction

__5__ A/D converter

7-16 register addresses 205 through 214 octal; that is, eight registers (205, 206, 207, 210, 211, 212, 213, and 214)

7-17 a–single-ended (all commons tied together), d–differential (all commons separate)

7-18 false; analog interfaces use rocker switches to select single-ended or differential input configurations

7-19 Shielded cable should be used because it keeps line impedance imbalances low and maintains a good common mode rejection ratio of noise levels, such as power lines.

7-20 *Analog input ratings:*

- +4 to +20 mA
- 0 to +1
- 0 to +5 volts DC
- 0 to +10 volts DC
- +1 to +5 volts DC
- ±5 volts DC
- ±10 volts DC

Analog output ratings:

- +4 to +20 mA
- +10 to +50 mA
- 0 to +5 volts DC
- 0 to +10 volts DC
- ±2.5 volts DC
- ±5 volts DC
- ±10 volts DC

7-21   true

7-22   __|__ pressure transducer sensor

   __O__ AC motor drive

   __O__ chart recorder

   __O__ control valve

   __|__ load cell

   __|__ potentiometer

7-23   digital-to-analog converter (D/A or DAC)

7-24   c–0111 1111 1111 or 12 mA (equal to a count of 2047)

7-25   Since the analog output module has a sign bit provision, it receives counts ranging from –4095 to +4095, proportional to the –5 to +5 VDC required by the transducer. The following diagram illustrates the relationship between the module count, the output voltage, and the percentage opening:

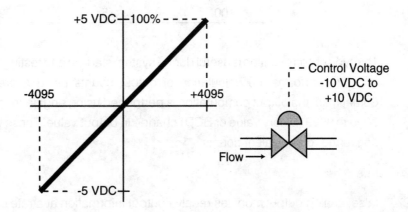

To formulate the desired table, first obtain the equivalent values corresponding to each variable. The changes in percentage opening, voltage, and counts are:

ΔPercentage	ΔVoltage (–5 to + 5)	ΔCounts (–4095 to + 4095)
100	10	8190

So the percentage changes as a function of voltage and counts are:

$$1\% \text{ as a function of voltage} = \frac{10 \text{ VDC}}{100} = 0.1 \text{ VDC}$$

$$1\% \text{ as a function of counts} = \frac{8190 \text{ counts}}{100} = 81.9 \text{ counts}$$

Note that these computations represent magnitude changes. To implement the table, add the offset values for the voltage and counts to the percentage function to account for the bipolar effect of the module and the negative-to-positive changes in counts. The term P is the percentage number to be used in the table.

$$\text{Percentage as a function of voltage} = (0.1)(P) - 5 \text{ VDC}$$

$$\text{Percentage as a function of counts} = (81.9)(P) - 4095 \text{ counts}$$

Therefore, the required table is implemented by multiplying each voltage and count relationship by the desired percentage of opening.

Opening(%)	Output Voltage (V)	Counts
0	–5	–4095
10	–4	–3276
20	–3	–2457
30	–2	–1638
40	–1	–819
50	0	0
60	+1	+819
70	+2	+1638
80	+3	+2457
90	+4	+3276
100	+5	+4095

This type of computation is useful during system start-up and testing. Generally, the software program performs the calculation of output counts using a predetermined algorithm. Sometimes, the output computation is performed using engineering units, which indicate a 0000 to 9999 (binary value or BCD) change in output value. These units must ultimately be converted to equivalent counts.

7-26   true

7-27   false; analog output modules receive output information at a rate of one channel per scan

7-28   _3_ holding register

   _6_ transducer

   _1_ data table

   _7_ voltage signal

   _5_ analog output module

   _8_ analog variable signal

   _2_ output instruction

   _4_ D/A converter

7-29   *(a)* The following illustration shows the relationship between voltage, percent opening, and counts. The X-axis can represent either output voltage or percentage opening. The Y-axis represents the number of counts output by the module for each X value (% or VDC). The equation of line Y, which takes the form $Y = mX + b$, represents equivalent counts as a function of voltage or percentage opening.

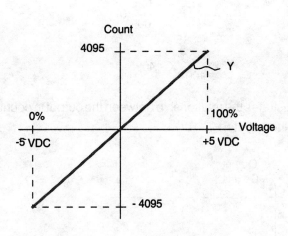

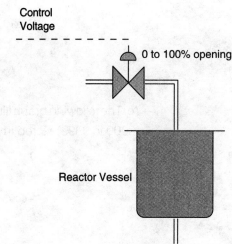

The equation of line *Y* as a function of voltage is expressed by:

$$m = \frac{\Delta Y}{\Delta X} = \frac{4095\text{ counts} - (-4095\text{ counts})}{5\text{ VDC} - (-5\text{ VDC})} = \frac{8190\text{ counts}}{10\text{ VDC}}$$

$$Y = mX + b$$

$$Y = \frac{8190}{10}X + b$$

The value *b*, which is calculated by replacing a known value for *Y* when *X* is 0 counts, is:

$$b = \left(\frac{8190}{10}\right)0$$

$$b = 0$$

Therefore, the equation of line *Y* showing counts as a function of voltage is:

$$Y = \frac{8190}{10}X + 0$$

$$Y = \frac{8190}{10}X$$

(b) This equation of line *Y* as a function of percentage is computed in a similar manner:

$$m = \frac{\Delta Y}{\Delta X} = \frac{8190\text{ counts}}{100\%}$$

$$Y = mX + b$$

$$Y = \frac{8190}{100}X + b$$

The value of *b* is computed by replacing *Y* with the count value when *X* equals 0. This *Y* value is –4095; therefore, the equation of line *Y* showing counts as a function of percentage opening is:

$$b = -4095 - \frac{8190}{100}(X)$$

$$= -4095 - \frac{8190}{100}(0)$$

$$= -4095$$

$$Y = \frac{8190}{100}X - 4095$$

(c) The following graph illustrates the relationship between the output in counts and the value (0000 to 9999) stored in the register:

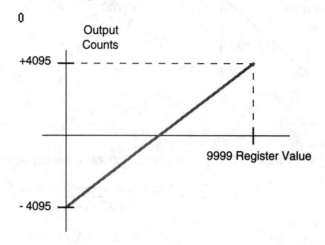

This graph is very similar to the one shown in part (a); the only difference is that the output equation must be recomputed to show counts as a function of register value. Thus, this new equation is:

$$m = \frac{\Delta \text{counts}}{\Delta \text{register value}} = \frac{8190}{9999}$$

$$Y = mX + b$$

$$Y = \frac{8190}{9999}X + b$$

The value of *Y* is –4095 when *X* is 0, so *b* equals:

$$b = -4095 - \frac{8190}{9999}X$$

$$= -4095 - \frac{8190}{9999}(0)$$

$$= -4095$$

Therefore, the equation of line *Y* showing counts as a function of register value is:

$$Y = \frac{8190}{9999}X - 4095$$

If this type of equation is implemented in a PLC using standard decimal arithmetic instructions with the 0000 to 9999 register values represented in BCD code, the PLC must convert from BCD to decimal. The PLC performs this conversion using software instructions.

7-30 *(a)*

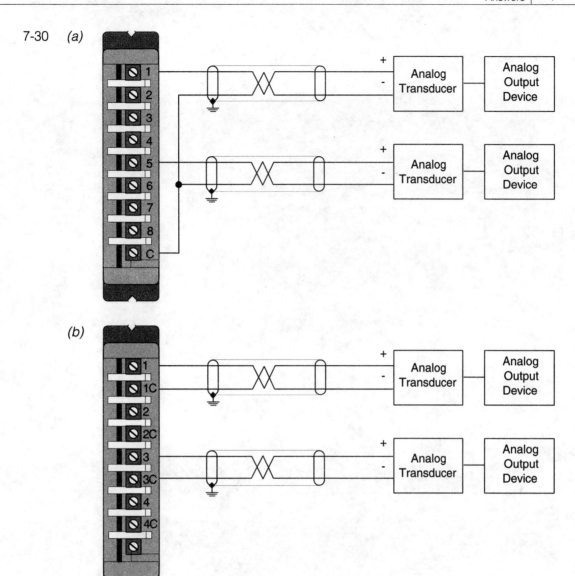

(b)

CHAPTER 8 ANSWERS

8-1   direct action modules

8-2   microprocessor

8-3   pulse stretcher, one scan

8-4   b–110 volts AC

8-5   Fast-input devices include:
-    proximity switches
-    photoelectric cells
-    any other instrumentation equipment that provides pulses in the range of 50 µsecs to 100 µsecs

8-6

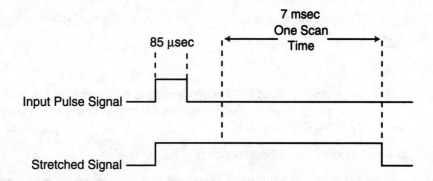

8-7   b–short-circuit, c–open-circuit

8-8   false; the module detects short circuits and open circuits by sensing changes in current sent by the module

8-9   A fast-response module is necessary whenever an input signal must create an output in a short time—generally within about 1 msec. The fast-response module responds to the fast input within 1 msec and also informs the processor that it has energized its fast-response output.

8-10   true

8-11   a–excitation voltage

8-12   d–millivolt

8-13   false; temperature data from a thermocouple is nonlinear

8-14   b–an ice-point reference

8-15   c–loss of signal due to wire resistance

8-16   A thermocouple module reports temperature data directly to the PLC in degrees Celsius or Fahrenheit in either BCD or binary format.

8-17   true

8-18   *(a)* The total lead resistance is the product of the thermocouple resistance and the length of the lead wire, which is:

$$\text{Total lead resistance } = (0.222)(750)$$
$$= 166.5 \text{ ohms}$$

(b) The compensation requirement is the difference between the module's compensation and the total resistance multiplied by the compensation error factor:

$$\text{Compensation in } °C = (166.5 - 25 \text{ ohms})(0.08°C / \text{ohm})$$
$$= 11.32°C$$

8-19   false; RTDs determine temperature by sensing resistance changes in their elements

8-20   An RTD module sends a small (mA) current through the RTD device and reads the resistance to the current flow. Changes in temperature are calculated based on resistance changes detected by the RTD module.

8-21   __b__ 100 ohms/–200 to 850°C

        __a__ 120 ohms/–80 to 300°C

        __c__ 10 ohms/–200 to 260°C

8-22   true

8-23   The most commonly used RTD configuration is the 3-wire, which is used in applications requiring long lead wires where wire resistance is significant in comparison to the ohms/°C sensitivity of the RTD element.

8-24   b–three-mode, closed-loop feedback control

8-25   The basic function of a PID module is to maintain certain process characteristics at desired set points.

8-26   Typical process variable inputs to PID modules include:
- liquid level
- temperature
- flow rate
- pressure

8-27 K_P is the proportional gain. This factor provides control action that is proportional to the instantaneous error value.

    K_I is the integral gain represented by K_P/Ti, where Ti is the reset time. This factor provides additional compensation to the control action, causing a change proportional to the value of the error over a period of time.

    K_D is the derivative gain represented by $K_P Td$, where Td is the rate time. This factor adds compensation to the control action, causing a change proportional to the rate of change of the error.

8-28   __e__ rate time

        __c__ desired output

        __a__ rate or period of update

        __d__ linearized scaled output

        __f__ reset time

        __b__ quantity compared to error signal

8-29

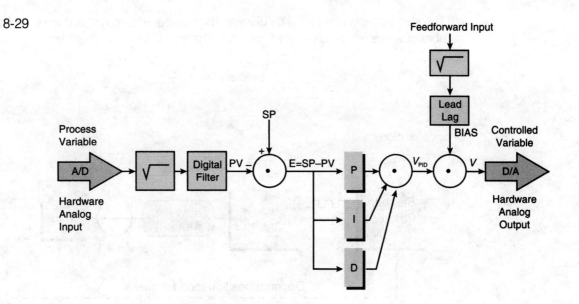

8-30   true

8-31   Encoder input module applications include:
 -   closed-loop positioning of machine tool axes, hoists, and conveyors
 -   cycle monitoring of high-speed machines, like can-making equipment

8-32   *(a)* Incremental encoders provide pulses that signify position as the encoder rotates. The encoder module receives and counts these pulses and then sends the information to the processor.

(b) Absolute encoders provide the processor with BCD or Gray code data that represents the angular position of the shaft.

8-33   d–independent of

8-34   one

8-35   a–bidirectional

8-36   true

8-37   d–all of the above

8-38   b–closed-loop

8-39   pulse trains

8-40   rate

8-41   *(a)* The linear displacement is computed by determining the number of threads it takes to move one inch. Each thread requires one revolution (rotational-to-linear displacement); therefore, moving one inch requires four revolutions and each revolution requires 400 steps:

$$1" \ \text{travel} = (4 \ \text{rev})(400 \ \text{steps} / \text{rev})$$
$$= 1600 \ \text{steps}$$

Thus:
$$1 \quad \text{step} = \frac{1}{1600}$$
$$= 0.000625 \ \text{inches}$$

(b) The step angle is computed by dividing the number of degrees in one revolution by the number of steps required to turn the motor. Therefore, the step angle is:

$$\text{step angle} = \frac{360°}{400}$$
$$= 0.9°$$

8-42   b–acceleration

8-43

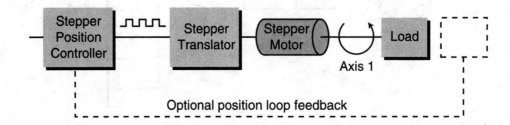

Optional position loop feedback

8-44   a–single-step (individual mode sequences), d–continuous (block instructions)

8-45   false; stepper motor loads with high inertia do require large amounts of power for acceleration and deceleration

8-46   In independent mode, each axis moves independently of the other axes. Each axis executes its own profile mode, which may be single step or continuous. The beginning and end of each axis motion may be different.

In synchronized mode, the beginning and end motion commands of each axis, based on time, are the same. A profile of one of the axes may start later or end earlier than the other axes, but the move that follows will not occur until all axes have started or ended their motions.

8-47   *(a)*

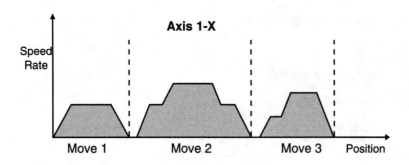

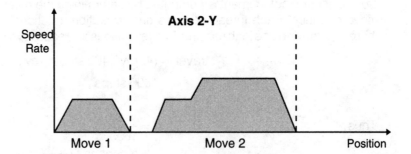

(b)

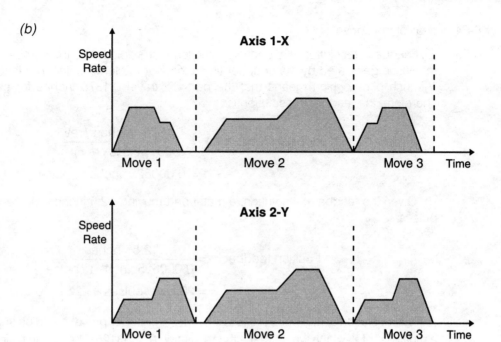

8-48   Servo interface modules provide the drive controller with a ±10 VDC signal, which defines the forward and reverse speeds of the servo motor.

8-49   c–axis positioning

8-50   The advantages of servo control over clutch-gear systems include:
- shorter positioning time
- higher accuracy
- better reliability
- improved repeatability

8-51   true

8-52   b–closed-loop, c–position

8-53

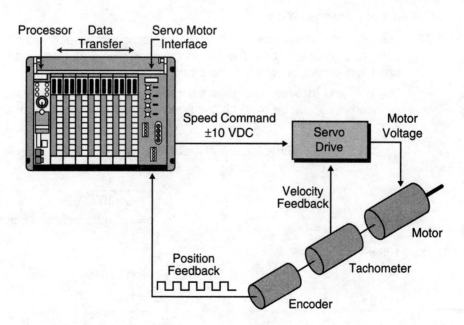

8-54   d–all of the above

8-55   *(a)* Feedback resolution is a function of the leadscrew pitch and the number of pulses per revolution generated by the encoder times the feedback multiplier. The leadscrew has a $^3/_{16}$ inch pitch, which means that the part will travel 0.1875 inches for every rotation. Therefore, the feedback resolution is:

$$\text{Feedback resolution} = \frac{0.1875 \text{ inches / rev}}{(300 \text{ pulses / rev})(1)}$$

$$= 0.000625 \text{ inches / pulse}$$

(b) Given the feedback resolution, a metal part moving 12.5 inches will generate 20,000 pulses:

$$\text{Position feedback} = \frac{12.5 \text{ inches}}{0.000625 \text{ inches / pulse}}$$

$$= 20,000 \text{ pulses}$$

(c) The resolution of 0.000625 inches (movement/encoder pulse) could be improved using a multiplier of 2, which would make the resolution 0.0003125. The ×2 multiplier allows both the quadrature pulses (A and B) to be counted, yielding twice as many pulses in one rotation.

8-56   d–travel of 0.0625 inches

8-57   An ASCII interface is an I/O module that sends and receives alphanumeric data between peripheral equipment and the processor. Devices that are typically interfaced with ASCII modules include:
- printers
- video terminals
- ASCII displays
- computers

8-58   c–parallel

8-59   a–faster than

8-60   c–every two characters

8-61   The scan time of 8 msec implies that a character cannot be received in less time than 8 msec. Each ASCII character has 10 bits (7 for the code plus start, stop, and parity bits), which are used during each character transmission.

The inverse of the scan time gives the minimum time that the processor will require to read an incoming character of 10 bits. Therefore, the time for one character (10 bits) is:

$$\text{Time for one character} = \frac{1}{\text{scan}}$$

$$= \frac{1}{8 \times 10^{-3}}$$

$$= 125 \text{ characters / scan}$$

Thus, the baud rate is:

$$\text{Baud rate} = (125)(10)$$

$$= 1250$$

The maximum baud rate is 1250, which transmits 125 characters per second. However, since this baud rate is not standard, the system would have to have a standard one, perhaps a 1200 baud.

8-62   data-processing modules

8-63   false; communication between a BASIC module and the processor generally occurs through move instructions

8-64   Network interface modules allow several PLCs and other devices to communicate over a high-speed local area communication network. When a processor sends a message, its resident network module transmits the message over the network, where another network module in another PLC receives and interprets it.

8-65   a–IF conditions, e–THEN actions

8-66   true

8-67   __P__ EIA RS-232C

        __P__ IEEE 488

        __D__ 20 mA current loop

        __P__ EIA RS-422

        __P__ EIA RS-485

8-68   ASCII

8-69   half-duplex, full-duplex

8-70   25

8-71   The electrical characteristics of the RS-232C standard include:

-   The signal voltages at the interface point should be a minimum of +5 V and a maximum of +15 V for logic 0. For logic 1, the signal voltages should be a minimum of –5 V and a maximum of –15 V.

-   The maximum recommended cable distance is 50 feet (or 15 meters). However, longer distances than this are permissible, provided that the resulting load capacitance measured at the interface point (and including the signal terminator) does not exceed 2500 picofarads.

-   The drivers used must be able to withstand open or short circuits between pins in the interface.

-   The load impedance at the terminator side must be between 3000 and 7000 ohms with no more than 2500 picofarads capacitance.

-   Voltages under –3 V (logic 1) are called mark potentials (signal condition), and voltages above +3 V (logic 0) are called space voltages. The area between –3 V and +3 V is not defined.

8-72   __c__ network compatible

        __a__ mechanical specification

        __e__ TTY serial interface

        __d__ balanced link

        __b__ unbalanced link

8-73

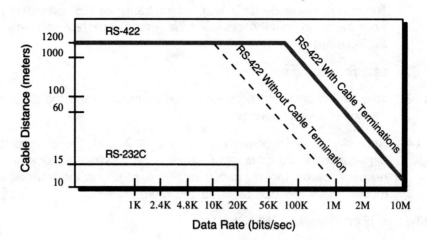

8-74   d–signal ground

CHAPTER 9 ANSWERS

9-1   ladder language

9-2   false; functional blocks are a part of enhanced ladder language

9-3   The seven ladder language instruction categories are:
- ladder relay
- timing
- counting
- program/flow control
- arithmetic
- data manipulation
- data transfer
- special function
- network communication

9-4   c–ladder diagram

9-5   Boolean language

9-6

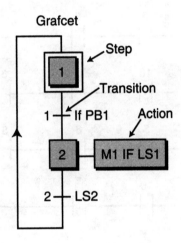

Grafcet

9-7   true

9-8   A ladder rung consists of a power line (L1) and a return line (L2) with input conditions and an output instruction located between them. The output instruction is located in the right-most position of the rung.

9-9   b–contacts, e–coils

9-10   true

9-11   b–coil symbols

9-12   a–left to right

9-13   A functional block without any conditional inputs should be connected directly to the left line of the ladder rung (L1) as follows:

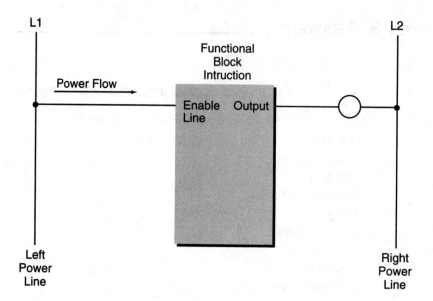

9-14   false; most PLCs do not allow reverse power flow

9-15   c—contacts 10, 11, 8, and 7 closed

9-16

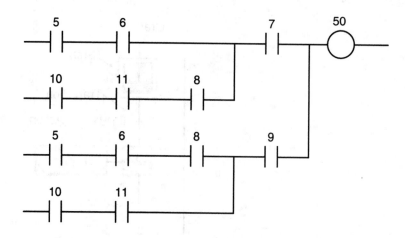

9-17   An output coil instruction controls either a real output or an internal output.

9-18   A latched coil is reset with an unlatch coil instruction.

9-19   The referenced trigger signal must make either an OFF-to-ON (leading-edge) or an ON-to-OFF (trailing-edge) transition for a transitional contact to provide a one-shot output.

9-20   true

9-21

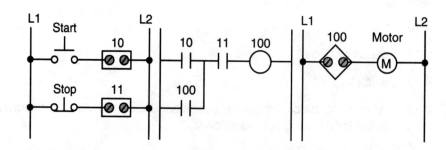

9-22   retentive ON-delay timer

9-23   The delay of 9 cycles at 60 Hz translates into a delay of 0.15 sec:

$$9 \text{ cycles} = \frac{9}{60} = 0.15 \sec$$

Therefore, using a time base of 0.01 seconds, the timer must count 15 ticks (0.15 sec ÷ 0.01 sec = 15 ticks) to create the delay.

9-24   *(a)* An ON-delay energize timer instruction provides time-delayed action of an event. When its rung has continuity, this instruction begins counting time-based intervals. When the accumulated value equals the preset value, it energizes the output.

(b) An ON-delay de-energize timer instruction de-energizes an output. When its rung has continuity, this instruction begins counting until the accumulated value equals the preset value, at which time, it turns OFF the output.

(c) An OFF-delay energize timer instruction provides time-delayed action when the rung's control line does not have continuity. When continuity does not exist, the timer begins timing, energizing the output when the accumulated and preset values are equal.

(d) An OFF-delay de-energize timer turns OFF an output when the control line does not have continuity and the accumulated value equals the preset value.

9-25   Using a normally closed contact with an ON-delay energize timer instruction will cause the instruction to act as an ON-delay de-energize timer instruction. The normally closed contact instruction will turn OFF the output when the ON-delay energize timer instruction times out.

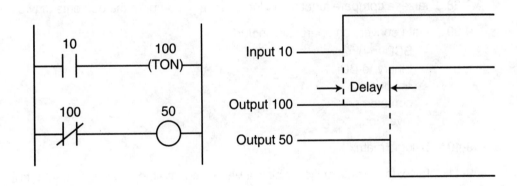

9-26   A retentive timer reset instruction is the only automatic way to reset the accumulated value of a retentive timer.

9-27   d–preset, a–accumulated

9-28   b–OFF-to-ON

9-29   A master control relay instruction activates or deactivates the execution of a group of ladder rungs. It is used with an END instruction to fence a group of rungs.

9-30   If a PLC does not have a reserved subroutine programming area, one can be created by programming a dummy rung that directly controls another dummy rung at the end of the programmed subroutines.

9-31   return

9-32   double-precision, single-precision

9-33

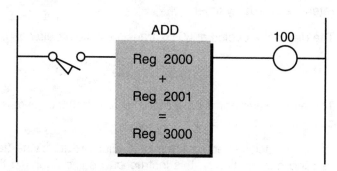

Reg 2000 = Ingredient A
Reg 2001 = Ingredient B
Reg 3000 = Sum of ingredients A and B

9-34   false; both are equally valid ways of expressing an arithmetic instruction

9-35   d–I/O transfer

9-36   If input 100 closes, the value in register 2001 will be multiplied by the value in register 2003 and the result will be stored in register 3000. Output 50 will be turned ON when the arithmetic operation is completed.

9-37   A division block's three possible outputs are done/enable (which signals the successful completion of the division), overflow (which indicates an error or overflow), and remainder (which signals whether the result has a remainder).

9-38   false; a compare functional block can only compare the contents of two registers

9-39   Data conversion operations include:
-   BCD-to-binary
-   binary-to-BCD
-   absolute
-   complement
-   inversion

9-40   b–logic matrix

9-41   false; the least significant bit will be moved into the most significant bit position

9-42   d–examine bit

9-43   The ladder program functions as follows:

(1) When input 10 (SS1) is enabled, the value (in BCD) of the thumbwheel switches in slot 3 will be stored in register 2000 via a block transfer in instruction. Then, output 30 will be energized.

(2) The second block transfer in instruction will read the analog input signal in slot 4 and store the value in register 3000. Output 31 will be energized when this block is enabled.

(3) The MOV BCD-D (move BCD to binary) instruction will convert the BCD value stored in register 2000 to a binary value and then store this value in register 2001. Output 32 will be energized when this block is enabled.

(4) The compare block (CMP) will compare the values in registers 3000 and 2001. If the value in register 3000 is greater than or equal to the value in register 2001, output 33 will turn ON, energizing output 20 (Sol1).

9-44   move block

9-45   c–ASCII transfer

9-46   The contents of register 1500 will be 0000 1010 0000 1110:

> Reg 1000 = 0011 1010 1000 1110
> Reg 1002 = 0000 1111 0000 1111   (mask)
> Reg 1500 = 0000 1010 0000 1110

9-47   b–diagnostic

9-48   PID

9-49   true

9-50   _c_ sends data to a specific network node

_e_ obtains data from a specific network PLC

_d_ captures status data from the network

_a_ obtains information from the network

_b_ sends one-bit status data to the network

9-51   *(a)* LD 1
AND 2
LD 4
AND 5
OR LD
LD 3
OR NOT 6
AND LD
OUT 100

(b) LD 1
AND 2
LD 4
AND 5
OR LD
AND 3
OR NOT 6
OUT 200

(c) LD NOT 1
AND 2
LD 5
AND 6
OR LD
AND 3
LD 4
OR NOT 7
AND LD
OUT 250

9-52   *(a)*

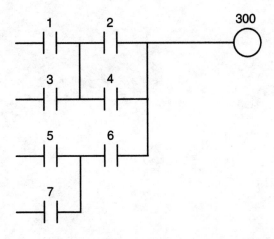

(b)

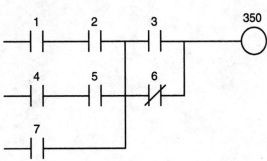

257

(c)

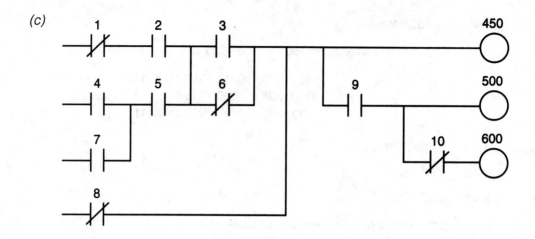

CHAPTER 10 ANSWERS

10-1   d—application guidelines

10-2   __T__ structured text

   __G__ ladder diagrams

   __F__ sequential function charts

   __G__ function block diagram

   __T__ instruction list

10-3   Data variable types include:
  - bit-based strings (Boolean)
  - integers
  - real
  - time
  - ASCII character string
  - vendor- and user-defined variables

   Data function types include:
  - bit-based
  - numerical/arithmetic
  - data function conversion
  - select functions
  - comparisons
  - ASCII string functions
  - vendor- and user-defined functions

   Function block types include:
  - set/reset (bistable)
  - edge trigger detection
  - timers
  - vendor- and user-defined blocks

10-4   Boolean, integer, real

10-5   true

10-6   b—encapsulation

10-7   instruction list

10-8   false; structured text supports conditional programming statements, as well as iterations

10-9

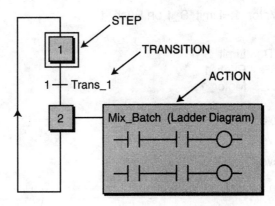

10-10

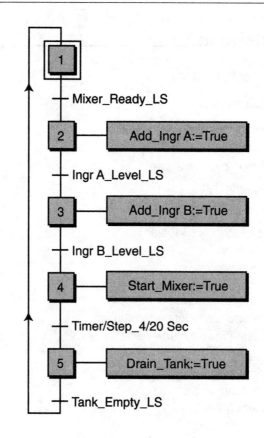

10-11   macrostep

10-12   *(a)*

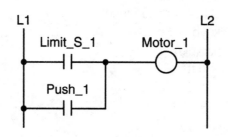

(b)

(c)   Motor_1:=Limit_S_1 OR Push_1

(d)   LD   Limit_S_1
        OR   Push_1
        ST   Motor_1

10-13   __c__ level 0

        __a__ level 1

        __b__ level 2

10-14   Boolean activity (or Boolean attribute)

10-15   false; the turning ON of a triggering signal will initiate a leading-edge transition, while the turning OFF of a triggering signal will initiate a trailing-edge transition

10-16   *(a)*   *(b)*

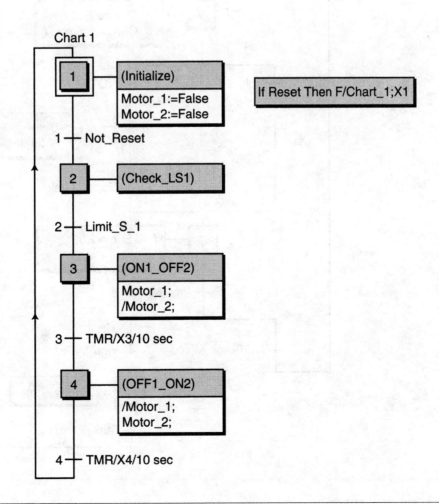

10-17   __c__   OR convergence

__b__   AND divergence

__d__   AND convergence

__a__   OR divergence

10-18   b–can communicate data with the main program

10-19   true

10-20

Chart 1

1   (Initialize)
Motor_1:=False
Motor_2:=False

If Reset Then F/Chart_1;X1

1 — Not_Reset

2   (Check_LS1)

2 — Limit_S_1

3   (ON1_OFF2)
Motor_1;
/Motor_2;

3 — TMR/X3/10 sec

4   (OFF1_ON2)
/Motor_1;
Motor_2;

4 — TMR/X4/10 sec

10-21   A stand-alone action triggers a transition to a specified SFC step once the stand-alone action's conditions are satisfied. A stand-alone action is not part of the SFC program itself; rather, it acts as an independent interrupt jump to instruction, specifying what part of the SFC program to jump to.

10-22   a–once, d–continuously

10-23   *(a)* A normal SFC action becomes active when the step becomes active. It is deactivated when the step is deactivated.

(b) A set SFC action becomes active when the step becomes active and remains active after the step is deactivated.

(c) A reset SFC action deactivates a set SFC action. It performs this deactivation when the step containing the reset action becomes active.

10-24   true

10-25

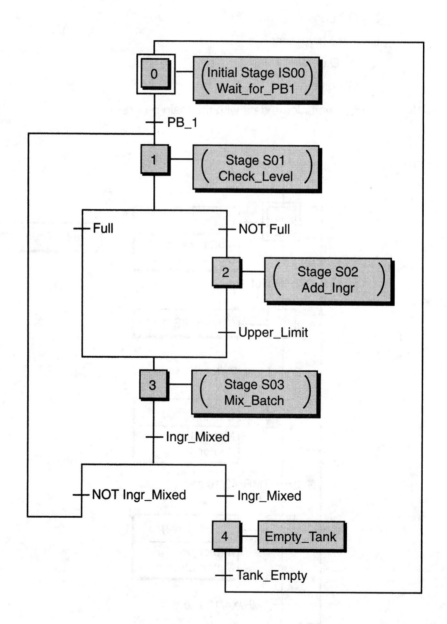

10-26   IEC 1131-3 programming guidelines include:

- Be consistent in the definition of the outputs and routines that will occur during actions.
- Define variables with proper, easy-to-reference names.
- Be consistent in the programming of transitions.
- Interlock program elements from within transitions, not actions.
- Document actions and transitions properly.

IEC 1131-3 troubleshooting guidelines include:

- Locate the step that was active when a malfunction occurred.
- Determine the status of the transition elements that form the logic after the step where operation halted.
- Investigate the active step and its following transitions first when diagnosing the location of a problem.

CHAPTER 11 ANSWERS

11-1   c–define the control task

11-2   algorithm

11-3   Guidelines for modernizing a control system include:
- understanding the actual process or machine function
- reviewing the machine logic and optimizing it when possible
- assigning real I/O addresses and internal addresses to inputs and outputs
- translating relay ladder diagrams into PLC coding

11-4   relay ladder diagram

11-5   b–specifications

11-6   flowchart

11-7   d–all of the above

11-8

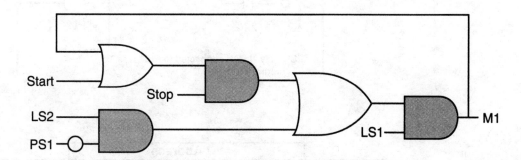

11-9

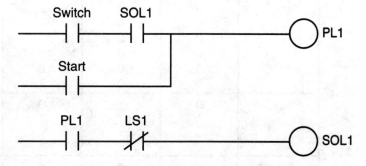

11-10   false; internal outputs are also documented during address assignment

11-11   octal, decimal, hexadecimal

11-12   I/O connection diagram

11-13   *(a)*

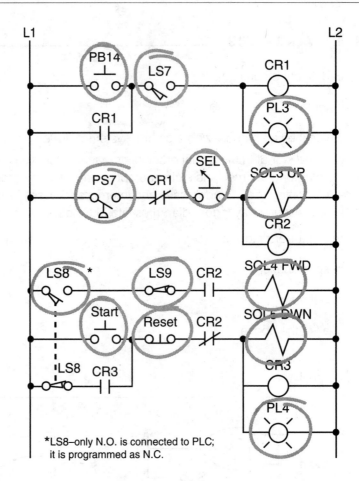

*LS8–only N.O. is connected to PLC;
it is programmed as N.C.

(b)

Module Type	I/O Address			Description
	Rack	**Group**	**Terminal**	
Input	0	0	0	PB14
	0	0	1	LS7
	0	0	2	PS7
	0	0	3	SEL
	0	0	4	LS8
	0	0	5	LS9
	0	0	6	Start PB
	0	0	7	Reset PB
Spare	0	1	0	Not used
	.	.	.	
	.	.	.	
	.	.	.	
	0	1	7	
Output	0	2	0	PL3
	0	2	1	SOL3 Up
	0	2	2	SOL4 Forward
	0	2	3	SOL5 Down
	0	2	4	PL4
	0	2	5	—
	0	2	6	—
	0	2	7	—

(c)

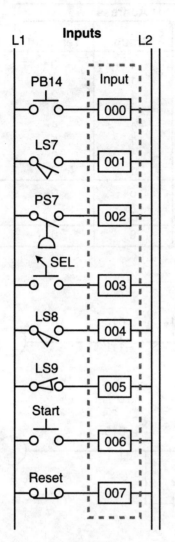

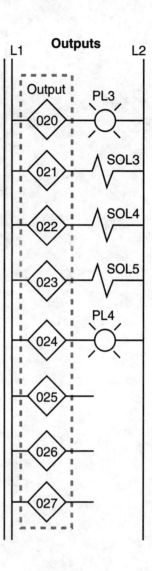

11-14   c–ensure safety

11-15   b–in series

11-16   d–to shut down the system if there is a PLC failure

11-17   A safety control relay is used to remove power from the I/O modules during a system error. When a malfunction occurs, the safety control relay will turn off, opening its SCR contact to stop the flow of power to the connected devices.

11-18   false; most of the time a normally closed input device is programmed as normally open; however, the programming of the input will depend on its function in the program

11-19   The normally closed PLC fault contacts are used to energize the PLC failure alarm. If the PLC fails, the PLC fault coil will not energize. Therefore, the normally open PLC fault contacts will not close to provide power to the connected devices. Instead, the normally closed PLC fault contacts will remain closed, sounding the PLC failure alarm.

11-20　*(a)*

Module Type	I/O Address			Description
	Rack	**Group**	**Terminal**	
Input	0	1	0	LS14
	0	1	1	SS3
	0	1	2	PS1
	0	1	3	S4
	0	1	4	LS15
	0	1	5	SS4
	0	1	6	—
	0	1	7	—
Output	0	5	0	SOL7
	⋮	⋮	⋮	
Internal	1	0	0	CR10

(b)

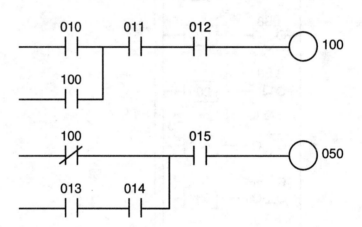

11-21　true

11-22　d–an internal output

11-23　There is a possibility of bidirectional power flow through the normally closed contact CR1 in line 3. A PLC will only allow power to flow in a forward path. Therefore, if the reverse path from line 4 to line 2 is meant to be followed, the circuit would have to be reconfigured so that the CR1 contacts are included in both lines 2 and 4.

11-24　coding

11-25　*(a)*

Device	Internal	Description
TMR1	100	Used to trap TMR1
CR1	—	Same as SOL1
CR2	—	Same as SOL2
CR3	101	Replace CR3
TMR1	200	Timer 1
TMR2	201	Timer 2

(b)

Module Type	I/O Address			Description
	Rack	Group	Terminal	
Input	0	0	0	PB1
	0	0	1	PS1
	0	0	2	FS1
	0	0	3	TS1
	0	0	4	LS1
	0	0	5	PS2
	0	0	6	—
	0	0	7	—
Output	0	3	0	SOL1
	0	3	1	SOL2
	0	3	2	SOL3
	⋮	⋮	⋮	

(c)

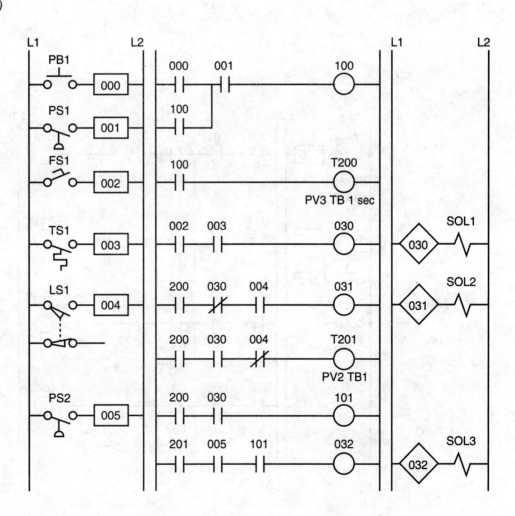

11-26   *(a)*

| | I/O Address | | | |
Module Type	Rack	Group	Terminal	Description
Input	0	0	0	Stop PB (wired NC)
	0	0	1	Forward PB (wired NO)
	0	0	2	Reverse PB (wired NO)
	0	0	3	Overload contacts
Input	0	0	4	Acknowledge OL/Reset PB
	•	•	•	
	•	•	•	
	•	•	•	
Output	0	3	0	Motor starter M1 (FWD)
	0	3	1	Forward PL1
	0	3	2	Motor starter M2 (REV)
	0	3	3	Reverse PL2

(b)

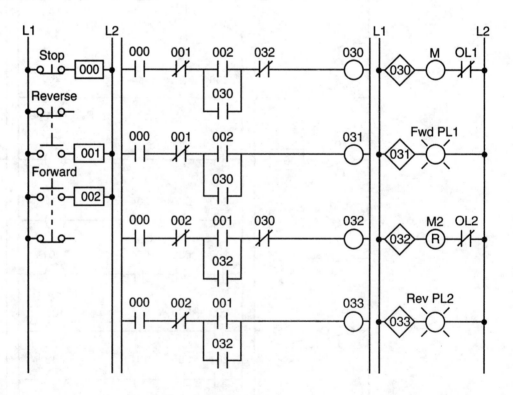

11-27

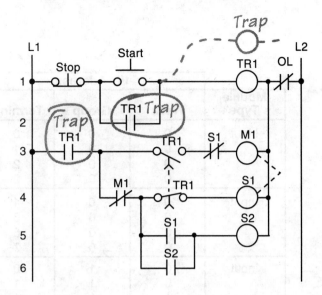

11-28 The field input devices are the start push button, stop push button, jog/run selector switch, and forward/reverse selector switch. The speed potentiometer will be replaced by an analog output in the PLC implementation.

11-29 *(a)*

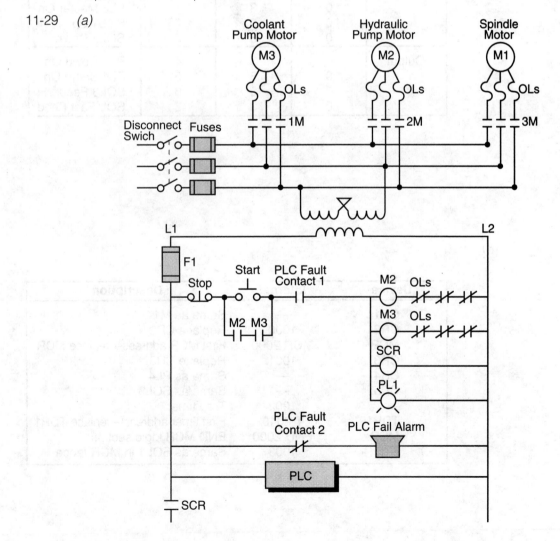

(b)

Module Type	I/O Address			Description
	Rack	Group	Terminal	
Input	0	0	0	Setup/Run
	0	0	1	Run PB
	0	0	2	Up LS1
	0	0	3	Enable SS
Input	0	0	4	Up PB
	0	0	5	LS2
	0	0	6	LS3
	0	0	7	Feed LS4
Input	0	1	0	LS5
	0	1	1	Not used
	•	•	•	•
	•	•	•	•
	0	1	7	
Output	0	3	0	M1 Starter
	0	3	1	PL2 Master On
	0	3	2	SOL1 Up
	0	3	3	SOL2 Down
Output	0	3	4	PL3 Down On
	0	3	5	PL4 Setup On
	0	3	6	SOL3 Feed
	0	3	7	SOL Fast Feed

(c)

Device	Internal	Description
CR1	—	Same as M1
CR2	1000	Replace CR2
MCR	MCR 2000	First MCR address—replace MCR
CR3	1001	Replace CR3
CR4	—	Same as PL4
CR5	—	Same as SOL3
—	1002	Trap timer
TDR1	T 2040	First timer address—replace TDR1
MCR	END 2000	END MCR logic section
—	1003	Same as SOL1 in MCR fence

(d)

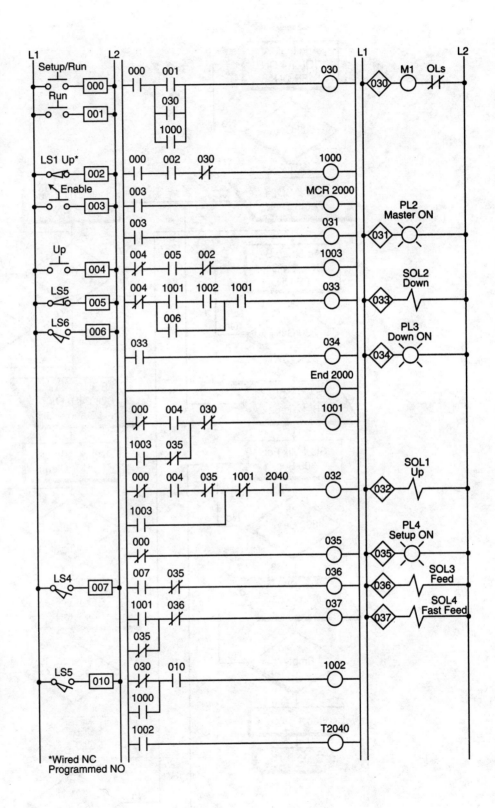

11-30   known measured values

11-31 *(a)*

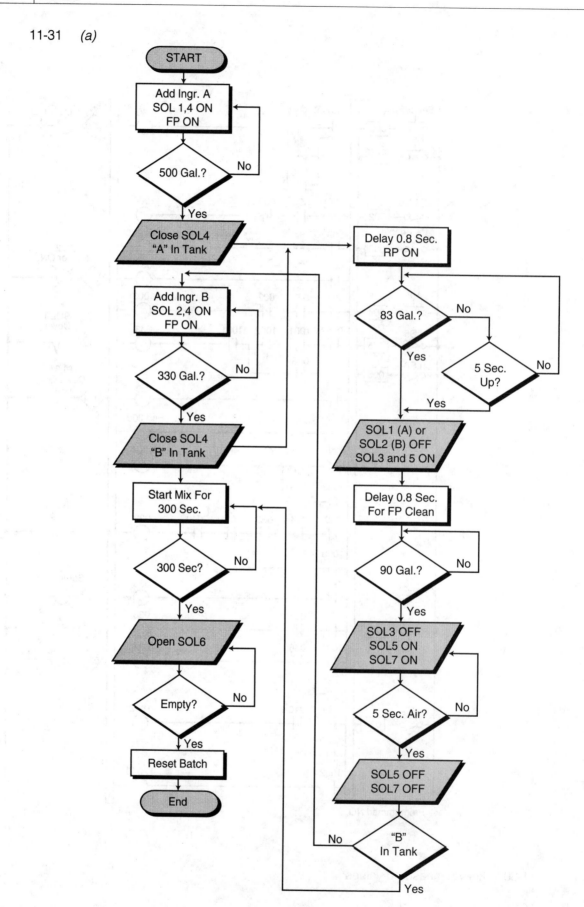

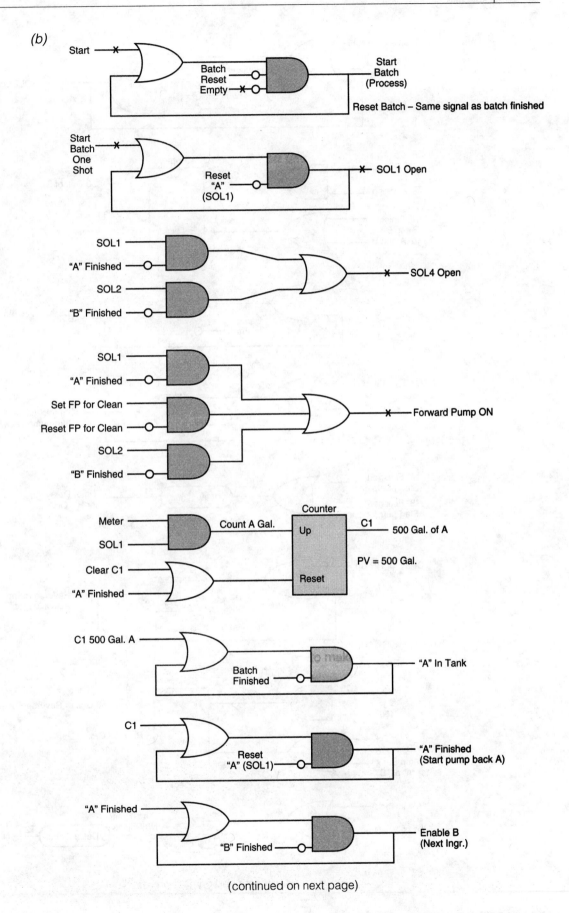

(b)

(continued on next page)

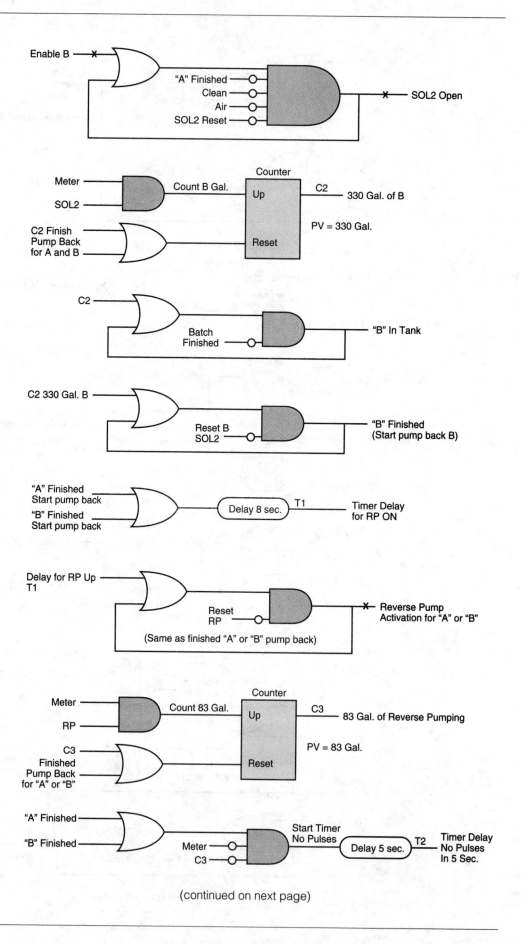

Enable B —✗

"A" Finished
Clean
Air
SOL2 Reset

✗— SOL2 Open

Meter
SOL2

Count B Gal.

Counter

Up

C2

330 Gal. of B

C2 Finish
Pump Back
for A and B

Reset

PV = 330 Gal.

C2

Batch
Finished

"B" In Tank

C2 330 Gal. B

Reset B
SOL2

"B" Finished
(Start pump back B)

"A" Finished
Start pump back
"B" Finished
Start pump back

Delay 8 sec.

T1

Timer Delay
for RP ON

Delay for RP Up
T1

Reset
RP

✗— Reverse Pump
Activation for "A" or "B"

(Same as finished "A" or "B" pump back)

Meter
RP

Count 83 Gal.

Counter

Up

C3

83 Gal. of Reverse Pumping

C3
Finished
Pump Back
for "A" or "B"

Reset

PV = 83 Gal.

"A" Finished
"B" Finished

Meter
C3

Start Timer
No Pulses

Delay 5 sec.

T2

Timer Delay
No Pulses
In 5 Sec.

(continued on next page)

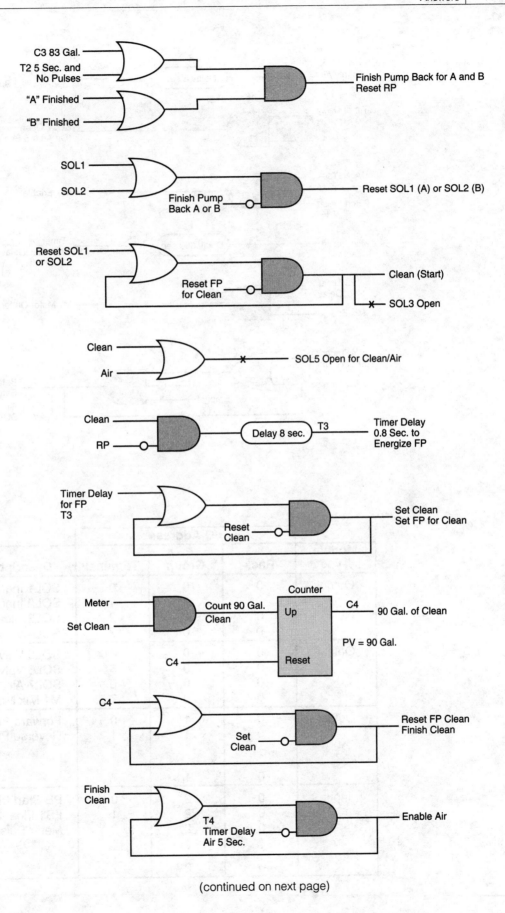

C3 83 Gal.
T2 5 Sec. and No Pulses
"A" Finished
"B" Finished

Finish Pump Back for A and B Reset RP

SOL1
SOL2
Finish Pump Back A or B

Reset SOL1 (A) or SOL2 (B)

Reset SOL1 or SOL2
Reset FP for Clean

Clean (Start)
SOL3 Open

Clean
Air

SOL5 Open for Clean/Air

Clean
RP

Delay 8 sec. T3

Timer Delay 0.8 Sec. to Energize FP

Timer Delay for FP T3
Reset Clean

Set Clean Set FP for Clean

Counter

Meter
Set Clean

Count 90 Gal. Clean

Up

C4

90 Gal. of Clean

PV = 90 Gal.

C4

Reset

C4
Set Clean

Reset FP Clean Finish Clean

Finish Clean
T4 Timer Delay Air 5 Sec.

Enable Air

(continued on next page)

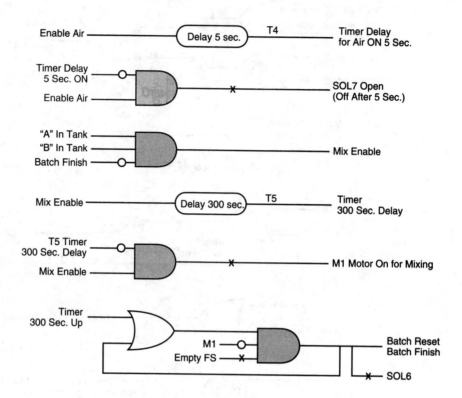

(c)

| | I/O Address | | | |
Module Type	Rack	Group	Terminal	Description
Output	0	0	0	SOL1 Ingr. A
	0	0	1	SOL2 Ingr. B
	0	0	2	SOL3 Cleanser
	0	0	3	SOL4 Valve
Output	0	0	4	SOL5 Valve
	0	0	5	SOL6 Valve
	0	0	6	SOL7 Air
	0	0	7	M1 Mix Motor
Output	0	1	0	Forward Pump
	0	1	1	Reverse Pump
	·	·	·	
	·	·	·	
	0	1	7	
Input	0	2	0	PB Start Batch
	0	2	1	FS1 Float Switch
	0	2	2	Meter Pulses
	·	·	·	
	·	·	·	
	0	2	7	

(d)

Device	Internal	Description
CR1	1000	Start batch
CR2	1001	Start batch one-shot
CR16	—	Reset batch—batch finished
CR17	—	Same as SOL6
CR9	1002	Reset A, SOL1; Reset B, SOL2
CR4	1003	A finished—start reverse pump A
CR7	1004	B finished—start reverse pump B
CR11	1005	Set FP for clean
CR12	1006	Finish clean—reset FP
C1	C2300	Count 500 gallons of A
CR3	1007	A in tank
CR5	1010	Enable B
CR10	1011	Clean (start)
CR13	1012	Air—enable air
CR15	1013	Reset SOL2
C2	C2301	Count 300 gallons of B
CR6	1014	B in tank
T1	T2000	Delay 0.8 seconds for RP
CR8	1015	Reset RP, finish RP for A or B
C3	C2302	Count 83 gallons in reverse pump
T2	T2001	No pulse in 5 seconds
T3	T2002	Delay 0.85 seconds for FP
C4	C2303	Count 90 gallons of cleanser
T4	T2003	Air on for 5 seconds
CR14	1016	Mix enable
T5	T2004	Motor on for 300 seconds

(e)

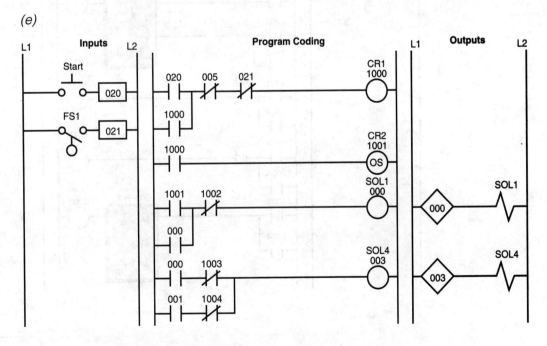

(continued on next page)

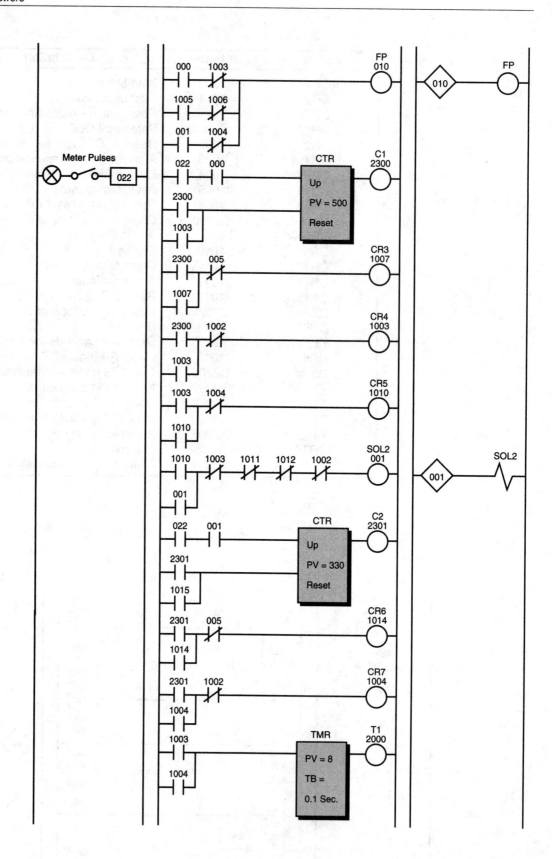

(continued on next page)

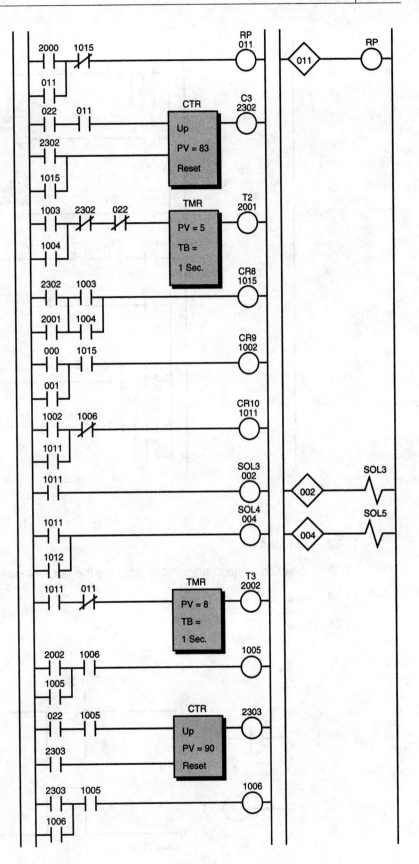

(continued on next page)

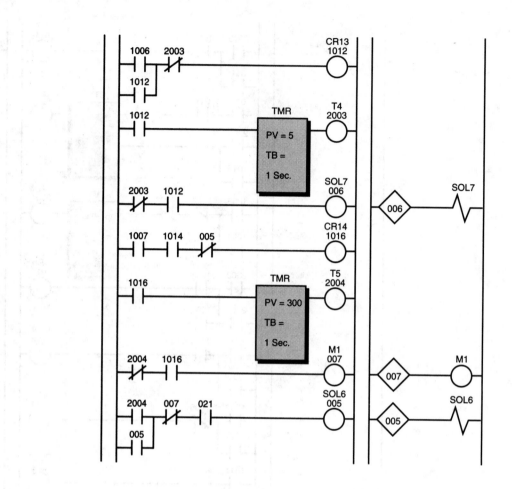

11-32   reduced

11-33   false; only one condition can activate the output in an exclusive-OR circuit

11-34   true

11-35

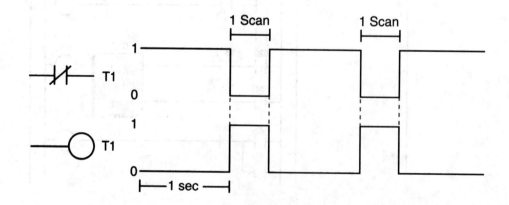

11-36

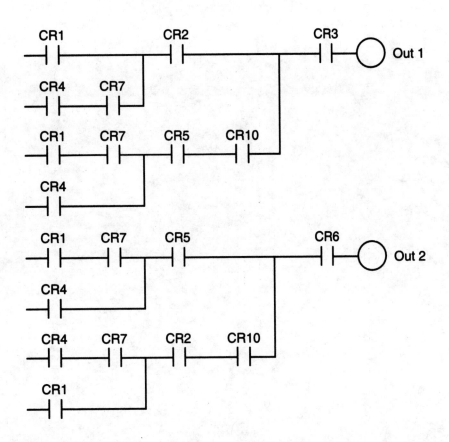

11-37   b–cascading two counters

CHAPTER 12 ANSWERS

12-1   documentation

12-2   false; the documentation process should start the moment the project starts

12-3   false; documentation includes descriptive details of the system hardware as well as the software

12-4   d–usage of ladder instructions

12-5

Address	I/O Type	Device
130	115 VAC in	PB10
131	115 VAC in	LS2
132	115 VAC in	TS7
133	115 VAC in	LS16 (wired NC)
134	115 VAC in	PS4
135	115 VAC in	Not used
136	115 VAC in	Not used
137	115 VAC in	Not used
320	115 VAC out	SOL3
321	115 VAC out	PL4
322	115 VAC out	PL5
323	115 VAC out	M4
324	115 VAC out	Not used
325	115 VAC out	Not used
326	115 VAC out	SOL7
327	115 VAC out	SOL10

12-6

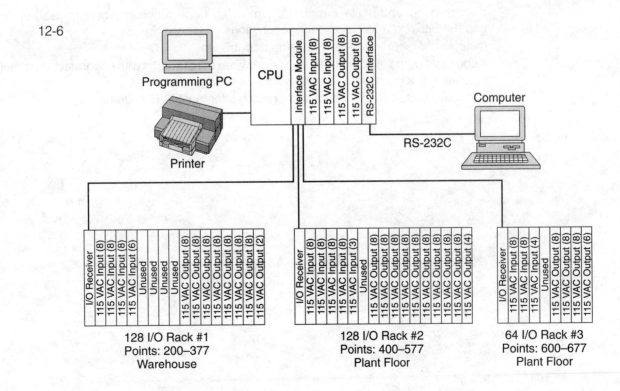

12-7   b–system abstract

12-8   false; to understand the control program, you must have the entire system documentation, not just the program printout

12-9   c–I/O wiring connection diagram

12-10   false; the documentation package is useful during system design, installation, start-up, debugging, and maintenance

12-11   c–a and b

12-12   The address, type of device, and function or description of each input and output should be included in the I/O address assignment document.

12-13   true

12-14   c–as the internals are used during system programming

12-15   b–improper reference to a register

12-16   c–the I/O connections for field devices

12-17   true

12-18   Media that are used to store and transport the control program are:
- cassette tapes
- floppy disks
- electronic memory modules

12-19   b–the latest ladder program printout

12-20   d–all of the above

12-21   The features of documentation systems include:
- electronic cut-and-paste capabilities, macros, copy functions, generic addressing capabilities, and address exchange functions
- multiple-character, wide-field labeling capabilities
- a complete range of I/O elements and hardwired I/O drawings with integrated, automatic cross-referencing of the logic program
- capability to upload and download programs for most PLC systems

CHAPTER 13 ANSWERS

13-1   false; the mean and the average are the same thing

13-2   ascending

13-3   mode

13-4   false; the standard deviation specifies how data is dispersed in relation to the mean

13-5   *(a)*

$$\text{Mean} = \frac{19+10+14+15.6+10+17+9+8}{8}$$
$$= 12.825 \text{ psi}$$

(b) The value 10 psi is the mode.

(c) The sample data listed in ascending order is 8, 9, 10, 10, 14, 15.6, 17, and 19 psi. Therefore, the median is:

$$\text{Median} = \frac{10+14}{2}$$
$$= 12 \text{ psi}$$

(d)

$$\sigma = \sqrt{\frac{\sum\limits_{n=1\,to\,i}(\overline{X}-X_n)^2}{n-1}}$$
$$= 4.115 \text{ psi}$$

13-6   95%

13-7   The sample data with a standard deviation of 0.04 psi has a distribution closer to the mean.

13-8   The three types of errors are gross errors, system errors, and random errors. Gross errors may be prevented by paying more attention to correct displays, having different people take the same readings, taking multiple instrument readings, and being aware of instrument capabilities. System errors may be prevented by calibrating instruments regularly, emphasizing regular maintenance of machinery and instruments, and monitoring the consistency of techniques. Random errors may be prevented by adjusting process line instruments, so that they can withstand disturbances.

13-9   By statistical analysis of the mean, mode, median, and standard deviation calculations of an operation, the user may predict future readings.

13-10   guarantee errors

13-11 *(a)*

$$V = \text{volume}$$
$$= \overline{X}\,\overline{Y}\,\overline{Z}$$
$$= (10)(12)(13)$$
$$= 1560 \text{ cm}^3$$

$$W_c = \text{weight of the cube}$$
$$= (V)(\overline{W})$$
$$= (1560)(0.30)$$
$$= 468 \text{ lbs}$$

(b)

$$\sigma_{W_c} = \sqrt{\left(\frac{\partial W_c}{\partial X}\right)^2 \sigma_X^2 + \left(\frac{\partial W_c}{\partial Y}\right)^2 \sigma_Y^2 + \left(\frac{\partial W_c}{\partial Z}\right)^2 \sigma_Z^2 + \left(\frac{\partial W_c}{\partial W}\right)^2 \sigma_W^2}$$

$$= \sqrt{(\overline{W}\,\overline{Y}\,\overline{Z})^2 (0.01)^2 + (\overline{X}\,\overline{Z}\,\overline{W})^2 (0.02)^2 + (\overline{X}\,\overline{Y}\,\overline{W})^2 (0.015)^2 + (\overline{X}\,\overline{Y}\,\overline{Z})^2 (0.0003)^2}$$

$$= \sqrt{\begin{aligned}&[(0.3)(12)(13)]^2 (0.01)^2 + [(10)(13)(0.3)]^2 (0.02)^2 + [(10)(12)(0.3)]^2 (0.015)^2 \\ &+ [(10)(12)(13)]^2 (0.0003)^2\end{aligned}}$$

$$= \sqrt{0.219 + 0.608 + 0.291 + 0.219}$$

$$= \sqrt{1.337}$$

$$= 1.156 \text{ lbs}$$

13-12 bridge circuits, LVDT mechanisms

13-13 bridge imbalance

13-14 c–is proportional to

13-15 a–accelerometer, c–load cell, d–Bourdon tube

13-16 RTDs, thermistors, thermocouples

13-17 RTDs

13-18 negative

13-19 false; thermocouples are widely used in industry

13-20 thermopile

13-21 displacement

13-22 body deformation of a rigid body as a result of force applied to the body

13-23 dummy gauge

13-24 true

13-25 false; they can also measure the rate of flow of gases and solids

13-26

$$Q = \frac{WV}{L}$$

$$= \frac{(45)(22)}{3}$$

$$= 330 \text{ kgs/min}$$

13-27 pressure

13-28 motion detection

13-29 Some common causes of vibration failures include:
- imbalance of a rotating member
- misalignment
- defective bearings and belts

13-30 Displacement, velocity, and acceleration are the three main motion parameters.

13-31 electric polarity

CHAPTER 14 ANSWERS

14-1 true

14-2 c–dynamic variable

14-3 error

14-4 b–regulated

14-5 control loop or feedback loop

14–6 true

14–7 false, positive feedback aggravates the error signal by magnifying the error and creating an unstable system

14–8 b–$E = SP - PV$

14–9 false, the controller reacts in a direct- or reverse-acting manner due to an increase or decrease in the process variable

14–10

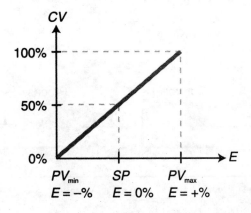 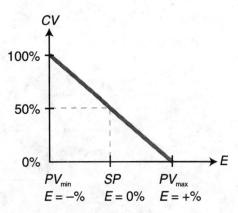

Direct Acting
As percentage of error *increases*, the control variable *increases*

Reverse Acting
As percentage of error *increases*, the control variable *decreases*

14–11

	Control Variable	
	Direct Acting	Reverse Acting
Error ↑	↑	↓
Error ↓	↓	↑

14–12 true

14–13   The controller will take action when the process variable passes the SP + DB and SP – DB values.

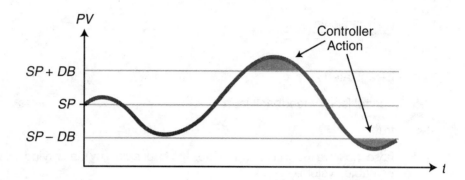

14–14   false; when the process variable is at the set point or within the error deadband, the process is at steady state

14–15   d–disturbances

14–16   b–an equation that describes the process in terms of response over time and the outcome of the process variable

14–17   true

14–18

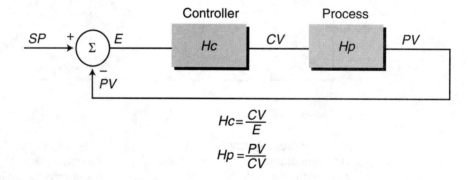

$$Hc = \frac{CV}{E}$$

$$Hp = \frac{PV}{CV}$$

14-19   c–the time it takes for the process variable to start reacting to a change in input

14–20   *(a)*

$$K = \frac{PV_{final} - PV_{initial}}{CV_{final} - CV_{initial}}$$

$$= \frac{81°C - 65°C}{75\% - 55\%}$$

$$= \frac{16°C}{20\%}$$

$$= 0.8°C / \%$$

(b) The transient response time is 20 minutes.

(c) The process gain term indicates that the process gains 0.8°C for each percentage change in input change. The transient response time indicates the time it takes the process variable to achieve a steady-state value.

14–21   true

14–22   false, a lag time delay can also occur when the control variable is decreased

14–23   c–first-order, d–second-order

14–24   true

14–25   b–Laplace transforms

14–26   response B

14–27

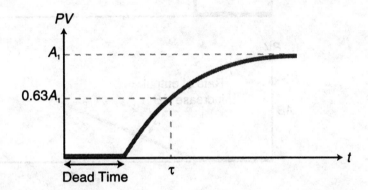

14–28   two (s^2)

14–29   <u>c</u> $sX_{(s)}$

       <u>d</u> $\dfrac{A}{s}$

       <u>b</u> $s^2X_{(s)}$

       <u>a</u> $X_{(s)}$

14–30   <u>b</u> $\dfrac{1}{(3s+4)(s+2)}$

       <u>a</u> $\dfrac{4}{3s+1}$

       <u>c</u> $\dfrac{8}{s^3+s^2+2s+1}$

14–31   true

14–32   d–ramping

14–33 The rate of increase of the integral response is the process gain A times the amplitude of the step B times t (i.e., $PV = ABt$).

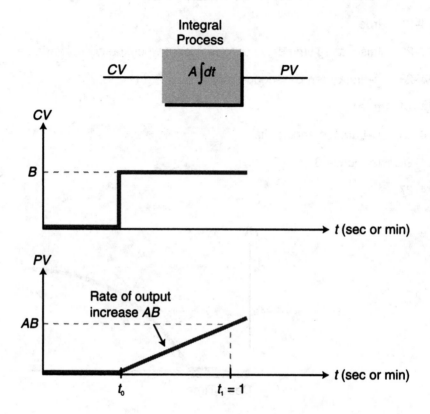

14–34 $CV_{(s)} = K_P E_{(s)} + \dfrac{K_I E_{(s)}}{s} + K_D E_{(s)} s$

14–35 b–$e^{-t_d s}$

14–36 b–one, d–two

14–37 c–63.2%

14–38 a–99.3%

14–39 c–14.9 minutes (the dead time simply adds to the response time to achieve 90% of the final value)

14–40

$$V_{out} = V_{in}\left(1 - e^{\frac{-t}{\tau}}\right)$$

$$\frac{V_{out}}{V_{in}} = 1 - e^{\frac{-t}{\tau}}$$

$$0.50 = 1 - e^{\frac{-t}{7.5}}$$

$$e^{\frac{-t}{7.5}} = 1 - 0.50$$

$$= 0.50$$

Solving for *t* by taking the natural logarithm of both sides of the equation yields:

$$e^{\frac{-t}{7.5}} = 0.50$$

$$\frac{-t}{7.5} = \ln 0.50$$

$$-t = (7.5)(\ln 0.50)$$

$$= (7.5)(-0.693)$$

$$= 5.2 \text{ minutes}$$

Therefore, the value of the output will be at 50% of the value of the input in 5.2 minutes.

14-41   true

14-42   d–ζ

14–43

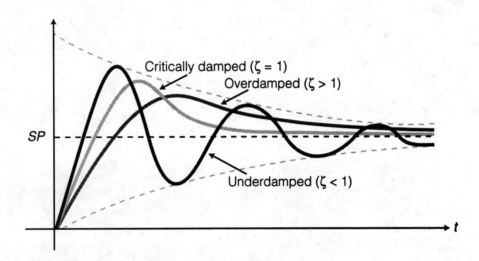

14–44   false; if $\tau_1 = \tau_2$, the second-order system is critically damped

14–45   false; if $\zeta = 0$, the response will be unstable, oscillating around the set point

14-46   c–a critically damped second-order system

14-47   c–first-order lag

CHAPTER 15 ANSWERS

15-1   d–conditionally unstable

15-2   true

15-3   _c_ stable response
       _a_ conditionally stable
       _b_ unstable response

15-4 $\dfrac{PV_{(s)}}{Input_{(s)}} = (Hc_{(s)})(Hp_{(s)})$

15-5

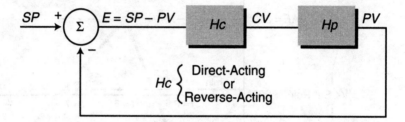

15-6   false; a closed-loop controller can provide direct or reverse action

15-7   c–As the control variable increases, the process variable decreases.

15-8   The two types of controller modes are discrete and continuous. Discrete-mode controllers produce discrete signals, while continuous-mode controllers produce analog signals.

15-9   b–ON/OFF controller, e–ON and OFF

15-10 a–two-position controller, c–direct and reverse

15-11 true

15-12 false; a two-position controller does not have hysteresis, causing the process variable to oscillate around the set point

15-13

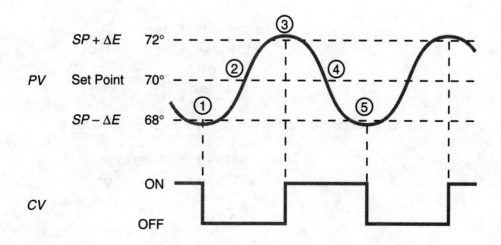

15-14   b–the finite warm up and cool off times (lag) of the heater system

15-15   *(a)* The following figure illustrates the response of the process variable over time, along with the controller's output status. The upper value of the deadband ($\Delta E = +5\%$) is 210°F, while the lower value ($\Delta E = -5\%$) is 190°F. This curve starts at 200°F *(SP)* and declines at a rate of 4°F/min until the temperature equals 190°F *(SP – ΔE)*. At 190°F, the controller turns ON and starts heating the system at a rate of 8°F/min until the temperature reaches 210°F *(SP + ΔE)*, at which point, the controller turns off the heater. The process variable starts to cool off again at the rate of 4°F/min until the temperature reaches *SP – ΔE*, where the cycle is repeated.

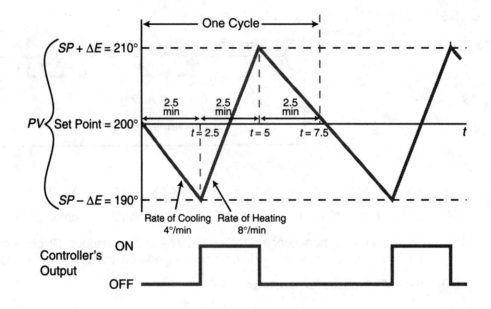

To calculate the time for each curve is to determine the difference between the temperatures and divide this difference by the rate required to get from one temperature to another. The time required for the first half of the curve, the OFF mode, to decline from the set point (200°F) to the lower limit of the deadband (190°F) is:

$$200°F \rightarrow 190°F \ @ \ \text{rate} - 4°F / \text{min}$$
$$-10°F \ \text{change} \ @ \ \text{rate} - 4°F / \text{min}$$
$$t = \frac{-10°F}{-4°F / \text{min}} = 2.5 \ \text{min}$$

The same calculation for the OFF-to-ON state of the controller is:

$$190°F \rightarrow 210°F \ @ \ \text{rate} \ 8°F / \text{min}$$
$$20°F \ \text{change} \ @ \ \text{rate} \ 8°F / \text{min}$$
$$t = \frac{20°F}{8°F / \text{min}} = 2.5 \ \text{min}$$

Finally, the time required for the next part of the curve is:

$$210°F \rightarrow 190°F @ \text{rate} - 4°F/\text{min}$$

$$-20°F \text{ change @ rate} - 4°F/\text{min}$$

$$t = \frac{-20°F}{-4°F/\text{min}} = 5 \text{ min}$$

However, to compute the oscillation period, the system only requires half of this last time calculation, 2.5 minutes, to complete the cycle (i.e., return to the set point). Thus, the total time for the oscillation response is 7.5 min (2.5 min + 2.5 min + 2.5 min).

(b) A lag of 60 seconds, or 1 minute, will cause the ON/OFF response to undershoot and overshoot the deadband, slightly affecting the frequency of oscillation. This 1-minute lag may be due to the cooling off and heating up times associated with the heating element. The oscillation frequency for the first part of the curve can be calculated as follows:

$$200°F \rightarrow 190°F @ \text{rate} - 4°F/\text{min}$$

$$t = \frac{-10°F}{-4°F/\text{min}} = 2.5 \text{ min}$$

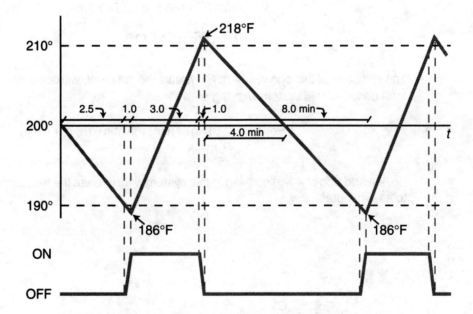

However, once the temperature reaches 190°F and the heater turns ON, another minute will elapse while the heating element heats up. Meanwhile, the temperature will continue to drop. So, during that 1-minute lapse, the temperature will drop another 4°F, making the final low-limit temperature 186°F:

$$t = \frac{\Delta \text{ temperature}}{\text{rate}}$$

$$1 \text{min} = \frac{\Delta \text{ temperature}}{-4°F/\text{min}}$$

$$\Delta \text{ temperature} = (1)(-4) = -4°F$$

$$190°F - 4°F = 186°F$$

This lag will cause an undershoot of the deadband. Once the controller is ON, it will heat the tank at a rate of 8°F/min, reaching the 210°F upper temperature level in 3 minutes:

$$186°F \rightarrow 210°F \text{ @ rate } 8°F/min$$

$$t = \frac{24°F}{8°F/min} = 3 \text{ min}$$

The 1-minute lag will cause an overshoot of 8°F:

$$1 min = \frac{\Delta \text{ temperature}}{8°F/min}$$

$$\Delta \text{ temperature} = (1)(8)$$

$$= 8°F$$

This will make the upper temperature 218°F (210°F + 8°F). The final period of oscillation, which is the last half of the curve, is the cooling off period between the upper temperature limit (218°F) and the lower limit (186°F):

$$218°F \rightarrow 186°F \text{ @ rate } 4°F/min$$

$$t = \frac{32°F}{4°F/min} = 8 \text{ min}$$

The half point of this curve, where *PV* equals the set point, will occur at 4 minutes. Thus, the total period of this system with lag is:

$$\text{Period} = (2.5 \text{ min} + 1 \text{ min}) + (3 \text{ min} + 1 \text{ min}) + 4 \text{ min}$$

$$= 11.5 \text{ min}$$

So, the addition of a 1-minute lag to this system will increase the frequency from 7.5 minutes to 11.5 minutes.

15-16

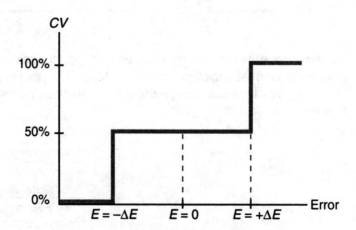

15-17

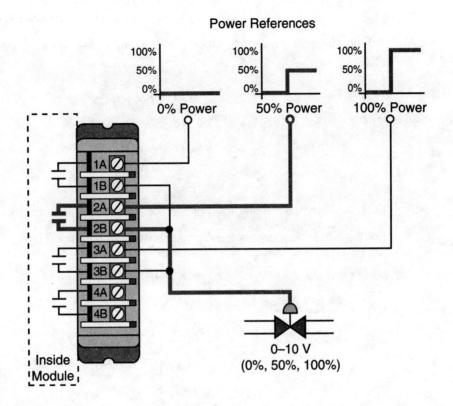

Power References

15-18   true

15-19   b–incremental

15-20   c–integral, d–reset

15-21   false; derivative action, which is never used by itself in a process application, is often combined with proportional and proportional-integral controller modes

15-22   a–the percentage change in *CV* for each percentage change in error

15-23

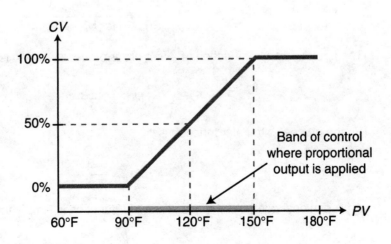

15-24   b–inversely

15-25   true

15-26   The equation for a proportional controller's output, taking into consideration the value $CV_{(old)}$ is:

$$CV_{(t)} = K_P E + CV_{(old)}$$

where:

$$CV_{(t)} = \text{the control variable}$$
$$K_P = \text{the proportional gain}$$
$$E = \text{the error}$$

15-27   false; the Laplace transfer for a proportional controller is a constant value, K_P

15-28   For the closed-loop system, the process variable is defined by:

$$PV_{(s)} = \left(E_{(s)}\right)\left(Hc_{(s)}\right)\left(Hp_{(s)}\right)$$

Replacing $E_{(s)}$ with $SP_{(s)} - PV_{(s)}$ yields:

$$PV_{(s)} = \left(SP_{(s)} - PV_{(s)}\right)Hc_{(s)}Hp_{(s)}$$
$$PV_{(s)} = \left(SP_{(s)}Hc_{(s)}Hp_{(s)}\right) - \left(PV_{(s)}Hc_{(s)}Hp_{(s)}\right)$$
$$PV_{(s)}\left(1 + Hc_{(s)}Hp_{(s)}\right) = SP_{(s)}Hc_{(s)}Hp_{(s)}$$

Solving for $PV_{(s)}$ over $SP_{(s)}$ yields the closed-loop transfer function of this process control system:

$$\frac{PV_{(s)}}{SP_{(s)}} = \frac{Hc_{(s)}Hp_{(s)}}{Hc_{(s)}Hp_{(s)} + 1}$$

15-29   d–all of the above

15-30   true

15-31   (a) The transfer function of a closed-loop system is expressed as:

$$\frac{PV_{(s)}}{SP_{(s)}} = \frac{Hc_{(s)}Hp_{(s)}}{Hc_{(s)}Hp_{(s)} + 1}$$

The Laplace transfer function of a first-order process with lag is:

$$Hp_{(s)} = \frac{A}{\tau s + 1}$$

So the process's transfer function is:

$$Hp_{(s)} = \frac{4}{20s + 1}$$

A proportional controller's Laplace transfer function is simply the value of its gain, so:

$$Hc_{(s)} = 10$$

Therefore, the closed-loop transfer function of the entire system is:

$$\frac{PV_{(s)}}{SP_{(s)}} = \frac{(10)\left(\frac{4}{20s+1}\right)}{\left[(10)\left(\frac{4}{20s+1}\right)\right]+1}$$

$$= \frac{\left(\frac{40}{20s+1}\right)}{\left(\frac{40}{20s+1}+1\right)}$$

$$= \frac{\left(\frac{40}{20s+1}\right)}{\left(\frac{40+20s+1}{20s+1}\right)}$$

$$= \frac{40}{40+20s+1}$$

$$= \frac{40}{20s+41}$$

This transfer function indicates that this is a first-order system. To express it in the form of a first-order system, we must divide the numerator and denominator by 41 to obtain:

$$\frac{PV_{(s)}}{SP_{(s)}} = \frac{\left(\frac{40}{41}\right)}{\left(\frac{20s}{41}+\frac{41}{41}\right)}$$

$$= \frac{0.976}{0.488s+1}$$

(b) The response to a unit step change in the set point is given by:

$$SP_{(s)} = \frac{1}{s} \quad \text{(unit step)}$$

Therefore, using the previous equation, the process variable response will be:

$$PV_{(s)} = SP_{(s)}\left(\frac{0.976}{0.488s+1}\right)$$

Thus:

$$PV_{(s)} = \left(\frac{1}{s}\right)\left(\frac{0.976}{0.488s+1}\right)$$

$$PV_{(s)} = \frac{0.976}{s(0.488s+1)}$$

This response is in the form of the inverse Laplace transform of a first-order response to a step input with lag:

$$\mathscr{L}^{-1}\left[\frac{A}{s(\tau s+1)}\right] = A\left(1-e^{\frac{-t}{\tau \sec}}\right)$$

Hence, in the time domain, the process variable response will be equal to:

$$PV_{(t)} = 0.976\left(1-e^{\frac{-t}{0.488\sec}}\right)$$

(c) The figure below illustrates the time response of the closed-loop system to a unit step change in the set point. Note that the gain of the system is 0.976, meaning that the process variable in the system will not reach the value of the unit step input. Instead, the system will respond only 0.976 to the unit step change of 1. The process variable steady-state value (PV_{ss}), which is the final value of *PV*, can be computed using the final value theorem:

$$PV_{ss} = \lim_{t \to \infty}\left[0.976\left(1 - e^{\frac{-t}{0.732}}\right)\right]$$

$$= \lim_{t \to \infty}\left[0.976(1 - 0)\right]$$

$$= 0.976$$

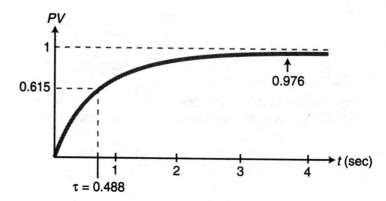

(d) The system time constant, $\tau_{sys} = 0.488$, indicates that the system will take 0.488 seconds to reach 0.615, or 63% of the steady-state value.

15-32   The closed-loop transfer function is represented by:

$$\frac{PV_{(s)}}{SP_{(s)}} = \frac{Hc_{(s)}Hp_{(s)}}{Hc_{(s)}Hp_{(s)} + 1}$$

where:

$$Hc_{(s)} = 3$$

$$Hp_{(s)} = \frac{1}{(10s + 1)(2.5s + 1)}$$

Therefore:

$$\frac{PV}{SP} = \frac{\left[\dfrac{3}{(10s + 1)(2.5s + 1)}\right]}{\left[\dfrac{3}{(10s + 1)(2.5s + 1)}\right] + 1}$$

$$= \frac{\left[\dfrac{3}{(10s + 1)(2.5s + 1)}\right]}{\left[\dfrac{3 + (10s + 1)(2.5s + 1)}{(10s + 1)(2.5s + 1)}\right]}$$

$$= \frac{3}{25s^2 + 12.5s + 4}$$

The final value of the process variable at steady state will be:

$$\lim_{t \to \infty} f_{(t)} = \lim_{s \to 0} sF_{(s)}$$

$$\lim_{s \to 0} sPV_{(s)} = (s)\left(\frac{1}{s}\right)\left[\frac{3}{25s^2 + 12.5s + 4}\right]$$

$$= \frac{3}{4}$$

$$= 0.75$$

Thus, the final value to a unit step input will be 0.75.

15-33   true

15-34   c–continue to ramp due to the integration of the error

15-35   The gain of curve K_{I1} is greater than the gain of curve K_{I2}, and both curves belong to a direct-acting controller.

15-36   d– $K_I = \dfrac{\% \text{ change in } \frac{dCV}{dt}}{\% \text{ error over full range}}$

15-37 $CV_{(t=4)} = K_I E(t - t_0) + CV_{(t=0)}$

$$= (0.6 \text{ sec}^{-1})(5\%)(4 - 0) + 50\%$$

$$= 62\%$$

15-38   true

15-39   a–fast response, d–eliminates offset error

15-40

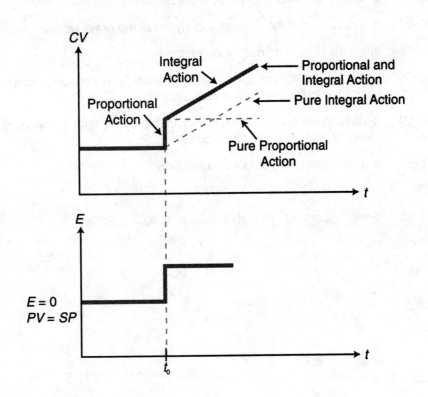

15-41   true

15-42   The proportional action of a PI controller starts to correct the error immediately by applying a large increase in the control variable. An integral-only controller slowly ramps its output to correct the error.

15-43   c–the integral gain is equal to the amount of proportional gain after the integral time period

15-44   true

15-45   b–proportion to the rate of change of the error

15-46   true

15-47   __b__ modified derivative controller

        __a__ standard derivative controller

15-48   d–anticipatory of the final error

15-49   true

15-50   c–a brake to the process variable

15-51   d–three-mode

15-52   true

15-53   g–all of the above

15-54   b–the frequency of how often a PLC reads and executes the integral and derivative terms in a PID algorithm

15-55   false; bumpless transfer does not eliminate error in an open-loop process

15-56   a–output, d–primary, b–input, e–secondary

15-57   c–a reduction of their overshoots by 1/4 of the previous one

15–58   false; the ITAE is an open-loop method

15-59   d–stepped by 10% of the *CV* and the results are charted to determine several parameters used to calculate the tuning constants

15-60   b–dividing the change in process variable by the time as calculated by the tangent of the steepest point in the reaction curve

15-61   a–open-loop, c–lag time and dead time

15-62   true

15-63   c–the proportional gain should be reduced

15-64   true

CHAPTER 16 ANSWERS

16-1   artificial intelligence

16-2   false; it was first developed in the early 1960s

16-3   diagnostic, knowledge, expert

16-4   true

16-5   *(a)* Diagnostic systems are the lowest level of AI system. They mainly serve as fault detectors for applications with small, simple knowledge databases. Diagnostics systems lack the ability to solve problems that occur. Most of the time, diagnostic systems make only go and no go decisions; however, these systems may provide some information about the fault's possible cause.

   (b) Knowledge systems are expanded diagnostic systems that can process larger amounts of information and rules. Knowledge systems detect process faults, as well as provide information about their causes.

   (c) Expert systems are top-of-the-line AI systems whose knowledge databases contain information that is readily available for real-time responses. These systems use statistical analysis to predict process outcomes. Expert systems can make control system decisions based on process data.

16-6   global database, knowledge database, inference engine

16-7   true

16-8

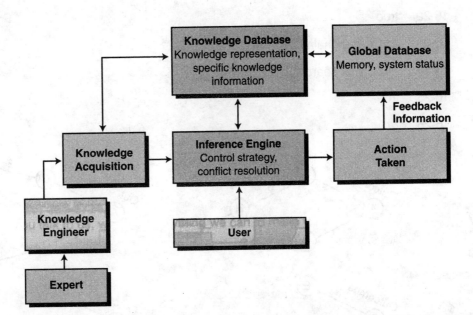

16-9   *(a)* The global database contains information about the system's status, that is, the conditions taking place at the given moment. This database updates information about the process, as well as records information about the actions executed for later use in statistical analysis.

   (b) The knowledge database stores the information extracted from the expert. This information covers all the knowledge that governs the complete process. This section also provides information about possible malfunctions, their implications, and possible solutions that will later be analyzed in the inference engine.

(c) The inference engine is where all decisions and actions are made. The inference engine works with the knowledge database to execute applicable rules. The inference engine is the section of the AI system where the control strategy is carried out.

16-10   true

16-11   data table

16-12   false; an AI system's decisions are made in the inference engine

16-13   true

16-14   rule-based

16-15   e–antecedent, a–consequent

16-16   false; in a rule-based system, a hierarchical structure exists as long as the programming sequence calls for it

16-17   c–Inferencing

16-18   false; knowledge inferencing occurs in the inference engine

16-19   blackboard architecture

16-20   false; depending on the magnitude of the decisions, some actions may be executed either on a local basis (subsystem level) or by the main controller

16-21   forward chaining

16-22   true

16-23   backward chaining

16-24   depth-first search

16-25   true

16-26   *(a)*   *(b)*

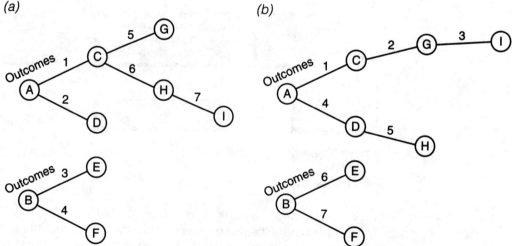

16-27   false; AI systems use statistical analysis to anticipate the outcomes of a process

16-28   Baye's theorem

16-29   The probability that the temperature regulator is faulty even though the batch temperature is correct is 21%, as given by the equation:

$$P(R/T) = \frac{(0.5)(0.3)}{(0.5)(0.3) + (0.8)(0.7)}$$
$$= \frac{0.15}{0.15 + 0.56}$$
$$= 0.21$$

16-30   true

CHAPTER 17 ANSWERS

17–1   c–reasoning algorithms used to emulate human thinking and decision making in machines

17–2   true

17–3   b–50% cool, 50% cold

17–4   false; fuzzy logic implements reasoning algorithms that are able to judge terms like "a little bit to the left"

17–5

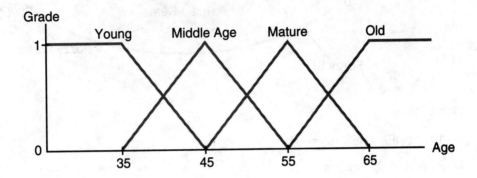

17–6   b–input, d–output

17–7   true

17–8   c–IF...THEN rules

17–9   c–IF normal, THEN normal speed and IF too cool, THEN less speed

17–10   The three components of the fuzzy logic process are fuzzification, fuzzy processing, and defuzzification.

17–11   __b__ evaluation of user-supplied information
        __c__ conversion of a fuzzy outcome into a real output value
        __a__ translation of an input variable into fuzzy form
        __d__ fuzzy input

17–12   true

17–13   *(a)* Z
        (b) S
        (c) Π
        (d) Λ

17–14   false; membership functions can be asymmetrical

17–15   c–Membership functions can have more than 3 line segments

17–16   c–labels, d–conditions

17–17

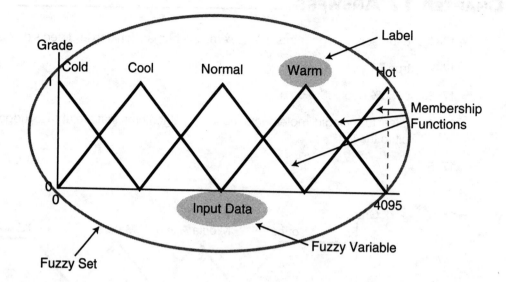

17–18   true

17–19   c–IF...THEN rules

17–20   d–IF, a–triggers

17–21   false; IF conditions can also have inputs linked by an OR condition

17–22   b–four

17–23   b–lowest, c–highest

17–24   c–0.25

17–25   c–nine

17–26   c–add

17–27   d–noncontinuous functions

17–28

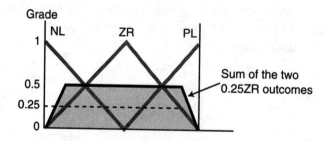

17–29   d–sum of the averages

17–30   true

17–31   b–2340 counts

17–32   a–1170 ,c–3510

17–33

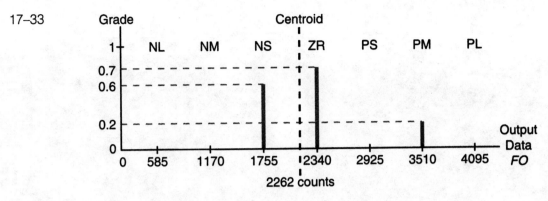

17–34 The approximate output as specified by the centroid will be 2048 counts.

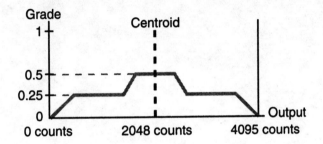

17–35 true

17–36 c–less

17–37 false; a fuzzy set can also have an even number of membership functions

17–38 c–there are points where no sensitivity exists between labels

17–39 true

17–40 d–an error condition

CHAPTER 18 ANSWERS

18-1 decentralize

18-2 node

18-3 Industrial network criteria include:
- capability to support real-time control
- high data integrity
- high noise immunity
- high reliability in harsh environments
- suitability for large installations

18-4 Business networks do not require as much noise immunity as industrial networks. They also have less stringent access time requirements because a business workstation can easily wait a few seconds for information, but a machine being controlled by a PLC may need information within milliseconds.

18-5 Before LANs, communication between PLCs was accomplished by connecting an output module of one PLC to an input module of another PLC. The amount of data to be transferred and the transmission speed would determine how many wires were required and whether the data would be transmitted in parallel or series. In another communication method, the PLCs communicated through their programming ports via a central computer that was customer supplied and programmed.

18-6 centralized data acquisition, distributed control

18-7 Three disadvantages of large applications that use a single PLC system for data collection and control are that they consume a large amount of memory, they tend to slow down the scan time, and they complicate the control logic program.

18-8 true

18-9 true

18-10 d–all of the above

18-11 c–tree

18-12 false; star topology does allow easy implementation of point-to-point protocol

18-13 c–failure of the central node will bring down the system

18-14

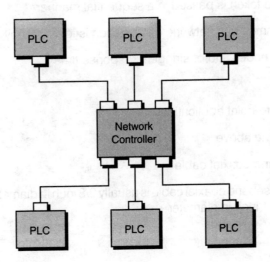

18-15   multidrop

18-16   a–high-speed throughput

18-17   false; since a break can affect at least one node, the communication of the entire network is deteriorated

18-18   true

18-19   In a master/slave configuration, the master sends data to the slaves. If the master needs data from a slave, the master polls the slave's address and waits for a response. No communication takes place unless it is initiated by the master.

18-20   b–Failure of a node brings down the system.

18-21   true

18-22   c–it requires twice as much wiring as ring networks

18-23   b–access method

18-24   polling

18-25   master

18-26   c–carrier sense multiple access with collision detection

18-27   In the collision detection access method, each node with a message to transmit waits until there is no traffic on the network and then transmits its data. While a node is transmitting, the collision-detection circuitry checks for the presence of another transmitter. If two nodes try to transmit at the same time, a collision will occur. When this happens, the node disables its transmitter and then waits a variable amount of time before resending its message.

18-28   c–there are not many nodes in the network

18-29   b–network throughput to drop off and access time to increase

18-30   false; collision detection is mainly used for business applications

18-31   c–contention among stations trying to gain access to the network

18-32   token

18-33   e–relinquish, c–next designated

18-34   false; the token is passed in a sequential manner

18-35   In a common bus network, each station is identified by an address.

18-36   c–many nodes and/or stringent response time

18-37   true

18-38   b–point-to-point applications

18-39   d–all of the above

18-40   broadband coaxial cable

18-41   false; baseband coaxial cable is usually 3/8 inch in diameter, while broadband coaxial cable is 1/2 to 1 inch in diameter

18-42   true

18-43   d–all of the above

18-44   true

18-45   The two span lengths that must be evaluated are the maximum length of the main trunkline cable and the maximum length of the drop between a node and the main line.

18-46   false; the transmission distance does affect the type of coaxial cable selected because broadband cable can transmit data farther than baseband cable

18-47   b–the maximum response time

18-48   gateway

18-49   a–information stored in the executive memory

18-50   A protocol is a set of rules that must be followed if two or more devices are to communicate with each other.

18-51   A protocol generally addresses the following network communication problems:
- communication line errors
- flow control to keep buffers from overflowing
- access by multiple devices
- failure detection
- data translation
- interpretation of messages

18-52   _e_ layer 7: application

  _a_ layer 6: presentation

  _g_ layer 5: session

  _c_ layer 4: transport

  _d_ layer 3: network

  _b_ layer 2: data link

  _f_ layer 1: physical

18-53   true

18-54   TCP, IP

18-55   b–common bus, e–token passing

18-56   _j_ broadband

  _f_ baseband

  _i_ local area networks

  _b_ polling

  _d_ twisted-pair cable

  _h_ ISO/OSI

  _k_ coaxial cable

  _e_ gateway

  _a_ node

  _g_ token passing

  _c_ fiber optics

CHAPTER 19 ANSWERS _____

19–1   c–network that allows direct communication between a PLC and intelligent I/O field devices

19–2   d–I/O bus scanner

19–3   _c_ I/O field devices

        _a_ device bus network

        _b_ process bus network

19–4   c–small amounts of, b–large amounts of

19–5   b–bit wide, c–byte wide

19–6   true

19–7   true

19–8   _d_ Profibus

        _a_ DeviceNet

        _e_ Fieldbus Foundation

        _c_ Seriplex

        _b_ InterBus-S

19–9   b–Phoenix Contact, d–nonintelligent field devices

19–10   five, two, two, one

19–11   a–SDS, e–DeviceNet

19–12   false; it uses three of the ISO layers—the physical, data link, and application layers

19–13   c–a high-density I/O concentrator

19–14   c–control area network bus, b–the automotive industry

19–15   true

19–16   false; the InterBus–S and the InterBus Loop share the same protocol, making it possible for them to communicate with each other

19–17   c–ASIC

19–18   true

19–19   true

19–20   false; process bus networks can transfer data at a fast rate, but the amount of data they transmit is large

19–21   c–communication stack

19–22   b–user layer

19–23   true

19–24   b–H1 (low speed of 31.25 Kbaud), d–H2 (high speed of 1 Mbaud or 2.5 Mbaud)

19–25   false; it is possible to connect networks at both speeds to only one host

19–26   a–cyclic, b–acyclic, e–scheduled, c–unscheduled

19–27   d–Function blocks

19–28   true

19–29   true

19–30   __c__ process automation version

__b__ performance-optimized version

__a__ communicates between upper-level, cell-level, and field-level devices

19–31   true

19–32   true

19–33   c–direct data link mapper (DDLM)

19–34   true

19–35   c–a combination of master-master and master-slave

19–36   d–EIA RS-485

19–37   false; the number of conductors and type of cable (shielded or unshielded) varies according to each individual device bus network

19–38   true

19–39   b–process bus–compatible, d–device bus–compatible

CHAPTER 20 ANSWERS

20-1   The system layout is the conscientious approach to placing and interconnecting the PLC's components not only to satisfy the application, but also to ensure that the controller will operate trouble free in its environment.

20-2   false; in a proper system layout, the components are easily accessible

20-3   Components other than the PLC that may be part of the system layout include:
   - isolation transformers
   - auxiliary power supplies
   - safety control relays
   - circuit breakers
   - fuse blocks
   - line noise suppressors

20-4   c–close to the machine or process

20-5   d–all of the above

20-6   b–vibration

20-7   General enclosure and I/O wiring guidelines include the following:
   - The enclosure should be placed in a position that allows the doors to be opened fully for easy access to wiring and components for testing or troubleshooting.
   - The enclosure should be deep enough to allow clearance between the closed enclosure door and either the print-pocket mounted on the door or the enclosed components and related cables.
   - The enclosure's back panel should be removable to facilitate mounting of the components and other assemblies.
   - An emergency disconnect device should be mounted in the cabinet in an easily accessible location.
   - Accessories, such as AC power outlets, interior lighting, and a gasketed plexiglass window to allow viewing of the processor and I/O indicators, should be considered for installation and maintenance convenience.

20-8   false; a power outlet is very convenient inside the enclosure to allow for a programming terminal to be plugged in during start-up

20-9   c–60°C inside the enclosure

20-10   fan or blower

20-11   condensation

20-12   false; it is a good practice to place a PLC system far away from high noise generating equipment, such as arc welders

20-13   b–vertical

20-14   power supply

20-15   c–directly above the CPU

20-16   c–the effects of noise are minimized

20-17   false; fans should be placed near hot spots

20-18   d–crosstalk

20-19   The duct and wiring layout defines the physical location of wireways and the routing of field I/O signals, power, and PLC interconnections within the enclosure.

20-20   true

20-21   a–separate from

20-22   a right angle

20-23   grounding

20-24   permanent

20-25   true

20-26   Paint and nonconductive materials should be scraped away to provide a good ground connection.

20-27   true

20-28   Isolation transformers are required in cases in where heavy equipment is likely to introduce noise onto the AC line.

20-29   false; emergency stop switches should not be wired to the PLC

20-30   false; emergency stops should be used when necessary to maintain the safety of the control system

20-31   a–Electromechanical MCRs

20-32   Outrush is a condition that occurs when output triacs are turned off by throwing the power disconnect, thus causing the energy stored in an inductive load to seek the nearest path to ground, which is often through the triacs. To correct this problem, a capacitor may be placed across the disconnect (0.47 µF for 120 VAC, 0.22 µF for 240 VAC).

20-33   c–60% of the inputs and 30% of the outputs are ON at one time

20-34   constant voltage transformer

20-35   b–every time there is a change

20-36   false; the input power and the AC and DC wire bundles should be kept separate

20-37   d–size matching

20-38   d–all of the above

20-39   true

20-40   Special wiring considerations may be necessary for:
   -   leaky inputs
   -   inductive loads
   -   output fusing
   -   shielding of low-level and analog signals

20-41   OFF

20-42   false; triacs leak more than transistors

20-43   bleeding resistor

20-44   true

20-45   (a) small AC load suppression

(b) large AC load suppression

(c) DC load suppression

20-46   true

20-47   true

20-48   false; in the static output wiring check, power is applied to both the controller and the output devices

20-49   c–disconnected

20-50   dummy rung

20-51   d–all of the above

20-52   Changes to the control logic should be documented immediately.

20-53   Preventive PLC maintenance should be performed during the scheduled maintenance of the machine.

20-54   Any build-up of dust or dirt can obstruct the heat dissipation of components in the system.

20-55   true

20-56   d–all of the above

20-57   d–all of the above

20-58   d–all of the above

20-59   A ground loop condition occurs when two or more electrical paths to ground exist in a ground line.

20-60   d–all of the above

20-61   The first step should be to check the input power and/or logic indicators.

20-62   __4__ check the wiring connection to the module

__3__ close the field device and measure the voltage to the input module

__1__ place the PLC in standby mode

__2__ evaluate the PLC's reading of the module

__5__ check the voltage at the field device

20-63   c–isolate the problem to the module, the field device, or the field wiring

CHAPTER 21 ANSWERS

21-1 relay replacers

21-2 d–large PLCs

21-3 The I/O count is the primary specification in categorizing PLCs.

21-4 false; as the I/O count increases, so does the complexity of the system and the amount of memory

21-5 true

21-6 d–32 or less

21-7 false; area A controllers can support more I/O than micro PLCs

21-8 b–the enhancements of the standard features of segment 2 controllers

21-9 c–32K of memory

21-10 Features of large PLCs include:
- all the software capabilities of a medium-sized PLC
- double-precision arithmetic
- more block transfers
- PID capabilities
- host computer communication modules
- more than one RS-232C communication port
- more memory
- subroutine capabilities

21-11 d–all of the above

21-12 false; future needs must also be considered

21-13 c–documentation

21-14 Factors that must be considered when evaluating discrete outputs include:
- fuses
- transient surge protection
- isolation between power and logic
- indicators
- cost per point

21-15 b–accessibility

21-16 c–isolated commons

21-17 __c__ bipolar

   __d__ special analog input

   __b__ 4 to 20 mA

   __a__ special I/O

   __f__ PID module

   __e__ analog I/O

21-18 d–reduce

21-19 *(a)*

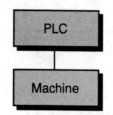

(b)

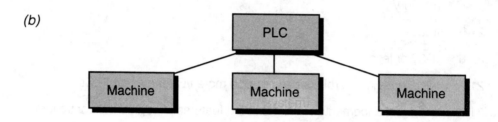

(c)

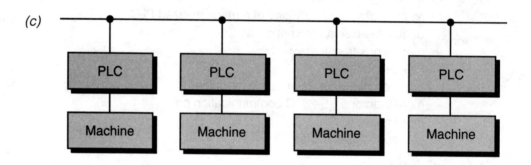

21-20 true

21-21 b–It is used to control more than one machine.

21-22 true

21-23 b–it can control one large process or several smaller processes

21-24 redundant

21-25 c–two PLCs that communicate with each other

21-26 local area network

21-27 false; different PLC manufacturers use different communication schemes, making communication between their PLCs difficult

21-28 type, amount

21-29 true

21-30 c–the number of inputs and outputs, d–the complexity of the control program

21-31 true

21-32 The programming device should be the first peripheral considered in a PLC system.

21-33 Peripheral requirements should be considered along with the CPU because the CPU determines the type and number of peripherals that can be interfaced and supported, as well as the method of interfacing.

21-34 false; physical and environmental characteristics significantly impact system reliability

21-35 b–operating parameters

21-36 true

21-37 The burn-in procedure involves operating the product at an elevated temperature to force an electronic board or part to fail. If a part passes the burn-in procedure, it has a very high probability for proper operation.

21-38 c–standardization

21-39 d–all of the above

21-40 __1__ the process to be controlled
__5__ memory type
__2__ type of control
__6__ memory capacity
__3__ I/O interface requirements
__7__ scan requirements
__4__ software language and functions
__10__ physical and environmental constraints
__8__ programming and storage devices
__9__ peripheral requirements
__11__ other PLC factors